The Southern Gourmet

by Virginia Clower Robbins

Published by

PRECISION FOODS, INC.
Tupelo, Mississippi

First Printing September 1973—10,000 Books
Second Printing December 1977—5,000 Books
Third Printing February 1980—5,000 Books
Fourth Printing February 1983—5,000 Books
Fifth Printing May 1988—5,000 Books
Sixth Printing October 1995—5,000 Books

Copies of *The Southern Gourmet* Cookbook may be obtained by addressing The Southern Gourmet Cookbook, P.O. Box 2067, Tupelo, Mississippi 38803. Price is $13.95 (see order blank in back of book).

ISBN: 0-9649067-0-8

Printed in the USA by

WIMMER
The Wimmer Companies, Inc.
Memphis

FOREWORD

Some thirty years ago, when I went into Country Club work as executive secretary and hostess, I found myself faced with the problems which try the patience of every club director. My previous experience had been feeding the football team hot tamales, and suddenly I found myself having to provide an endless stream of new menus.

Since both club functions and parties given by club members brought together guests who were largely the same, month after month, new and different recipes were necessary in order to maintain the club's longstanding reputation of a distinctive cuisine. In addition, my menus had to be flexible enough to accommodate groups ranging from half a dozen to several hundred in number. My duties included serving refreshments following committee meetings and lectures, planning luncheons and receptions for the large club membership, and arranging parties of all sizes and types for members who wished to entertain at the club.

For my salvation, I brought my own personal recipe file, together with a number of my mother's treasured family recipes and many good recipes of generous friends who were noted for their ability to entertain and were willing to part with their secrets.

In the succeeding years I have been constantly on the alert to add to this nucleus of tested recipes. As a result, I have accumulated a tremendous number of recipes which I believe will be helpful both to the club hostess and to the woman who is entertaining in her own home. While the majority of my suggestions unquestionably have a Southern flavor, I have included a number of recipes gleaned from other localities as well. Therefore, I hope that some of my ideas will add zest to the menus of hostesses in all parts of the country, and thus fulfill the expectations of the club members and personal friends who have suggested that I compile them in book form.

I consider myself lucky to have found such a rewarding profession. This book will have accomplished its real purpose if I have been able to share with you not only some of my favorite recipes, but also some of my enthusiasm for the joy and fun of creative cooking.

Virginia Clower Robbins
Tupelo, Mississippi
1973

DEDICATION

To my Mother and Mother-in-law and, of course, to my children, who have inspired me, given me courage to write this book and shown me the real art of cooking.

Virginia Clower Robbins

TABLE OF CONTENTS

Appetizers
Ices
Hors D'Oeuvres
Canapés
Dips

Appetizers
Ices
Hors D'Oeuvres
Canapés
Dips

I always think of the appetizer or hors d' oeuvre course as being like the first act of a play. It should whet the appetite for something wonderful to follow, and yet it should be provocative enough to keep everyone interested while they wait.

The only basic rule I follow when preparing my first course is that it must be as good to look at as it is to eat, because I believe the eye should eat as well as the stomach. Also, the portions should be small enough to stimulate but never quite satisfy the appetite.

As long as food is well prepared and attractively served, I believe a good cook can be as daring as he or she chooses in the selection of what dishes go together. I've found that much of the satisfaction and fun of creative cooking and entertaining is in the unexpected. Don't worry about what is "right" and what is "wrong". Let the dishes you prepare reflect your personality.

Avocado Appetizers

1 Avocado
1 firm tomato
¼ head of lettuce, shredded
4 strips bacon cooked until crisp
Russian dressing

Cut avocado and tomato into small cubes; marinate in French dressing. When ready to serve, combine with lettuce and bacon, which has been crumbled in bits, add Russian dressing. Serve on small curled lettuce hearts placed in cocktail glass. Use as first course. Serves 6.

Avocado and Shrimp Cocktail

½ pound cooked shrimp
1 avocado

Cut avocado into cubes; sprinkle with lemon juice; clean shrimp; combine with the same cocktail sauce that is given for "artichoke and egg appetizer".

Artichoke and Egg Appetizers

1 No. 2 can artichoke hearts, diced
6 hard boiled eggs, chopped
1 c. finely diced celery
2 slices crisp bacon, crumbled

Mix with Russian dressing made of:

½ cup mayonnaise
1 tablespoon Worcestershire sauce
1 tablespoon chili sauce
1 tablespoon tomato catsup
1 tablespoon horseradish

Mix all ingredients in a jar and shake well. Serves 6.

Artichoke Appetizer or Salad

1 can baby artichokes
1 diced pimento
1 small diced cucumber
2 Tbsp. lemon juice
1 Tbsp. gelatin
¼ c. cold water
1 c. boiling water
¼ c. sugar

Make cucumber aspic of gelatin, lemon juice, water, sugar and cucumber; tint green with a few drops of green coloring; add other ingredients; mold in very small molds. Serves 8.

Bacon Roll-Ups

Cut slices of bacon in four pieces; wrap around olives, cocktail sausages, oysters or pecan halves put together with Roquefort cheese spread; dip in burgundy wine and broil; serve hot, speared on cocktail picks.

Stuffed Beets

Scoop out centers of tiny rosebud beets; fill with highly seasoned, diced, hard-boiled eggs; bound together with a bit of cooked dressing or with seasoned and sweetened vinegar. Put cocktail picks in sides of the beets and serve on relish tray.
Tiny pickled beets stuffed with cottage cheese make tasty garnishes for sliced cold meats.

Chipped Beef and Cheese Rolls

Season cream cheese with onion juice, minced parsley, Worcestershire sauce, and horseradish; shape into narrow cylinders, size of little finger; roll in thin slices of chipped beef; trim the ends evenly. Chill and use to garnish salads or on hors d'oeuvre tray. Thin slices of baked ham can be used the same way.

11

Cereal Crunchies

1 lb. margarine
1 Tbsp. Worcestershire sauce
2 tsp. salt
1 teaspoon garlic powder
1 box Rice Chex cereal (12 oz.)
1 box Cheerio cereal
1 box pretzel bits
½ lb. each almonds and pecans

Blanch almonds; cut in half lengthwise and toast in oven to a light brown. Melt margarine; add seasonings; combine with cereals, pecans and toasted almonds. Put in a large, flat pan and toast slowly for 2 hours at 250 degrees. Thin pretzel sticks can be substituted for the bits. Peanuts can be substituted for almonds. These can be served at cocktail parties or with tomato juice. They keep well in air-tight containers.

Cheese Puffs

1½ c. grated American cheese
2 egg whites
2 egg yolks
1 tsp. Worcestershire sauce

Grate cheese; add beaten yolks and Worcestershire sauce; beat egg whites very stiff; combine with cheese. Toast rounds of bread on one side; spread untoasted side with cheese mixture. Put in hot oven until puffed and brown. Serve at once.

Cheese Wafers

2 c. grated sharp cheese
2 c. plain flour
2 sticks soft oleo
2 c. Rice Krispies
1 tsp. red pepper
½ tsp. paprika

Mix all together; form into small balls. Place balls on ungreased cookie sheet and press down with a fork. Bake 10 minutes at 350 degrees.

I Cheese Straws

2 c. plain flour
1 lb. extra sharp cheese
½ tsp. red pepper
1½ tsp. salt
1 stick butter

Melt butter and pour over grated cheese. Let stand several hours. Gradually work dry ingredients into cheese mixture. If cheese mixture is too stiff, a little water may be added. Put in cookie press and press through to an ungreased cookie sheet. Bake in 325 degree oven about 20 minutes. Do not brown. Makes 50 straws.

12

II Cheese Straws

½ lb. extra sharp Cheddar cheese
2 sticks oleo
1¾ c. flour
1 tsp. salt
½ tsp. red pepper
1 tsp. Tabasco sauce

Grate cheese; blend with butter; add Tabasco. Sift flour; add salt and pepper. Mix the two mixtures thoroughly. Squeeze through pastry tube in 3½ inch strips on ungreased cookie sheets or roll on floured board; cut in desired shapes. Bake 375 degrees. Yields about 6 dozen.

III Cheese Straws

1 lb. grated sharp cheese
1 stick butter
2 c. flour
1 tsp salt
½ tsp. red pepper

Grate cheese, melt butter, pour over cheese, work in flour and pepper; let cool. Press from cookie press on cookie sheet and bake at 375 degrees. Variation: Cream 2 sticks oleo; add 1 c. grated sharp cheese; add 1 tsp. red pepper, 1 tsp. garlic salt, and 2 c. sifted flour together and roll in waxed paper. Chill thoroughly. Slice ¼ inch thick. Bake 350 degrees for 15 minutes.

Cheese Whirls

1 stick butter
1 lb. grated cheese
2 c. flour
¼ tsp. red pepper
Apple jelly

Cream butter and cheese together, add flour and red pepper. Roll out on board and spread with apple jelly. Roll as a jelly roll and wrap in wax paper. Store in ice box until ready to use. Slice in ¼ inch slices and bake in 400 degree oven until slightly brown. Cooks fast, so watch it!

Cocktail Bite Size Ribs

3 lbs. young loin ribs 1¼"
¼ c. prepared mustard
¼ c. white karo
¼ c. soy sauce
3 Tbsp. vinegar
2 Tbsp. Lee and Perrin sauce
2 tsp. Tabasco sauce
1 Tbsp. M.S.G.

Place ribs in shallow baking pan. Marinate overnight. Bake for 3 hours at 350 degrees. Before serving, spoon sauce over ribs.

Deviled Ham Puffs

1 8-oz. pkg. Philadelphia cream
  cheese
1 egg yolk
Salt
1 tsp. onion juice
½ tsp. baking powder

Toast 24 bread circles on one side. Spread with 2 cans deviled ham. Cover each circle with mound of above mixture. Bake 10 minutes in 375 degree oven until puffed.

I Cheese Roll

2 small pkgs. Velveeta cheese
2 small pkgs. cream cheese
1 c. pecans
Chili powder

Run pecans through food chopper first, then cheese. Cream together. Make roll 1½ inches in diameter. Chill. Roll in chili powder. Slice and serve on round crackers.

II Cheese Roll

½ lb. yellow cheese
½ lb. Philadelphia cream cheese
¼ lb. Roquefort cheese
1 small onion
1½ c. chopped pecans

Grind onion, yellow cheese and Roquefort cheese together, knead with cream cheese; add ½ c. pecans, form into 2 narrow cylinders, roll in the rest of the finely chopped pecans. Chill for 24 hours; slice and put on crackers. You can make into balls and serve as a spread. Makes 2 good size balls.

To keep cheese, dip a cloth in vinegar water, wring it out, and wrap cheese in it. Wrap in waxed paper and store in refrigerator.

Cheese Dreams

1 lb. Old English Cheese, grated
Dash of Tabasco
Dash of Worcestershire sauce
Dash of paprika
½ c. cream

Mix ingredients well. Cut very thin slices of bread. Remove crusts, spread a thin layer of mixture on slices, sprinkle with paprika; roll into blanket roll, brush with melted butter and sprinkle with paprika. Run in 400 degree oven for a few minutes to brown lightly. Serves 30.

Cheese Balls

1 c. chopped cheese
  (New York State, if possible)
1 c. grated cheese
1 c. thick white sauce
2 eggs
Cracker crumbs
1 slightly beaten egg

Mix cheese, white sauce and 2 eggs. Refrigerate overnight. Make into balls, dip in slightly beaten egg, then roll in very fine cracker crumbs. Fry in deep fat.

Cheese Biscuits

1 lb. New York Cheese, grated
1 stick oleo
2 c. self-rising flour
2 Tbsp. cream
½ tsp. red pepper

Mix well together and make 2 rolls; chill thoroughly, then slice and brush with slightly beaten egg yolks. Place pecan half on each biscuit. Bake until light brown in 350 degree oven.

Cheese Ball

Mix carefully in blender:
  1 pkg. cottage cheese
  1 pkg. (8 oz.) cream cheese
  1 lb. Cheddar cheese
  ½ lb. any other cheese
  1 pkg. Blue cheese salad mix
    (dry)

Place in mixing bowl. Add ½ bottle chopped olives. Add chopped nuts, hot sauce, garlic salt, and Worcestershire to taste. Add enough mayonnaise to make into a workable ball. Roll in chili powder and then in chopped nuts.

15

Cheese Sausage Rolls

Cook 16 sausage links. Cut crusts from 16 slices of bread. Roll bread flat. Mix 1 c. shredded American cheese and 4 Tbsp. butter. Spread on both sides of bread. Roll sausage in each slice. Bake on greased sheet, at 400 degrees F. for 10-12 minutes. Slice and serve or freeze.

Cheese Bites

¾ c. flour
½ stick oleo (room temperature)
1 6-oz. glass jar Ole English
  Cheese spread

Combine soft oleo with cheese spread. Work in sifted flour. Form mixture into balls to refrigerate for several hours. Just before serving, put in a 450 degree F. oven for 10 minutes. Makes about 33 small balls.

Cheese Crackers

2 c. flour
2 c. sharp cheese, grated
2 c. Rice Krispies
2 sticks oleo
1 tsp. salt or ½ tsp. garlic salt
1 tsp. Tabasco sauce or
  1 tsp. cayenne pepper
1 tsp. Worcestershire sauce
Imitation bacon bits (optional)

Mix ingredients well. Work into small balls and press with fork. Bake at 300 degrees until golden brown.

Salsa and Chips

1 pkg. corn tortillas
1 large can tomatoes
1 small can dried green chilies
1 small onion, diced
Seasoning

Cut tortillas into 6ths and fry until crisp. Salt and let cool. Drain tomatoes and cut up into small pieces. Add chilies and onion. Season to taste (salt, pepper, garlic, oregano). Serve chilled as dip for tortilla chips.

16

Onion Pinwheels

2 Tbsp. instant minced onion
2 c. biscuit mix
2 Tbsp. melted butter or
 margarine
1 c. shredded Cheddar cheese
Paprika

Add onion to biscuit mix and prepare dough as package directs. Roll into 13 X 9-inch rectangle. Spread with butter and sprinkle with cheese and paprika. Roll as for jelly roll; pinch seam tight. Cut into 13 (1-inch) slices; arrange cut side up in greased 8-inch round pan. Bake in 425 degree F. oven 12 to 15 minutes, until light brown. Rolls may be frozen after baking and reheated in foil. Makes 13 pinwheels.

Tamale Treats

1 lb. ground beef
1 lb. ground pork
4 cloves garlic, minced
1½ c. yellow corn meal
½ c. flour
1 tsp. chili powder
2 tsp. salt
1 tsp. seasoned pepper
¾ c. tomato juice

Combine all the above, mixing with your hands. Shape into small marble-sized balls. Place in the Mexicali Sauce and simmer for 2 hours. Serve in a chafing dish with colorful tooth picks.

Mexicali sauce:
2 large cans tomatoes
1 tsp. chili powder
1 onion, grated
2 tsp. salt
2 tsp. sugar
1 tsp. seasoned pepper

Mash tomatoes or whiz in blender for 2 seconds. Add rest of ingredients in a heavy pot and simmer until desired thickness.

Red-Devil Balls

1 8-oz. pkg. cream cheese
1 4½-oz. can deviled ham
1 c. chopped walnuts or pecans

Blend before time the cream cheese and ham. Refrigerate until easy to handle; then shape into 30 small balls. Roll in chopped nuts. Chill until firm. Serve balls on toothpicks alone or with olives and crackers.

17

Salted Nuts

Put a small amount of salad oil into a pan. Pour in the nuts and stir until they are well coated. There should be no excess oil. Set the pan in a moderate oven (350 degrees F.) and stir frequently until they are a light brown. Drain on brown paper a few minutes. Spread on wax paper and sprinkle with salt.

Hot Cream Cheese Canapés

1 3-oz. pkg. cream cheese
1 egg
1 tsp. onion juice
1 Tbsp. lemon juice
1 tsp. salt
Chutney for topping

Blend ingredients until smooth and airy. Pile high on well-buttered toast rounds; spread chutney on top and place on buttered cookie sheet and bake 5 or 6 minutes at 450 degrees F. Serve immediately.

Antipasta

½ head cauliflower broken into
    small pieces
2 carrots, halved and cut
    lengthwise in strips
2 stalks celery, cut in
    1 inch pieces
1 green pepper, cut in
    1 inch strips
1 red pepper, cut in 1 inch strips
1 can (3¾-oz.) black olives
6 small white onions, peeled
¼ lb. fresh green beans, cut in half
¾ c. water
¾ c. wine vinegar
¼ c. vegetable oil
1 tsp. olive oil
2 Tbsp. sugar
1 garlic clove, pressed
1 tsp. dried oregano
Dash salt and freshly ground
    pepper

In a large frying pan combine all the ingredients and bring to a boil. Simmer covered for approximately 5 minutes. Cool, and refrigerate mixture in a large jar for a day or two. This is a good antipasto dish to eat while watching TV or for a bedtime snack, rather than serving it as a first course. Serves 8.

18

Pâté.

2 lbs calf liver
½ lb. chicken liver
¼ lb. pork liver
1 clove garlic, crushed
Dash salt and pepper
4 Tbsp. brandy
2 eggs beaten
¼ c. heavy cream
2 Tbsp. fresh lemon juice
Pinch powdered bay leaf
½ lb. sliced bacon

Preheat oven at 325 degrees F. Mince the livers, or have your butcher put them through a grinder twice, using the finest blade. Add all other ingredients to the livers except bacon and brandy. With a fork mash into a paste. Warm the brandy in a sauce pan, light and pour slowly over the liver mixture. Mix well. Line a pâté mold or a bread loaf pan with strips of bacon, pack in the liver and cover with remaining bacon strips. Cover the mold or pan with aluminum foil and set it in a large shallow roasting pan that contains one or two inches water. Let stand in oven for about 2 hours. Remove from oven, discard the foil, and "weight" the pâté with any heavy object that will cover the entire loaf. Chill overnight, unmold and serve with a favorite garnish. I don't think any collection of hors d'oeuvres and first course recipes would be complete without a pâté. I have several ways of preparing this fine dish but I'm particularly fond of this one.

Wilma's Olive Surprise

¼ c. soft oleo
1 c. grated sharp cheese
3 doz. med. size stuffed olives
¼ tsp. salt
¼ tsp. paprika
½ c. sifted plain flour

Cream oleo and cheese in mixer until well blended; add rest of the ingredients except olives. Chill dough 15 to 20 minutes. Dip end of fingers in flour. Roll dough into marble size balls. Punch hole in center of ball and insert olive and close up. Bake 15 to 20 minutes in 400 degree oven. Serve hot. These can be prepared and frozen to be baked later.

Four or five whole cloves and a teaspoon of
sugar added to a quart of prunes
while soaking gives them a delicious flavor.
Cook prunes in the same water used for soaking.

Anchovy and Pepper Stuffed Tomatoes

1 pt. cherry tomatoes
5 small tins of flat anchovy
  fillets
2 Tbsp. finely chopped parsley
2 Tbsp. finely chopped Bermuda
  onions
1 Tbsp. olive oil
1 jar hot peppers
1 Tbsp. juice from hot pepper

Wash tomatoes, cut off tops, and hollow them out with a demitasse spoon or a tiny scoop. Invert them to dry on a paper towel. Wash anchovy fillets individually to remove all saltiness and put them in a bowl with parsley, onion and olive oil. Put hot peppers with juice through a blender for 15 seconds, add one tablespoon pepper mixture to other ingredients and mix well. Stuff tomatoes with the mixture and refrigerate. Serves 12.

Stuffed Mushrooms

1 lb. medium size mushrooms
1 Tbsp. sweet butter
1 Tbsp. finely chopped parsley
1 garlic clove, chopped fine
1 tsp. finely chopped shallots
Dash salt and pepper

Wash mushrooms and remove stems. Reserve 10 or 12 of the best caps for your stuffing. Finely chop the remaining mushrooms and stems and brown in butter with parsley, shallots, garlic, salt and pepper for about 5 minutes. Put the mixture aside. Brown the mushroom caps on both sides, about 2 minutes. Stuff mushrooms with mixture and put under the broiler for about 5 minutes or until brown. The mushrooms may also be refrigerated until ready to use, and put under the broiler just before serving. Makes 4 servings. Stuffed mushrooms are a great favorite for cocktail parties, but I prefer to serve them as a first course for dinner. They can be made ahead of time.

Bess's Marinated Brussel Sprouts

2 10-oz. pkgs. frozen Brussel
  sprouts
½ c. tarragon vinegar
½ c. wesson oil
1 small clove garlic, chopped fine
1 Tbsp. sugar
1 tsp. salt
Dash pepper sauce
2 Tbsp. sliced green onions

Cook sprouts according to directions. Drain and add other ingredients. Chill 8 hours or overnight. Drain before serving.

Caviar Mold (Spread)

Dissolve 1 envelope gelatin in ½ c. cold sweet milk; when solid put in double boiler to melt. Slightly cool, and add 1 c. Miracle Whip, juice of one lemon, one large jar caviar (about the size of 1 lb. jar peanut butter), fold in ½ pt. whipped cream. Put in a quart size melon mold that has been oiled. Serve surrounded by crackers. So easy and so delicious.

Delicious Spread

(Use two ring molds)

4 cans chicken consomme
5 envelopes of Knox gelatin

Season this with lemon juice, onion juice, Lea and Perrin and Tabasco. Let this congeal in ring molds. Take 2-8 oz. packages of Philadelphia cream cheese, 2 cans of anchovies or anchovy paste, season and add sherry just enough to moisten. Now to build it. You scoop out the inside of the congealed mixture and put the cheese mixture on inside the ring, leaving about 1 inch of gelatin mold for lining. Take the scooped out part, reheat and pour over all. Let set. Delicious and so pretty. Use Melba toast rounds or crackers with this spread.

Seafood Spread

1 3-oz. pkg. cream cheese,
  softened
1 stick butter, room temperature
½ c. cottage cheese
2 tsp. anchovy paste
1 tsp. caraway seeds, crushed
  (optional)
1 tsp. dry mustard
1 tsp. paprika
1 tsp. grated onion
Sandwich bread slices
Pimento, parsley, anchovy,
  shrimp or sardine fillets

In a small mixing bowl beat together cream cheese, butter, cottage cheese, anchovy paste, caraway, mustard, paprika and onion. Cover and chill to blend flavors. Serve at room temperature as a spread. Makes 1½ cups spread. To make canapés: Remove crusts from slices of sandwich bread. Cover each slice with spread. Garnish with pimento and parsley. Cut in two. Place anchovy, shrimp or sardine fillet on each, if desired.

Cheese Spread
(sandwich)

1 Tbsp. flour
½ c. milk
½ lb. chopped sharp or
  mild cheese
1 egg or 2 egg yolks
1 small jar pimento
salt and pepper to taste

Beat eggs; add flour and milk, salt and pepper to taste. Cook until thick and add cheese. Stir until cheese melts and add pimento. If you freeze the pimentos, they will crush easily with a fork. Store for sandwiches.

Shrimp Spread

1 lb. boiled shrimp
2 pkgs. 8-oz. Philadelphia cream
  cheese
2 slices bacon, fried crisp and
  crumbled
½ onion grated
1 green pepper, chopped fine
1 small bottle capers
2 Tbsp. lemon juice, fresh

Add mayonnaise to make a spread and to spread smoothly on crackers or melba toast. Serves 10-12.

Avocado Spread

Mash well one ripe avocado and sprinkle with lemon juice. Salt to taste. Chopped onion is optional. I usually add a little mayonnaise. Serve on wheat wafers or salted crackers. One large avocado will make enough spread for about 50.

Condiment Cream Cheese

1. This is simple, easy and tasty. Just pour 57 sauce and Lea and Perrin generously over a plain package of cream cheese. Serve with crackers.
2. Use 3-oz. pkg. Cream and mix 2 tablespoons anchovy paste with softened cheese. Grate hard boiled egg over top.
3. Mix 1 carton sour cream with 2 small jars of red caviar. Sprinkle parsley flakes on top.
4. Mix 8-oz. cream cheese with ½ bottle or more of chutney.

22

Sardine Pâté

3¾-oz. can sardines
1⅓ c. margarine
1 Tbsp. lemon juice
¾ c. finely chopped olives
½ tsp. minced onion
½ clove garlic
¼ tsp. dry mustard
2 tsp. paprika
⅛ tsp. pepper
¼ tsp. Worcestershire sauce
Dash cayenne

Cream the margarine and sardines to a smooth paste and add the rest of the ingredients, mixing well. Chill and serve with crackers.

Eggplant Caviar

1 large eggplant
1 large onion, chopped
1 green pepper, chopped
1 bud garlic, crushed
Salt and pepper to taste
½ c. olive oil
2 fresh tomatoes, peeled and
  chopped
2 Tbsp. dry white wine

Put a whole eggplant in a 400 degree F. oven and bake until soft, about 1 hour. Sauté onion, garlic and pepper in olive oil until tender, but not brown. Peel and chop eggplant; mix with tomato; add to sauteed seasoning. Add salt and pepper to taste. Add dry white wine. Mix everything thoroughly and continue to cook gently until the mixture is fairly thick. Cool, then refrigerate. Serve well chilled with pumpernickel or thin pieces of ice box rye bread.

Millie's Marinated Carrots

5 c. sliced carrots
1 medium sliced onion
1 small green pepper
1 (10¾ oz. can) cream of tomato
  soup
½ c. salad oil
1 c. sugar
¾ c. vinegar
1 Tbsp. prepared mustard
1 Tbsp. Worcestershire sauce
1 Tbsp. salt
1 Tbsp. pepper

Cook carrots until tender. Drain and cool. Cut other vegetables and mix with cooled vegetables. Mix other ingredients and pour over. Marinate for at least 12 hours. Will keep 2 weeks or longer in refrigerator.

Chili-Tamale Dip

1 can chili (no beans)
1 can hot tamales
1 stick sharp Kraft cheese
1 stick garlic cheese

Heat cheese slowly in skillet. Mash tamales and add chili and tamales to cheese. Season with Tabasco and Worcestershire. Serve hot in chafing dish and sprinkle top with chopped green onions and grated cheese. Serve with tortillas or tostadas.

Crabmeat Dip

2 large pkgs. cream cheese
1 c. frozen crabmeat (or canned)
½ Tbsp. Worcestershire
½ Tbsp. lemon juice
Chives chopped fine
Red pepper and salt to taste

Melt cream cheese in double boiler. Add other ingredients. Serve very hot in chafing dish with melba toast rounds.

Clam Dip

2 3-oz. pkgs. cream cheese
1 7-oz. can minced clam, drained
½ clove garlic, pressed
½ tsp. Worcestershire sauce
2 tsp. lemon juice
2 Tbsp. clam juice

Allow cheese to soften at room temperature. Drain juice of clam. Blend garlic, lemon juice, Worcestershire sauce and cream cheese. Mix in minced clam. Season with salt and pepper to taste. Serve with potato chips.

I Curry Dip

1 pt. mayonnaise
3 Tbsp. catsup
3 tsp. curry powder
1 Tbsp. Worcestershire
1 tsp. onion juice
Salt and pepper to taste

Mix first 5 ingredients together until well blended. Add salt and pepper to taste. Wonderful dip for shrimp, raw cauliflower, carrots, celery hearts, carrot sticks.

Marbles can be used as a safety alarm to let you know when the pot is running dry. The marbles, when the water gets low, will make a fearful racket.

24

II Curry Dip

1 c. mayonnaise
3 Tbsp. catsup
2 to 3 tsp. curry powder
2 tsp. lemon juice
1 Tbsp. Worcestershire sauce
Salt, pepper, garlic to taste

Combine all ingredients, mixing well. Goes well with ham. May be made ahead of time and kept in the refrigerator.

Pink Shrimp Dip

1 pkg. (8-oz.) cream cheese
⅔ c. salad dressing
6 Tbsp. chili sauce
4 Tbsp. lemon juice
½ c. Worcestershire sauce
1 tsp. onion juice or
2 Tbsp. grated onion
2 5-oz. cans shrimp finely cut or
1 lb. fresh boiled shrimp

Blend cheese with seasonings; mix in shrimp. Chill. Can be made the day before. Add a few drops of red food coloring if you want it a bit pinker.

Shrimp or Clam Dip

2 c. shrimp or clam, minced
   (fresh or canned)
¼ c. French dressing
6 Tbsp. salad dressing
1 tsp. Worcestershire sauce
1 large pkg. cream cheese
Grated onion if desired

Blend well and chill. Serve with potato chips, crackers, etc. Makes about 3 cups of dip.

Bleu Cheese Tasty Dip

1 8-oz. pkg. cream cheese
3 oz. Bleu Cheese
3 Tbsp. cream
1 tsp. chives
½ tsp. Worcestershire
Paprika

Combine cheeses and blend until smooth. Add cream, chives, Worcestershire and mix well. Sprinkle with paprika and serve with potato chips.

I Avocado Dip

1 large ripe avocado
1 tsp. grated onion
3 tsp. lemon juice
4 Tbsp. mayonnaise
Few drops of Tabasco
Dash of salt

Mash avocado to smooth paste. Add lemon juice, grated onion, mayonnaise, salt and Tabasco. Refrigerate until ready to serve.

II Avocado Dip

¾ c. sieved avocado
1 clove garlic
1½ tsp. lemon juice
3 Tbsp. parsley, minced
¾ tsp. celery seed
¼ tsp. salt
Few drops Tabasco sauce
1 tsp. grated onion
½ tsp. prepared mustard

Cut avocado in half and remove seed and skin. Force fruit through a sieve. Rub bowl with cut garlic and discard garlic. Add avocado and other ingredients. Blend well. Chill. Yields 1 cup.

California Avocado Dip

1 8-oz. pkg. cream cheese
1 avocado, mashed
3 Tbsp. lemon juice
1 tsp. finely cut onion
1 tsp. salt
Dash of Worcestershire sauce

Allow cream cheese to soften at room temperature. Add avocado a little at a time, blending until smooth. Stir in lemon juice, onion, salt and Worcestershire sauce.

Chili Dip

2 cans chili (without beans)
1 large can tamales (mashed)
1 large onion, grated
1 Tbsp. Worcestershire sauce
2 pods crushed garlic
1 lb. sharp yellow cheese, grated
Tabasco to taste

Heat thoroughly in a double boiler. Use fritoes for a dip. This is a large amount and may be cut in half for smaller amount.

26

Lobster-Cucumber Dip

1 c. lobster meat, chopped fine
Melted butter to sauté
1 cucumber, chopped fine
Mayonnaise to spread
Salt and pepper to season

Sauté lobster meat in melted butter. Cool. Add cucumber, mayonnaise and salt and pepper. Chill. Especially good on whole wheat bread.

Exotic Cheese Dip

1 c. cream cheese
½ c. dairy sour cream
1 pkg. Good Seasons Salad Mix, any one of them (Exotic Herb and Blue Cheese mix)

Mix thoroughly and chill. Dip with potato chips, crackers, etc. Cottage cheese may be substituted for sour cream. Refrigerate for a few days or freeze for later use.

Seafood Dip in Chafing Dish

Cream sauce base
½ c. butter
1 c. flour
2 c. sweet milk
1 small can evaporated milk
1 bunch finely chopped green onions or shallots
1 tsp. paprika
1 tsp. white pepper
½ tsp. salt
2 c. crab meat
1 lb. diced cooked shrimp
1 large can mushrooms
1 c. chopped parsley

Make the cream sauce. Add rest of ingredients. Put in chafing dish. Serves 30 or more. Serve on toast points. If too thick add a small amount of warm milk.

Oyster Dip

1 qt. oysters (chopped and muscle removed)
1 heart of celery chopped
16 green onions chopped very fine
½ bunch parsley chopped
Soy sauce
Red pepper
Bread crumbs
½ stick butter
½ stick butter

Mix butter and sauté chopped oysters. Add onions, celery and parsley and cook about 5 minutes. Add soy sauce until the juice looks brownish. Add enough bread crumbs for spreading consistency. Serve hot in chafing dish with melba rounds.

Rumaki

Marinate chicken livers several hours or over night in wesson oil, garlic, soy sauce and honey. Cut liver in two and wrap around a water chestnut which has been cut into ¼" pieces. Wrap a piece of bacon around liver and water chestnut and secure with a tooth pick. Broil until brown and crisp.

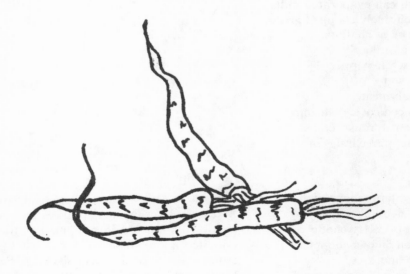

To make carrots curl, sliver very thin lengthwise.
Drop into ice and water. The curl is natural
and permanent.

ICE'S AND FRUIT COURSES

Orange and Berry Ice

2 oranges, grated rind
2 c. berry juice
2 lemons, grated rind
2 c. water

Mix ingredients, sweeten to taste and freeze.

Cranberry Frappé

3 pts. cranberries
1½ pts. sugar
1 c. cream
3 pts. water
1½ lemons - made into juice

Boil cranberries in water. When soft, strain. Add sugar to the juice. Bring to brisk boil. Cool. Add lemon juice and freeze to a soft mush. Then stir in the cream and finish freezing. Serve with meat course. The juice and grated rind of 2 oranges improves this.

Bess Mount's Slush

1 c. sugar
3 c. water

Bring to a quick boil for 2 or 3 minutes cool:

Add:

1 can (#2) crushed pineapple
1 12-oz. can unsweetened
  frozen orange juice
6 ripe bananas, mashed

Mix this to the cooled syrup and freeze but *do not stir.* About 1 hour before serving take out and let it get to a slushy consistency. You may have to watch and return to freezer to keep it icy or slushy. Serve in parfait glasses. Garnish with an orange slice and mint.

If a dish is cracked, but not broken, put it in a
pan of milk and boil it for 45 minutes to
obliterate the crack and strengthen the dish.

Water Melon Baskets

Cut your melon for a basket. Cut the meat with a melon cutter and put in a bowl to chill with ginger ale. Then put back into the melon basket. Leave about 1 inch rind around the edges so it will be durable to handle. Very attractive for patio parties.

Honeydew Melons

Select melon just ripe enough to eat and still pretty and green. Chill and cut into wedges. Put cantaloupe balls in the wedge and garnish with frosted green grapes and then slices of lime. Delicious and pretty.

Bea's Frosted Strawberries

Wash strawberries with the stems and caps on. Let dry on paper toweling until dry. Make fondant: In a saucepan melt 4 cups sugar with 1⅓ cups water and 2 tablespoons glucose or light corn syrup, covered, over low heat until the sugar is dissolved. Lift the lid a few times and with a brush dipped in cold water wash down any sugar crystal clinging to the sides of the pan. Put a candy thermometer in the pan and cook the syrup over moderately high heat until 240 degrees F. Pour the syrup onto a damp smooth surface, preferably marble, and let it cool for 5 minutes. With a metal or wooden scraper work the syrup from the edges toward the center until it becomes opaque. Cover it with a damp towel and let it cool. Knead the fondant, a portion at a time, until it is smooth. At this point the fondant may be covered and refrigerated indefinitely. Transfer the fondant to the top of a double boiler and soften it over hot water. Add ¼ cup kirsch and 3 or 4 drops of red food coloring. Do not let the fondant get too warm or it will lose its shine. If it is too thick to pour easily, thin it with sugar syrup, or stir in a little unbeaten egg white. Dip the pointed ends of the strawberries in it, letting excess run off the berries. Let the fondant dry. These are delicious to eat as well as to garnish.

Fruit Grenadine

1 can (13½ oz.) pineapple chunks drained and chilled or
1 c. fresh pineapple wedges (chilled)
1 pkg. frozen melon balls or
1 c. fresh melon balls, chilled
2 whole oranges, sectioned and chilled
1 grapefruit, sectioned
6 Tbsp. grenadine
6 tsp. kirsch

In a large bowl, lightly toss fruit until well combined. Spoon into 6 dessert dishes. Sprinkle 1 Tbsp. grenadine and 1 tsp. kirsch over each serving. Serve at once. Makes 6 servings.

Cranberry Ice

1 qt. cranberries
4 c. water
2½ c. sugar
Juice of 1 lemon

Heat sugar and water until sugar is dissolved. Remove from heat. Barely cover berries with water and cook until soft. Put through a strainer and add to liquid. Add lemon juice and freeze. When frozen, scrape to give a frosted appearance and return to freezer. Serve with turkey course. This is a delightful starter. Serves 12.

Fruit Juices

Always save fruit juices, both fresh and canned. Some excellent uses for these leftover juices are as follows:

Colored Ice Cubes—Freeze fruit juices in refrigerator tray. Use fruit juice in concentrated form for bright colors. Dilute with water for pastel colors. Serve with lemonades or other fruit drinks.

Fruit Lemonades—Add fruit juices to lemonade for attractive color and flavor.

Appetizers—Serve fruit juices in combination for the first course of luncheon or dinner. The following are suggested combinations:

Pineapple and strawberry juice
Grape, lemon and pineapple juice
Grapefruit, pineapple and orange juice
Grape, orange and lemon juice
Stewed rhubarb and pineapple juice
Loganberry or raspberry and pineapple juice

31

Frozen Appetizers - Freeze sweetened fruit juices in refrigerator tray for 1 hour, stirring every 20 minutes. Loganberry, pomegranate, raspberry or cherry juice are especially good frozen.

Sherbets - Use fruit juices for sherbet or ices. Citrus fruits in combination with other juices are best.

Miscellaneous

Citrus Fruit Rinds - Dry out, grate and keep in covered jars; sprinkle over crumb cake or coffee cake batter before baking. These may also be used for candied orange or grapefruit peel baskets.

Cake Frostings or Icings - Use orange icing for orange rolls; marshmallow or orange rind for gingerbread; whipped cream garnishes for fruit desserts; meringue for lemon or orange pie (or tarts); creamy rice or puddings; orange or lemon fluffs.

Cooked Peach and Pear Halves - Drain fruit, arrange in baking dish with a marshmallow in each center. Combine syrup from the fruit with ⅔ cup sugar and 2 tablespoons lemon juice. Boil for 5 minutes. Pour over fruit; dot with butter and bake in hot oven, basting with syrup. Serve with meat. Use leftover halves of cooked fruits for garnishes or meat platters.

Beverages

Beverages

Fruit Punch
(For 50 People)

4 large cans frozen orange juice
6 large cans frozen lemonade
1 qt. pineapple sherbet

Rinse cans with just a little water and add to juices. Let stand overnight in refrigerator. 4 quarts of Canada Dry Ginger ale (also refrigerated). At the time of serving divide the juice in half; add 2 quarts of ginger ale to ½ of the juice. Just before serving add half the sherbet. Then use other half ingredients the same way. This is good for teas, weddings and church functions, etc.

Instant Spiced Tea

1 lb. 2-oz. jar Tang
1 c. instant tea
2¼ c. sugar
1 pkg. lemonade mix
2 tsp. ground cinnamon
1 tsp. ground cloves

Mix well and place in tightly covered container. Use 1 teaspoon full to cup of boiling water. This will keep for weeks if kept in jars air tight.

Bill's Iced Tea

Dissolve in 2 cups boiling water
   1¾ c. sugar
   9 tea bags

Steep for 5 minutes. Remove tea bags and add juice of 5 lemons, 2 or 3 sprigs of mint. Add enough water to make 1 gallon. It's so refreshing and keeps in ice box several days.

Frozen Daiquiris

Into blender put:
   1 can frozen limeade
   1 limeade can of light rum

Fill blender with ice. Blend well. "Wonderful on a hot day!"

To save daily washing of ash trays, wax them.
Ashes won't linger and disposable tissues
will wipe them clean.

Russian Tea

Tie 1 stick cinnamon and ¼ teaspoon whole cloves in a bag and bring to a boil in 6 cups water. Let simmer 10 minutes before adding 4 teaspoons tea. Strain tea; add juice one lemon, 2 oranges and sweeten to taste. Serves 8.

Mama's Egg Nog
(Merry Christmas)

2 dozen egg yolks, beaten until very light and thick, (it takes a long time). 24 rounded tablespoons sugar beaten in slowly. 3 pints 100 proof whiskey beaten in slowly. 3 pints whipped cream folded in. You may make a day in advance. Put in refrigerator. Beat up by hand each time before serving as the cream rises to top. Serves 24.

Summer Fizz

12 sprigs of fresh mint
1 c. boiling water
1 c. currant jelly
3 c. orange juice
½ c. lemon juice
1 c. cold water
1 qt. ginger ale

Crush the mint in a bowl. Add the boiling water and the cup of jelly. When jelly is melted, cool and strain out the mint. Add the fruit juice and cold water; just before serving, add the ginger ale. Serve real cold with halves of fresh strawberries and sprigs of mint.

Mama's Osceola Chilled Coffee

½ gal. chocolate ice cream
½ gal. vanilla ice cream
1 pt. whipping cream
1 c. sweet milk
1 small jar instant Maxwell House coffee
½ gal. soft ice cream like you get from dairy bar

Bring sweet milk to boiling point; stir in jar of instant coffee; set aside to cool. Mix chocolate and vanilla ice cream until it is consistency of custard; fold in coffee mixture; then fold in whipped cream. Chill thoroughly (not frozen, but slushy) until time to serve. Pour in chilled punch bowl about half; add 1 quart soft ice cream on top; garnish with dash nutmeg. Very rich but so good. Serves 46. Serve in punch cups.

Bea's Coffee Punch

Make regular pot of coffee; add cream and sugar to taste. Chill thoroughly; then add rum to taste. Float whip cream on top. Extra good.

Yucca Flat

1 gal. jug
4 lemons
1½ c. sugar
1 39¢ bottle red cherries

Mix real well until dissolved. Add 1 fifth Vodka. Finish filling jug ¾ full of crushed ice and 2 bottles of 7-Up. Shake well. Finish filling jug with crushed ice. Wrap real well with a towel; shake until all is dissolved.

Whiskey Sour

1 can pink frozen lemonade
1 can whiskey (Bourbon)
1 can water
1 egg white
8 ice cubes

Blend together. Serves 4.

Tom Collins

Blend
  2 Tbsp. frozen lemon juice
  2 tsp. sugar

Put mix in glass and add 1½ oz. gin, 1½ oz. soda. Fill remainder of glass with 7-Up, orange slice and cherry. One drink.

I Champagne Punch

4 bottles champagne
1 bottle brandy
4 qts. soda
1 bottle pale dry sherry
4 oz. orange curacao liqueur
4 oz. marchinico liqueur

Chill thoroughly and put in punch bowl. 2½ gal. - 75 cups.

II Champagne Punch

2 bottles sauterne
1 bottle champagne
1 bottle soda
½ c. lime juice (I have used lemon)
3 tsp. sugar

Dissolve sugar and juice together. All other ingredients should be chilled thoroughly and mixed the last 30 minutes before serving time. 1 Gal. 25 to 30 cups.

Fruit Punch

10 pkg. Kool-Aid, the color
    desired
6 small cans frozen orange juice
6 small cans frozen lemonade
3 46-oz. cans pineapple juice
1 large can crushed pineapple
3 qts. water
5 lb. sugar

Mix all ingredients and put in freezer until you are ready to serve. Take out and let get slushy. Add 5 large bottles ginger ale before putting in punch bowl.

Cranberry Punch

1 16-oz. bottle cranberry
    juice cocktail (2 c.)
1 12-oz. can pineapple juice
    (1½ c.)
1 18-oz. can grapefruit juice
    (2½ c.)

Combine well and chill juices. Makes 8 to 10 servings.

Hot Spiced Apple Juice

1 qt. apple juice
½ lemon, sliced thin
1 stick cinnamon
½ c. brown sugar
1 c. water
½ orange, sliced thin
¼ tsp. nutmeg

Combine all ingredients and heat to the boiling point. Let simmer for 10 minutes. Strain. Serve garnished with sprigs of mint. Serve hot.

38

Coffee Ice Cream Float

1 gal. fresh, strong coffee, cooled
½ gal. vanilla ice cream
1 can (1 lb.) chocolate syrup
1 bottle (12 oz.) sparkling water
  or ginger ale

Mix coffee and syrup. Mash and add one-half of ice cream. Stir until melted. Just before serving, add sparkling water. Pour into chilled punch bowl, containing about a six inch cube of ice. Top with spoonsful of the remainder of ice cream. Will serve 50 persons. Served at a tea given at Governor's Palace in Santa Fe. Delicious!

Cranberry Julep

¼ c. sugar
¾ c. water
1 can frozen orange juice
1 pt. bottle cranberry juice
2 Tbsp. lemon juice
1 c. ginger ale

Add water to sugar; place over heat and simmer five minutes. Cool. Add orange juice, cranberry and lemon juice. Mix well and chill. Add ginger ale just before serving. Serves 15.

Hot Pineapple Egg Nog

8 eggs
1 c. sugar
6 c. pineapple juice
1 pt. whipping cream

Separate egg yolks and whites. Add ½ cup sugar to egg yolks and beat thoroughly. Bring pineapple juice to boil. Add cream. Pour over egg yolks and heat, stirring constantly. Beat egg whites with ½ cup sugar and fold into hot mixture. Serve with grated orange peel. Serves 10 or 12. Delicious chilled, too.

39

Pink Punch

2 pkg. (10-oz. each) frozen sliced
  strawberries
1 bottle 4/ 5 qt. sauterne (chilled)
  Ice block (made in a 2 or 3 c.
  mold)
6 oz. (¾ c.) cognac
1 bottle (26 oz.) champagne
  chilled

Shortly before serving, turn the strawberries into a large punch bowl with the sauterne, lemon and orange slices. Allow to thaw at room temperature just enough to separate the berries. Add the ice block, cognac and champagne. Stir gently and serve.

*A pinch of pepper rolled in cotton and saturated
in oil will stop earache.*

*For a toothache use equal quantities of alum
and salt and apply to tooth.*

*To relieve a sprain, bathe and
wrap in hot vinegar.*

Breads
Biscuits
Rolls
Muffins
Sandwiches
Cornmeal
Cookery

Breads
Biscuits
Rolls
Muffins
Sandwiches
Cornmeal Cookery

Delicious Biscuit Variations

Biscuits are popular three times a day the year around and few tire of them, yet variations from the standard recipe are welcomed even by the most confirmed biscuit-and-jelly eater. Cheese biscuits are particularly pleasing for evening meals and are also excellent accompaniments for the salad luncheon. For Sunday evening supper, afternoon tea, luncheon, or any other occasion when a hot bread plays a leading role on the menu, lemon-filled biscuits are delightful.

Butterscotch "rolls" are easily contrived from ordinary biscuit dough by sprinkling the dough with brown sugar, rolling it jelly-roll fashion and cutting it into slices to be baked in muffin pans. Fruit-filled biscuits are another version of the biscuit formula which will meet with a happy reception at the family dining table.

Cheese Biscuits

2 c. soft wheat flour
2 tsp. baking powder
1 tsp. salt
2/4 Tbsp. shortening
¾ c. milk
4 Tbsp. butter (softened)
⅔ c. nippy cheese (grated)

Sift flour; add baking powder and salt. Sift together, cut fat into mixture; add milk. Mix into a soft dough. Place on floured board. Knead lightly. Roll very thin; spread with softened butter and sprinkle liberally with cheese. Roll as for a jelly roll. Cut into one inch slices. Place on baking sheet, brush with melted butter. Bake 12 to 15 minutes in a hot oven (400 degrees F.). Serve hot with salads.

Lemon Tea Biscuits

2 c. soft wheat flour
2 tsp. baking powder
1 tsp. salt
2-4 Tbsp. Butter
¾ c. milk
2 tsp. grated lemon rind

Mixture #2:

4 Tbsp granulated sugar
2 Tbsp. lemon juice
2 Tbsp. butter
1 tsp. grated lemon rind

Sift flour, measure; add baking powder and salt. Sift together. Cut butter into mixture. Add milk. Mix into soft dough. Toss on floured board. Knead lightly. Roll very thin. Cut with small cutter. Spread half of biscuits with Mixture #2. Top with the remaining biscuits. Bake 12 to 15 minutes in a hot oven 425 degrees F. Serve hot with tea.

Angel Biscuits

1 pkg. yeast
2 Tbsp. lukewarm water
1 c. shortening
5 c. unsifted flour
3 tsp. baking powder
¼ c. sugar
2 tsp. salt
1 tsp. soda
1½-2 c. buttermilk at room
  temperature

Dissolve yeast in water. Sift all dry ingredients together. Cut shortening in ½ of dry ingredients. Add remaining dry ingredients. Pour yeast in buttermilk; add to dry ingredients. Roll on floured board. Cut biscuits with cutter (not too thin). Better if dough has been chilled. If you like, freeze cut biscuits and bake later allowing time for biscuits to thaw and rise in a warm place (possibly 2 to 3 hours). Bake in 400 degree oven for 20 minutes. Delicious!

Pastry Biscuits

2 sticks butter
2⅓ c. flour
Ice water

Slice butter into bowl and work flour in with hands until consistency of cornmeal. Add ice water to moisten, as little as possible, working with a fork. Shape dough into ball, wrap in waxed paper and chill. Roll dough thin and cut into small biscuits. Bake in hot oven, 450 degrees on ungreased griddle. This dough may be prepared ahead and will keep in the refrigerator for a week. It is delicious to serve with coffee or sherry, and also makes good strawberry shortcake. This recipe came from Louisiana and I have used it for years. You can use it for so many dishes.

Pork Sausage Biscuits

Use regular biscuit dough and make into tiny biscuits and cook golden brown. Fry sausage into tiny cakes, place one in each biscuit and serve piping hot.

44

Mary Elizabeth's Cheese Biscuits

1 stick butter
1 roll garlic cheese
1 c. flour
Pinch of cayenne

Cream softened butter and cheese; add flour and cayenne. Roll into balls about ½ inch in diameter. Bake in a 275 degree oven 6 to 8 minutes. Freeze the balls, bag them, and cook as needed. Serves 4 dozen.

Cora's Sausage Drops

2 c. Bisquick
1 lb. hot pork sausage
½ lb. extra sharp cheese

Grate cheese and mix the Bisquick, cheese and sausage. Drop small balls on cookie sheet from a teaspoon. Bake 350 degrees until brown. Serve hot.

Corn Meal Rolls

1½ c. flour
¾ c. cornmeal
2 Tbsp. sugar
1 tsp. salt
3 Tbsp. baking powder
¼ tsp. soda

Sift these ingredients together.

2 heaping Tbsp. shortening
1 egg, well beaten

Sweet milk to make soft dough. Chop shortening into dry ingredients and add well beaten egg and milk to make a soft dough. Roll on a board floured with corn meal and shape as for Parker house rolls. Let rise 20 minutes before baking in 350 degree oven.

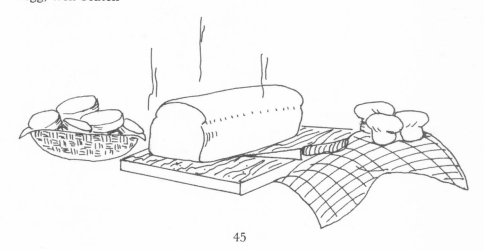

45

Buttermilk Rolls

2 c. buttermilk
3 c. all-purpose flour
3 tsp. baking powder
1 tsp. baking soda
1 Tbsp. sugar
1 tsp. salt
1 pkg. dry yeast
4 Tbsp. shortening

Allow buttermilk to stand until it reaches room temperature. Sift together dry ingredients. Stir in dry yeast. Add shortening and mix well. Stir in buttermilk and beat well. Knead lightly on a lightly floured board and roll out to ½ inch thickness. Cut with small biscuit cutter and place in greased pans, placing close together. Let rise 2 hours; then bake at 450 degrees for about 20 minutes. Makes about 4 dozen rolls.

Rolls

6 c. enriched flour
1 c. milk
4 Tbsp. sugar
4 tsp. salt
6 Tbsp. shortening
1 c. cold water
2 pkgs. yeast,
  (dry granular)
1 egg

One mixing, not a bit of kneading and only one rising. Sounds too good to be true; but, believe me, that's all there is to making these fresh baked feathery yeast rolls. Makes three dozen rolls.

Mama's Rolls

Heat nearly to boiling point:
  1 qt. milk or 2 c. water and
  2 c. milk
Add:
  1 c. sugar
  1 c. oleo or 2 sticks
Stir until dissolved. Let cool
  to lukewarm.
Mix:
  3 yeast cakes in 1 c.
  lukewarm water. Add to
  liquid mixture when cool.
Mix well:
  8 to 10 c. plain flour
  2 tsp. baking powder
  1 tsp. salt
  1 tsp. soda

Add to liquid mixture, making a medium stiff batter. Cover with cloth; let rise until double in bulk. Then add flour to make a stiff dough. Knead for about 10 minutes. Roll out and cut to your desire; let rise before baking. Will keep for a few days in ice box. Use as you need it.

Mama's Ice Box Rolls

1 c. lard
1 mashed potato
1 qt. water
2 qts. flour
⅔ c. sugar
1 Tbsp. salt
1 yeast cake
1 egg

Cream lard and sugar, add potato; dissolve yeast cake in water and let set 1 hour. Add beaten egg, then 2 to 3 qts. of flour and put in ice box. Pinch off what you need; roll out and cut; let rise 1½ hours before baking.

Hot Rolls

1 qt. sweet milk
1 c. sugar
1 c. Crisco

Bring to boiling point and let cool. Add 2 pkgs. yeast dissolved in ½ c. warm water; beat in 6 c. flour and *let rise 1 hour* or until double in size.

Then add:
  3 c. flour
  1 Tbsp. salt
1 tsp. soda
1 heaping tsp. baking powder

Mix well into other mixture; knead well; make into rolls; let rise until double in size and bake or place in refrigerator and use when needed. Just pinch off what you need, roll and cut; let rise and bake.

Mammy's Three Hour Rolls

Crumble 2 yeast cakes in a large bowl; sprinkle 3 tablespoons sugar over yeast. Mix well and pour over this 1 cup milk mixed with 1 cup warm water. Sift in enough self-rising flour to make a soft dough. Work in ½ cup shortening. Knead well and let rise 2 hours. Make into rolls; let rise 1 hour. Bake in moderate oven. This will make 48 dinner rolls.

Toasted Ham Finger Rolls

Slice bread very thin and spread with softened horseradish butter. Place a slice of paper thin baked ham on each slice. Roll and toast under broiler. Turn to brown evenly on all sides.

47

Butter Rolls

Heat milk in shallow pan. Roll biscuit dough thin and sprinkle with sugar, dots of butter and cinnamon, (nutmeg if desired). Roll and cut into small slices and drop in hot milk; then cook in oven until done and light brown. Extra good!

Never Fail Dumplings

1½ c. flour
Salt
3 Tbsp. shortening
1 egg, beaten
5 Tbsp. water

Mix flour and other ingredients. Divide into ball and roll thin. Let dry 20 minutes; cut. Drop into broth and cook 15 minutes.

Fluffy Dumplings

1 egg
¾ c. milk
2 c. flour
3 tsp. baking powder
½ tsp. salt
1 tsp. melted shortening

Mix well; roll very thin; cut in small squares. Drop in hot boiling broth or liquid.

Fritter Batter
(Joyce Cleveland)

1⅓ c. flour
1½ tsp. baking powder
¼ tsp. salt
⅔ c. milk
1 egg well beaten

Sift together flour, salt, baking powder; blend milk and egg together; add gradually to dry ingredients. Stir in desired fruit or meat. Drop from teaspoon into hot fat 365 to 375 degrees 2 to 5 minutes. Drain on paper toweling.

For apple fritters: reduce flour and milk ⅓ cup. Add 3 teaspoons confectioners sugar, enough for 2 medium size sour apples; peel, core and cut in narrow strips about ¾ inch long (1½ cups cut). Sift over with confectioners sugar. Serves 4 to 6.

For banana fritters: Peel bananas cut in havles lengthwise and then crosswise. Roll in powdered sugar, then dip in fritter batter. (To make ½ fritter batter increase milk to ½ cup). Drop in hot deep far; sift over with confectioners sugar.

For corn fritters: Increase salt and pepper; use whole kernel corn (1½ cups). Serve with maple syrup.

Mama Bates' Doughnuts

My mother made these by the dozens and dozens. She fed her three sons and their friends for every occasion.

4 c. flour
4 tsp. baking powder
½ tsp. salt
Flavoring to taste
⅓ c. melted shortening
4 egg yolks
1 c. sugar
1 c. milk

Roll to ½ inch thick. Cut with doughnut cutter. Fry in deep hot shortening. As they brown and come to the top, take out and drain on brown paper. Roll in sugar.

Mama's Drop Doughnuts

1 c. sugar
2 eggs
1 Tbsp. melted butter
3 c. plain flour
1 c. sweet milk
2 tsp. baking powder
1 tsp. vanilla

Cream sugar and eggs; then add the other ingredients. Drop from a teaspoon into hot shortening and cook until brown. Drain and roll in powdered sugar.

Peabody Vanilla Muffins

4 c. flour
2 c. sugar
1 pt. milk
4 tsp. baking powder
1 stick butter
4 eggs
4 Tbsp. vanilla
Pinch salt

Sift dry ingredients into mixing bowl, make well in center. Add slightly cooled melted shortening to beaten eggs, milk, vanilla and salt mixture; at once, add this to dry ingredients. Stir quickly, only 15-20 seconds. (The batter will appear lumpy.) Immediately pour into greased muffin tins (fill ⅔ full). Bake in 325 degree oven 15-20 minutes. Remove at once from pans. Makes 48 muffins.

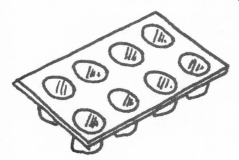

Blueberry Muffins

2 c. flour (plain)
1 tsp. salt
3 tsp. baking powder
2 Tbsp. sugar
¾ c. blueberries
¾ c. milk
3 Tbsp. melted shortening
1 beaten egg

Add milk mixture to flour mixture. Stir until dry mixture is moistened, but not enough to make batter smooth. Fill greased muffin pans ⅔ full and bake in hot oven 400 degrees for 15 minutes or until done.

Plain Muffins

2 c. cake flour
¾ tsp. salt
¼ c. sugar
2 tsp. baking powder
2 eggs
2 Tbsp. melted butter
¾ c. milk

Measure sifted flour. Re-sift with remaining dry ingredients. Beat eggs until light; blend in melted butter and milk. Stir liquid into dry ingredients with a few swift strokes. Batter will be lumpy but do not attempt to beat out lumps. Overhandling makes muffins tough and soggy. Pour batter into greased muffin tins, filling them about half full. Bake 15 to 20 minutes at 425 degrees. Remove from pans as soon as baked. Makes 24 muffins.

Variations for Plain Muffins

1. Apple muffins: Add ½ cup chopped apple and ½ teaspoon cinnamon.
2. Blueberry muffins: Increase sugar to ⅓ cup, butter to 4 tablespoons and add 1 cup of flour-coated blueberries.
3. Ham muffins: Add ½ cup of chopped, cooked ham.
4. Pineapple muffins: Add ½ cup well drained, crushed pineapple.
5. Orange-Pecan muffins: Make batter, using juice of 1 orange and decrease milk to ⅜ of a cup. Add ⅔ of a cup of chopped nuts.
6. Bacon muffins: Add 3 tablespoons of diced, cooked bacon.
7. Date muffins: Add ½ cup of sliced, pitted dates.

When driving a nail into plaster, dip nail into hot water or melted paraffin; this will prevent plaster from cracking.

Sesame-Cheese Bread

1 long loaf French bread
¼ c. sesame seed
½ c. grated sharp cheese
¼ c. butter or oleo

Split bread lengthwise. Combine remaining ingredients. Spread on cut side of bread. Cut diagonally in serving size pieces through to crust. Place on baking sheet and heat in moderate overn (350 degrees F.) 15 minutes. Serve at once. Makes 6 servings.

Dilly Casserole Bread

1 pkg. active dry yeast
¼ c. warm water
1 c. creamed cottage cheese
  heated to lukewarm
2 Tbsp. sugar
1 Tbsp. minced onion
1 Tbsp. butter
2 Tbsp. dill seed
1 tsp. salt
¼ tsp. soda
2¼ to 2½ c. flour
1 egg

Soften yeast in lukewarm water. Combine in mixing bowl the cottage cheese, sugar, onion, butter, dill seed, salt, soda, unbeaten egg and the softened yeast. Add flour to form a stiff dough, beating well after each addition. Cover; let rise in warm place (85 to 90 degrees F.) until light and double in size (50 to 60 minutes).
Stir dough down. Turn into well greased 1½ or 2-quart casserole and let rise in warm place until light (30 to 40 minutes). Bake at 350 degrees F. 40 to 50 minutes or until golden brown. Brush with soft butter and sprinkle with salt. Makes one round loaf.

Onion-Cheese Supper Bread

Absolutely delicious. Serve hot with cold cuts, sliced and tossed salad

½ c. chopped onions
1 Tbsp. fat
1 beaten egg
½ c. milk
1½ c. pkg. Bisquick
1 c. grated cheese
1 Tbsp. poppy seed
2 Tbsp. melted butter or oleo

Cook onions in fat till tender and light brown. Combine egg and milk; add to Bisquick and stir only till dry ingredients are just moistened. Add onion and half of cheese. Spread dough in greased 8 X 1½ inch round baking dish (like pie pyrex). Sprinkle top with remaining cheese and poppy seed. Drizzle melted butter over all. Bake in hot oven 400 degrees 20 to 25 minutes. Serve hot. Serves 6.

51

Irish Soda Bread

4 c. sifted flour
¼ c. sugar
1 tsp. salt
1 tsp. baking powder
1 tsp. baking soda
2 Tbsp. caraway seeds
¼ c. butter or margarine
2 c. seedless raisins
1⅓ c. buttermilk
1 egg

Sift flour, sugar, salt, baking powder and soda together; stir in caraway seeds. With a pastry blender or 2 knives (scissor fashion) cut in butter till mixture looks like coarse cornmeal; stir in raisins. Combine buttermilk with egg and stir into flour mixture till just moistened. Turn dough onto lightly floured surface and knead lightly till smooth. Shape into round loaf and place in a greased 2 quart casserole. With a sharp knife cut a cross in the top about ½ inch deep. Brush top with a slightly beaten egg yolk or cream. Bake at 375 degrees for about 1 hour and 10 minutes or until done when tested with a toothpick. Turn out and cool on rack. Serve warm or cold with butter. Makes good toast. Probably the easiest foods to prepare in honor of St. Patrick are corned beef and Irish soda bread. Hardly anything could be simpler - or please your man more. Irish soda bread is a quick bread made with caraway seeds and raisins which has a nutty sweetness all its own. It is similar to a biscuit dough (not yeast dough) and just as easy to make. Serve while still warm from the oven.

Southern Spoon Bread

1 qt. sweet milk
1½ c. cornmeal
4 Tbsp. butter
1 tsp. salt
4 eggs

Boil milk and add cornmeal. Cook to a mush; add beaten yolks and last beaten egg whites. Cook in a hot oven about 40 minutes. You can add 1 cup of grated cheese before adding egg whites; if so, then add more milk. This recipe was handed down from my great grandmother.

Quick Light Bread

1 yeast cake
1 egg
2 c. warm water
7 c. flour
3 Tbsp. butter or Crisco
1 Tbsp. salt
3 Tbsp. sugar

Soften yeast in cup lukewarm water. Put warm water, sugar, salt, and beaten egg in mixing bowl. Add 4 cups flour and beat until smooth; then, add remaining flour and beat until well mixed. Let rise until double in bulk. Beat down and pour into two well greased loaf pans. Let come to top of pans and bake in quick oven. Grease with melted butter when done. Bake at 350 degrees about 30 minutes. Makes 2 loaves.

French Bread

Scald ½ c. milk.
Boil 1 c. water.
Combine and cool
   to lukewarm.
Dissolve 1 cake yeast in
   ¼ c. lukewarm water
and add to milk-water
mixture with:
   1½ Tbsp. shortening
   1 Tbsp. sugar
Measure into a large bowl:
   4 c. all-purpose flour
   2 tsp. salt
   ½ Tbsp. sugar

Make a hole in center and pour in the liquid mixture. Stir thoroughly but do not knead. The dough will be soft. Cover with damp cloth and set in warm place to rise, (about 2 hours). Break down the dough and place on lightly floured board and pat into two equal oblongs. Form each into a French loaf by rolling dough toward you. Continue rolling, pressing outward with the hands and tapering the dough toward the ends until a long, thin roll is achieved. Place the 2 loaves on a buttered cookie sheet, cut diagonal slits across the top with sharp-pointed scissors to form customary indentations. Set in warm place to rise to somewhat less than double in bulk. Preheat oven to 400 degrees F. On bottom of oven place a pie tin filled with ½ inch of boiling water. Bake 15 minutes at 400 degrees F.; then 30 minutes at 350 degrees F. Five minutes before bread has finished baking, brush loaves with melted butter and return to oven.

Golden Batter Bread

1 c. milk
½ c. warm water
2 pkgs. dry yeast
¼ c. margarine or butter
¼ c. sugar
2 tsp. salt
1 egg, beaten
4½ c. sifted plain flour
1 can (3½ oz.) onion rings, crumbled

Scald milk till it bubbles; remove from heat and add margarine, sugar and salt; cool to lukewarm and sprinkle yeast in warm water. Stir till dissolved; add to milk mixture. Stir in beaten egg and 3 cups flour; spoon beat till smooth. Stir in rest of flour, making stiff batter. Let rise. Stir in crumbled onion rings; put in 2 well greased round or loaf pans. Let rise again. Bake at 350 degrees F. for 30-40 minutes.

Yeast Bread
(8-10 loaves)

¾ c. sugar
½ c. shortening
2½ Tbsp. salt
⅓ c. warm water
1 egg
1 qt. scalded milk
1 qt. boiling water
3 pkgs. dry yeast
20 to 25 c. flour

Dissolve yeast in ⅓ cup warm water. In a large bowl put sugar, shortening and salt. Stir in milk and water. Cool this to lukewarm and let stand 5 minutes. Add yeast mixture. Gradually add flour until mixture is stiff. Add egg while working in flour. Work in remaining flour with hand. Let stand 5 minutes. Knead on floured board for 10 minutes. Form in a big ball and put in greased bowl; turn over so top will be greased. Cover and let stand until rises to double. Then knead 5 minutes more. Divide into 8 to 10 pieces. Shape on floured board into 7 X 14 inch loaves. Put into greased pans and let rise to double. Bake 30 minutes at 400 degrees F.

Mama's Homemade Bread

1 yeast cake
½ c. lukewarm water
⅔ c. shortening
1 tsp. salt
½ c. sugar
1 c. mashed potatoes
1 c. scalded milk
2 eggs
6-8 c. sifted flour

Mash the potatoes and measure. Add shortening, sugar, salt, eggs and cream well. Dissolve yeast in lukewarm water. Add to scalded milk. Add this to the mashed potatoes; add sifted flour to make a stiff dough. Toss on floured board and knead well. Divide in half and place in well greased loaf pans. Let rise to top of pan. Start bread to cooking in preheated 250 degree oven. Increase to 350 degrees as bread cooks. Cook 30 to 40 minutes. When it begins to brown, brush top with melted butter.

54

Nut Bread

1 pkg. dates
1 c. pecans
1 c. brown sugar
1 c. boiling water
½ tsp. soda
1½ c. flour
Pinch salt
1 egg
1½ tsp. baking powder

Put soda on dates, over which pour the boiling water and let stand until cold. Add egg yolk, sugar, pecans, flour, salt and baking powder. Fold in well beaten egg white and one half teaspoon vanilla. Put in greased loaf pan. Cook in slow oven.

Orange Nut Bread

2¼ c. sifted plain flour
2 tsp. baking powder
½ tsp. soda
¾ tsp. salt
⅞ c sugar
¾ c. chopped nuts
½ c. raisins
¼ c. ground orange rind
1 egg, well beaten
½ c. milk
½ c. orange juice
2 Tbsp. melted oleo or Crisco

Sift flour once; measure, add baking powder, soda, salt and sugar and sift together. Add nuts, raisins and orange rind. Combine beaten eggs, milk and orange juice. Add to flour mixture with melted oleo or Crisco; mix until all flour is dampened and fruit and nuts are well distributed. Turn the batter into greased 9 X 5 X 3 loaf pan. Bake 1 hour at 350 degrees or until done. Let cool in pan 10 minutes; turn out, let cool completely before wrapping and storing.

Date Nut Pumpkin Bread

1 c. butter
1½ c. sugar
4 eggs
2 c. canned pumpkin
3 c. sifted flour
1 tsp. salt
2 tsp. baking powder
½ tsp. baking soda
1 Tbsp. cinnamon
1 8-oz. pkg. diced dates
½ c. raisins
1 c. chopped nuts

Cream butter and sugar. Add eggs, one at a time, beating after each addition. Add pumpkin and mix well. Sift flour, salt, baking powder, soda, and cinnamon together. Add to pumpkin mixture and beat well. Add dates, raisins, and nuts; mix until well coated and mixed well through mixture. May be baked in regular loaf pans or in one lb. coffee cans, 13 oz. salted peanut cans, or any other baking container. Fill container ¾ full with batter. Bake at 375 degrees for 60-75 minutes. Makes 2 5 X 9-inch loaf pans or one 3-quart casserole or 2 pound size coffee cans.

I Wilma's Pumpkin Bread

3½ c. plain flour
2 tsp. soda
1½ tsp. salt
2 tsp. cinnamon
1½ tsp. nutmeg
½ tsp. cloves
4 eggs
⅔ c. water
3 c. sugar
2 c. cooked pumpkin
1 c. oil
1 tsp. vanilla
⅔ c. raisins or dates
½ c. nuts

Sift flour and measure; add soda, salt and spices. Toss nuts and fruits lightly into flour mixture. Beat sugar and oil in mixer at slow speed. Add eggs one at a time; add pumpkin; add flour mixture, water and vanilla. Beat until mixed thoroughly. Bake at 350 degrees in 4 one pound coffee cans for 1 hour or 2 greased loaf pans for 1 hour. Serve warm with butter or cold.

II Betty's Pumpkin Bread

Sift:
   3 c. flour
   1 tsp. cinnamon
   1 tsp. nutmeg
   1½ tsp. salt
   2 tsp. soda
Cream:
   3 c. sugar
   1 c. oil

Combine and beat in 4 eggs, 1 cup canned pumpkin and ⅔ cup water. Grease and flour 3 one lb. coffee cans. Divide into equal parts; cook 1 hour at 350 degrees.

III Mary's Pumpkin Bread

3 c. sugar
1 c. salad oil
3 c. plain flour
1 tsp. nutmeg
2 c. canned pumpkin or
   fresh cooked
1 tsp. salt
1 tsp. soda
1 tsp. cinnamon
1 tsp. cloves
2 eggs

Cream sugar, oil and eggs; add pumpkin. Sift other ingredients together and mix well with creamed ingredients. Mix real well. Bake in stem pan or bundt pan 1 hour 15 minutes at 350 degrees.

I Florence's Banana Nut Bread

1 box yellow cake mix
½ tsp. soda
2 large or 3 small ripe bananas
Less: ¼ c. water called for on cake mix.
1 c. chopped nuts

Mash bananas; add soda; mix well and set aside. Mix cake mix, less ¼ c. water called for on the box. Then add to banana mixture. Add nuts. Bake in oven 300-325 degrees in tube pan or loaf pan. Bake 1 hour or more until tested done. Cake freezes nicely.

II Mama's Banana Quick Bread

⅓ c. Crisco
⅔ c. sugar
2 eggs, slightly beaten
1¾ c. sifted plain flour
2¾ tsp. baking powder
½ tsp. salt
1 c. mashed ripe bananas

Preheat oven to 350 degrees. Beat shortening until creamy and glossy or 2 minutes at medium speed with electric mixer. Gradually add sugar, beating until light and fluffy after each addition. Add eggs and beat until thick and pale lemon in color. Sift dry ingredients; add alternately with bananas; blend thoroughly. Grease bottom only of a loaf pan 4½ X 8½ X 3 inches. Turn batter into pan. Bake 60 to 70 minutes or until done. Let bread partially cool in pan before turning on rack.

III Banana Bread

¾ c. (6 oz.) butter
1¼ c. sugar
4 eggs
2 c. mashed bananas (5 or 6 bananas)
3½ c. sifted plain flour
4 tsp. baking powder
1 tsp. baking soda

Cream butter and sugar. Beat in the eggs. Sift dry ingredients together and add alternately with mashed bananas, blending well. Dust 2 loaf pans with flour and turn half of batter into each. Bake in moderate oven 350 degrees for one hour or until tested done. Makes 2 loaves 8¼ X 4½ inches.

Beep's Homemade Banana Bread

Cream:
  ½ c. Crisco or 1 cube oleo
  1 c. sugar
  2 eggs beaten well
Add:
  2 c. sifted flour
  1 tsp. baking soda
  1 pinch salt

Mash 3 ripe bananas (blender or by hand). Add nuts (and dates, optional). Mix all well. Bake in tube pan or loaf pan for 1 hour at 350 degrees.

Banana Nut Bread

Sift together:
  1½ c. flour
  1 tsp. baking powder
  ½ tsp. soda
  ½ tsp. salt
Cream well:
  1 stick butter
  ¾ c. sugar
  2 egg yolks beaten well
  3 bananas (mashed)
  1 c. chopped pecans
  1 tsp. vanilla

Fold dry ingredients into creamed mixture and blend well. Fold in 2 egg whites that have been beaten stiff. Pour in loaf pan and bake at 350 degrees for 1 hour.

Orange Bread

3 c. flour
4 tsp. baking powder
¾ tsp. salt
1 c. sugar
1 beaten egg
¼ c. orange rind grated
1 c. orange juice
⅓ c. salad oil or Crisco

Sift flour; measure; add baking powder, salt and sugar. Sift again. Combine egg, orange rind, juices and salad oil. Pour into flour mixture and stir just enough to moisten the dry ingredients; *do not beat*. Turn into a greased loaf pan 9½ X 5½ X 3 and bake in 350 degree oven about 1 hour or until done. Remove from pan. Cool. Best to wait a day to slice it and serve.

58

Apricot Bread

4 c. sifted, plain flour
2 tsp. baking soda
1 lb. dried apricots
1¾ c. water
1 tsp. salt
2 eggs, beaten
2 c. sugar
¾ c. Crisco
1 tsp. cinnamon
½ tsp. cloves
½ tsp. nutmeg

Line 2 9 X 5 inch loaf pans with waxed paper. Sift together flour and soda. Cut apricots in small pieces. Combine apricots, water, sugar, Crisco, spices and salt in sauce pan. Cook 5 minutes. Cool. Add eggs and flour mixture to apricot mixture, mixing until blended. Divide equally into loaf pans. Bake in moderate oven 350 degrees for 1 hour or until done.

Apricot Nut Bread

½ c. dried apricots, diced
1 egg
1 c. sugar
2 Tbsp. melted butter
2 c. sifted flour
3 tsp. baking powder
¼ tsp. soda
¾ tsp. salt
½ c. orange juice, strained
¼ c. water
1 c. blanched almonds, sliced

Soak apricots ½ hour. Drain and grind. Beat egg until light. Stir in sugar and mix well. Stir in butter. Sift flour with baking powder, soda and salt. Add alternately with orange juice and water. Add nuts and apricots. Mix well. Bake in loaf pan 1½ hours at 350 degrees F. This bread when spread with cream cheese and candied ginger makes a delightful tea sandwich.

Pineapple-Date Bread

1 beaten egg
⅓ c. milk
⅓ c. salad oil or melted Crisco
1 9-oz. can or 1 c. crushed
   pineapple
1 c. chopped walnuts
1 c. chopped dates
3 c. sifted plain flour
3 tsp. baking powder
¾ tsp. salt
¼ tsp. soda

Combine egg, milk, oil, pineapple, nuts and dates. Sift together dry ingredients; add to first mixture and stir just to moisten. Bake in greased 9½ X 5 X 3 loaf pan in 350 degree oven for 55 minutes.

Cranberry Bread

2 c. flour
½ tsp. salt
1 c. sugar
1¼ tsp. baking powder
½ tsp. baking soda (scant)

Sift above twice; then put juice and finely chopped rind of 1 orange in cup with 2 tablespoon shortening. Fill cup with boiling water to ¾ cup full. Add with above and 1 beaten egg to dry ingredients. Also, 1 cup chopped nut meat (preferably pecans) and 1 cup raw cranberries cut in half. Bake 1 hour at 350 degrees. Nice for morning entertaining. Makes 2 loaves.

Peanut Butter Bacon Bread

1 c. sugar
1 Tbsp. melted shortening
1 c. milk
1 egg, well beaten
1 c. chopped unsalted peanuts
1 c. peanut butter
½ tsp. salt
2 c. flour
3 tsp. baking powder
1 c. crisp bacon chips

Mix sugar, shortening and milk with beaten egg. Add peanut butter. Mix in salt, flour and baking powder. Add nuts and bacon chips and let stand in greased, floured pan for 20 minutes. Bake at 350 degrees for 1 hour or until done.

Quick Coffee Cake

2½ c. sifted flour
1¼ c. brown sugar
½ tsp. salt
½ c. shortening
2 tsp. baking powder
½ tsp. soda
1 egg, well beaten
¾ c. buttermilk
½ tsp. cinnamon
½ c. chopped pecans

Mix the flour, sugar and salt. Cut in the shortening with a blender until it looks like cornmeal. Take out ¾ cup. To the remaining mixture add the baking powder, soda, and mix well. Stir in the egg and buttermilk. Pour into 2 greased square cake tins. Mix the ¾ cup of flour mixture with ½ teaspoon cinnamon and nut meats. Sprinkle over the top of the batter and bake at 400 degrees for 20 to 25 minutes. Serve hot or reheated, but not cold.

Helen Corbitt's Coffee Cake

1¾ c. sugar
¾ c. butter
1⅛ c. milk
3 c. sifted flour
4 tsp. baking powder
1 tsp. salt
4 egg whites
2 c. chopped pecans
1⅛ c. brown sugar
2 Tbsp. cinnamon
¾ c. flour
¾ c. butter

Cream the sugar and butter until soft and smooth. Add the milk alternately with the flour, baking powder and salt. Fold in the beaten stiff egg whites. Pour into a buttered pan and cover with topping made from remaining ingredients.
Mix together until it looks like cake crumbs. Spread over the top and bake at 350 degrees for 40 to 45 minutes. Cut in squares. If any are left over, use them for crumb pudding or roll balls of vanilla ice cream in the crumbs and serve with butterscotch sauce.

Cheese Puff

Place 4 slices of bread, with crust trimmed off, in the bottom of a buttered baking dish. Sprinkle with 1 cup grated cheddar cheese; add 2 beaten eggs, 1½ cups milk, ½ teaspoon salt and pepper and dry mustard to taste. Top with 4 more slices of trimmed bread and another ½ cup grated cheese, ½ cup milk. Let this set for 3 or 4 hours. It can be made the night before and put in the ice box. Then take out and set dish in a pan of water and bake at 350 degrees until custard is set and bread is puffy, like a souffle. Bake about 40 minutes. This is a good dish for breakfast, lunch or supper. If it is a main dish, a green tossed salad or a tomato salad and a vegetable is a delightful meal.

Southern Waffles

1½ c. sifted flour (self-rising)
1½ c. self-rising cornmeal
¼ c. brown sugar
1½ c. sweet milk
3 eggs
¾ c. melted fat

Sift flour, sugar and meal. Beat eggs and combine with milk and fat. Add to dry ingredients and stir only to moisten and mix ingredients. Bake in hot waffle irons until golden brown and steam no longer escapes.

Note: For extra lightness beat the egg whites separately and fold in last.

Variations: Cheese waffles. Add 1 cup ¼ lb. grated cheese to batter. Serve topped with creamed vegetables, creamed ham or creamed chicken.

Shrimp Creole: Top crisp waffles with your favorite shrimp creole. Serve with tossed green salad.

Chili Bean Stack: Spoon hot chili between two crisp waffles. Sprinkle lightly with cheese.

Waffles

2 eggs, well beaten
1 pt. sweet milk
2½ c. flour
1 Tbsp. sugar
1 Tbsp. cornmeal
1 tsp. salt
4 tsp. baking powder
¾ c. Wesson oil

Beat eggs well and add the sweet milk. Sift with 2½ cups flour, (measure after sifting) sugar, meal, salt and baking powder; beat this into egg and milk mixture. Add oil and bake in hot waffle irons.

I Popovers

1 c. sifted flour
¼ tsp. salt
1 c. milk
1 Tbsp. shortening
2 eggs slightly beaten

Place flour and salt in mixing bowl. If shortening is used, cut it into flour and salt mixture until mixture resembles cornmeal. Blend eggs and milk. Add dry ingredients. Beat with rotary beater until smooth. Fill muffin cups ⅓ full (grease cups well). Bake at 375 degrees until well browned, about 40 minutes. Makes 8 to 12.

II Popovers

1 c. flour
½ tsp. salt
2 eggs
1 c. milk

Sift flour and salt together; add well beaten eggs; add milk gradually. Beat batter 5 minutes with rotary egg beater. Bake in hot greased muffin pans or unheated greased custard cups in a hot oven 450 degrees for 30 to 35 minutes.

Puffs

Makes fine breakfast surprise. Banana Puffs are an easy to make breakfast surprise or snack food. Cut unbaked refrigerator biscuits horizontally into two thin rounds. Place a slice of banana in the center of each half and bring edges up and around, pinching together with fingers to seal. Fry in preheated 375 degree deep fat until golden brown. Drain on absorbent paper. Sprinkle with confectioners sugar.

French Toast

¾ c. flour
½ tsp. soda
2 heaping tsp. baking powder
1 egg
1 c. buttermilk
½ tsp. salt

Beat egg and add buttermilk. Then sift together the ½ teaspoon salt, ¾ cup flour, ½ teaspoon soda and 2 teaspoons baking powder. Add this to the egg-milk mixture and mix well. Dip bread. Fry in deep fat only, Crisco or Snowdrift, not oil. This is a wonderful batter for fried onion rings.

Gingerbread

2 c. sifted flour
1½ tsp. soda
½ tsp. salt
1 tsp. cinnamon
½ tsp. cloves
½ c. butter or Crisco
½ c. brown sugar firmly packed
2 eggs well beaten
¾ c. molasses
1 c. boiling water

Bake in 8 X 11 pan in 350 degree oven about 40 minutes.

Gingerbread Topping

½ c. brown sugar
¼ c. flour
2 tsp. cinnamon
¼ c. soft butter
½ to 1 c. chopped nuts

Spread this topping made from the above ingredients over the gingerbread for last 10 minutes of baking. Serve with whipped cream.

Melba Toast Baskets

Use slices of fresh bread. Trim crusts. Butter and press in muffin tins with fingers. Brown in moderate oven.

Toasted Cheese Boxes

½ lb. grated American cheese
½ pt. mayonnaise
1 Tbsp. Worcestershire sauce
1 tsp. mustard
1 Tbsp. Durkee
Salt and pepper to taste

Mix cheese and mayonnaise. Add seasoning. Cut rounds or squares of bread. Spread bottom square with cheese mixture. Then top with another square and spread with mixture. When ready to serve, toast in moderate oven (400 degrees). Mixture will keep in refrigerator. Will make one pint. A little onion juice or garlic may be added to mixture if desired.

Lois's Cooked Pimento Cheese

In a double boiler put:
  ⅓ c. milk
  1 lb. Kraft's American cheese
When melted add:
  1 Tbsp. sugar
  1 small can pimento
  1 egg

Cook about 5 to 10 minutes. Add one pint of salad dressing.

Chicken Salad Sandwiches

Chop enough cooked chicken to make desired number of sandwiches. Add chopped celery, pickles, boiled eggs and homemade mayonnaise. Cut bread any desired shape and spread the chicken salad on. Season to taste. (1 chicken 2 to 3 lbs. boiled, cooled and cut up will make 4 dozen sandwiches.)

Cucumber Sandwiches

2 Tbsp. softened butter
2 Tbsp. bleu cheese
Cucumber slices
2 tsp. lemon juice
Salt, vinegar and red pepper
  to taste

Mix butter and cheese well; add lemon juice and red pepper to taste. Spread on rounds of bread, cut with small cutter. Top with a thin slice cucumber which has been chilled in ice water, to which a small amount of vinegar and salt has been added. Decorate with a dash of paprika. Serves 20.

Rolled Sandwiches

Roll each slice of bread that has been trimmed with a rolling pin to make thinner. This will make the bread easier to roll without breaking.

1 lb. American cheese
4 Tbsp. onion juice
Tabasco according to taste
1 Tbsp. Worcestershire sauce
1 Tbsp. mustard
1 loaf thin sliced bread

Grate cheese; add other ingredients and mix well until of consistency to spread. If necessary, add a little cream. Spread the bread with cheese mixture; add 2 whole small gherkins lengthwise, on end of bread slice and roll up. Wrap rolls individually in wax paper, twisting ends securely. Let set in deep freeze or refrigerator until hardened. Take out and cut into slices. Variation: 3 stuffed olives, 2 Vienna sausages, 3 cherries may be used instead of gherkins.

Double-Decker Shrimp and Cream Cheese Triangles
(Sandwiches)

Shrimp Layer;
  2 cans shrimp
    or
  1 lb. cooked shrimp
  1 piece celery, finely cut
  1 cup bought mayonnaise
  2 pkgs. cream cheese
  ¼ tsp. dry mustard
  ½ tsp. mace
  ½ tsp. onion juice
  Salt and Tabasco to taste
Cream cheese layer:
  2 large pkgs. cream cheese
    (8 oz. each)
  ½ c. cream
  Juice of small onion
  Salt, Tabasco and
  Worcestershire to taste

Soften cheese and blend with mayonnaise. Add seasonings, celery and shrimp, which has been mashed. Add red coloring to make desired shade of pink.

Soften cheese with cream and blend until smooth. Add seasonings and green coloring to make light shade.

Spread slice of trimmed bread with shrimp mixture. Cover with slice of bread and spread cheese mixture. Top with third slice. Wrap in wax paper and refrigerate for several hours. When ready to serve cut in 4 triangles. Makes 32 double-decker sandwiches or 128 triangles.

Sandwich Filling Suggestions

Date-nut filling: Mix 7½ oz. pkg. pitted dates, cut fine, ½ cup chopped nuts, two 3 oz. pkgs. cream cheese, ⅓ cup light cream.

Egg salad filling: Mix 2 finely chopped boiled eggs, 2 tablespoons minced ripe or stuffed green olives, ½ teaspoon salt, ½ teaspoon prepared mustard, 2 tablespoons mayonnaise and a little onion juice, finely cut celery. Or hard boiled eggs chopped fine, chopped bell pepper, onion juice, mayonnaise, and a little mustard.

Bleu cheese filling: Spread thin slices nut bread with Bleu cheese mixture, and add a thin slice cold chicken. Cut in small triangles. Delicious.

Open Faced Sandwiches

Cucumber-radish flowers: Butter 1¾ inch bread rounds. Make a border of thin unpeeled sliced radishes around edge. Top with cucumber slice, which has been marinated in cold, seasoned vinegar and patted dry. Dot center with a drop of mayonnaise and a parsley bit.

Olive scallops: Spread bread with seasoned cream cheese. Halve stuffed olives lengthwise, then slice across. Place rounded side in, around edge of bread round.

Spotted pinwheels: Spread bread with softened seasoned cream cheese. Arrange alternate strips of green pepper and pimento across bread. Roll up. Follow directions of cheese rolled sandwich recipe. Grated hard-boiled egg and finely cut parsley make attractive borders for open-faced sandwiches.

Pimento Cheese

Everyone has a different look for pimento cheese sandwiches, my favorite is very simple.

Grate 1 lb. of hoop cheese
1 small can pimento (2 or 3)
½ small onion grated (optional)
Dash garlic powder (optional)
Salt and white pepper to taste
Dash Lea and Perrin
1 c. mayonnaise, more if needed
   to make a good spread.

This will keep for weeks in refrigerator. I don't put pickle in unless I know if the party wants it. I serve ice cold dill pickles with it.

CORNMEAL COOKERY

Cornsticks   **Muffins**   **Cornbread**

Star of the Hot Breads — Quick to Make — Great in Variety

Sweetheart's Chili Corn Pone

2 c. plain cornmeal
1 tsp. salt
1 tsp. pepper
1 Tbsp. chili powder

Bring water to a boil and add to the above mixture; add enough to make a stiff batter. Make little pones and pat the size of a hot cake - fry in deep fat.

Corn Fried Onion Rings

3 large white onions
Milk to cover
1 c. self-rising flour
2 eggs, beaten slightly
Deep fat
½ c. sweet milk
  (in which onions were soaked)
2 c. self-rising cornmeal

If plain cornmeal and flour are used, add ½ teaspoon salt with flour and 1 teaspoon salt with cornmeal. Slice onions, separate into rings and cover with cold milk. Let stand 30 minutes, preferably in refrigerator. Drain well, saving milk to mix with egg. Dip onions first in flour, then in beaten egg mixed with ½ cup milk and again in cornmeal. Fry in deep fat heated to 365 degrees for about two minutes or until golden brown. Drain on brown paper. Idea: Tomatoes, green or ripe, sliced, sprinkle with a thin cornmeal coating and pan fried are crunchy and delicious. Makes an attractive garnish for meat dishes. Try French fried carrots, cauliflower and squash. Good!

Jack's Cornbread (Original)

3 heaping Tbsp. self-rising meal
2 heaping Tbsp. self-rising flour
1 tsp. vinegar
1 egg
1 tsp. sugar
2 Tbsp. Wesson oil
1 Tbsp. Karo

Sufficient milk to make mixture thin. Pour into small muffin rings. Bake at 400 degrees until brown. Makes 12 muffins. Delicious!

Old South's Best Cornmeal Muffins

2 c. cornmeal
3 tsp. baking powder
1 tsp. salt
3 Tbsp. melted fat or oil
1 Tbsp. sugar
1 egg
1¼c. sweet milk

Set oven to 450 degrees to preheat. Sift together the dry ingredients. Mix together egg, milk and fat. Add all at once to dry ingredients. Stir just to blend the ingredients. Pour batter into hot greased muffin tins, filling about ⅔ full. Pop quickly into oven. Bake for 15 to 20 minutes. You may use cornsticks mold or shallow pan 9 X 9 X 2.

Main Dish Suggestions With Cornmeal

Short cake: The crunchiness of tender stay-light corn bread muffins is just the right base for meat or vegetable short cake. Split hot muffins or squares of corn bread. Top or stack as for short cake with your favorite recipe for cream ham, eggs, chicken hash or barbecue and sauce. For special occasions bake the cornbread seasoned with herbs, in a ring mold and fill the center with creamed meat.

Tomato Supreme: Place half a tomato on square of corn bread which has been split, buttered and toasted. Pour a tangy cheese sauce over the tomato and top with 2 strips of bacon. Place on broiler rack and broil about 6 inches from heat.

Cornmeal Griddle Cakes

½ c. sifted flour
*1 tsp salt
*3 tsp. baking powder
1½ c. cornmeal
1 Tbsp. brown sugar
2 eggs beaten
1½ c. milk
4 Tbsp. melted fat
*Omit when using self-rising corn-meal and flour.

Sift flour, salt, baking powder and sugar together. Add cornmeal and mix well. Combine beaten egg, milk and fat. Add to dry ingredients. Pour batter on hot griddle; making cakes about 3" across. (It is hot enough when drops of water dance about.) Turn griddle cakes when they are puffed and full of little bubbles. Turn only once.

Cornbread or Corn Sticks

1 c. buttermilk
½ tsp. soda
1 egg
¼ c. flour
1 Tbsp. melted fat
1 c. cornmeal

Sift salt, soda and meal together. Break egg into this and add buttermilk and fat. Add flour. Mix and bake in cornstick or shallow pan. Bake in 425 degree oven. Preheat baking pans before putting batter in.

Cornbread

1½ c. cornmeal mix
Sweet milk
2 eggs
¼ c. Crisco oil

Mix together and beat real well to make a medium stiff batter. Pour into piping hot skillet or muffin irons. Bake in hot oven 425 degrees.

Hush Puppies

1 egg
1½ tsp. sugar
1 tsp. salt
1½ tsp. baking powder
1½ c. sweet milk
1 c. sifted meal
2 c. flour

Mix above ingredients and add the onions to taste, you can use more or less If too stiff add a little milk. Fry in deep hot fat. Make into balls about the size of a half dollar.

Mexican Corn Bread

1½ c. corn meal
1 c. cream style corn
1 c. sour cream or buttermilk
⅔ c. salad oil
2 eggs
2 Tbsp. minced bell pepper
3 tsp. baking powder
1 tsp. salt
1 c. grated cheese
2 Jalapena peppers or hot peppers
  from pepper sauce, chopped

Mix in order listed, except cheese. Pour half mixture in hot, greased pan. Sprinkle half cheese over mixture. Add remaining mixture and cover with remaining cheese. Bake in oven 350 degrees for 35 to 40 minutes.

*To prevent flour from lumping add a little
salt before mixing with water or milk.*

Cakes
Frostings
Candies

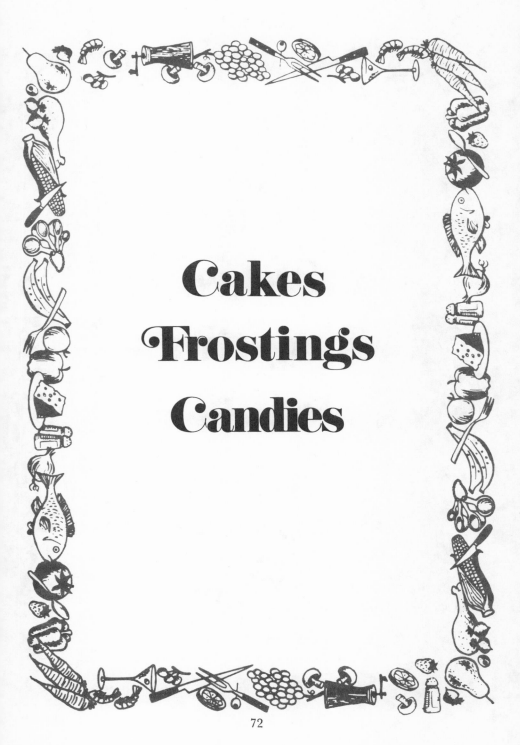

Cakes
Frostings
Candies

Net Williford's White Cake
Christmas Coconut Cake

A cake that makes Christmas delight.

⅔ c. Crisco
2 c. sugar
3 c. flour
½ tsp. salt
3 tsp. baking powder
1 c. warm water
1 tsp. orange extract
8 egg whites, beaten

The first thing to do when starting a cake is to cut 2 pieces of plain white paper the size of your layer cake pan. Grease the paper and pans well, place the paper on the bottom and dust well with flour. Sift flour, baking powder and salt together and sift twice. Cream Crisco and sugar until light and fluffy. Begin to add warm water, ¼ cup at a time, alternate with sifted flour mixture and beaten egg whites; flavoring last. Divide batter equally by pouring into 2 layer cake pans, and bake in moderate oven. Place layers in cold oven, if you are using gas oven and keep gas very low for first 15 minutes, then increase gradually. Remove cake layers from oven when they are just well done, not brown. You want all white cakes the lightest brown possible after becoming done. Turn cake out on rack to cool. Then turn on plate to ice.

Icing for Cake:
  3 large egg whites, beaten
    real stiff
  1½ c. sugar
  4 Tbsp. of white vinegar
  ¾ c. water
  Orange flavoring

Cook syrup (sugar and water and vinegar) until it forms hard ball. Pour over beaten whites. Do not mix coconut into icing. It destroys delicate flavor of the icing as well as flavor of the grated nut. Place layer of icing on top of first layer of cake; spread well, one inch thick. Now spread 1 inch of grated coconut and do the second layer the same way. Cover sides and put a 1 inch layer of coconut.

Coconut Balls For Tea Time

Double your recipe if you wish to have batter enough to make coconut balls also. Bake extra batter in a flat cake pan one inch thick. Cut into round balls; don't try to trim cake into tiny rounds, (the soft icing will shape easily when you are dabbing on icing).

Clyde's Pound Cake

3 sticks butter or margarine
1 box confectioners sugar
6 eggs
3 c. flour
1 tsp. lemon extract

Cream butter or margarine; add sugar slowly, beating after each addition. Add eggs one at a time, beating after each addition. Add flour slowly; then last add lemon extract. Bake in greased tube pan for 55 minutes at 350 degrees. Turn off heat and let stay in oven 10 minutes more. Take out of oven and let stand 10 minutes more in pan.

Pound Cake

½ c. Crisco
¼ lb. butter
¼ lb. oleo
3 c. sugar
6 eggs
3 c. plain flour
1 c. milk
1 tsp. each vanilla, lemon, almond, brandy flavoring

Cream shortening, oleo, butter and sugar. Add eggs one at a time. Add flavoring to milk and combine with creamed mixture, alternating with flour. This makes a large tube pan cake. Put in a cold oven and bake 2 hours at 325 degrees. Let cool about 15 minutes before turning out.

Whipping Cream Pound Cake

3 c. sugar
2 sticks butter
6 eggs
3 c. cake flour
1 c. whipping cream
2 tsp. vanilla
2 tsp. lemon flavoring
Dash of salt

Cream butter and sugar well; add eggs one at a time, beating well after each addition. Add flour and cream alternately. Add flavoring. Pour into a greased and floured tube pan. Put into cold oven. Set temperature at 350 degrees. Bake 1 hour or until well brown and done.

Pound Cake—Never Fail

1 stick oleo
1 stick butter
2 c. sugar
2 c. flour
7 eggs
1 Tbsp. vanilla
1 Tbsp. bourbon
1 tsp. almond
1 tsp. fresh lemon juice

Cream oleo, butter and sugar. Add a little flour first, then eggs one at a time with flour, a little at a time. Add vanilla, bourbon, almond and lemon juice. Bake at 325 degrees for 1 hour 15 minutes or until done.

Angie's Pound Cake for Bundt Cake Pan

4 eggs
2 Tbsp. vanilla or
　1 Tbsp. vanilla and
　1 Tbsp. lemon flavoring
1 c. butter (not oleo)
3 c. sugar
3 c. sifted flour
1 c. buttermilk
¼ tsp. soda

Cream butter and sugar; add alternately flour and buttermilk to which the soda has been added. Add eggs one at a time and vanilla. Bake at 350 degrees for 1 hour.

Sour Cream Pound Cake

¼ tsp. soda
1 8-oz. carton sour cream
1 tsp. vanilla, (You may vary
　almond or lemon
3 c. sugar
½ lb. butter
6 eggs
3 heaping c. cake flour

Cream sugar and butter well; then add eggs one at a time. Alternately add flour and sour cream (with soda). Add flavoring. Use a bundt cake pan. Bake at 350 degrees for 1 hour and 15 minutes or until done.

75

Chocolate Pound Cake

3 c. sugar
½ c. shortening
2 sticks oleo
5 eggs
3 c. sifted flour
½ tsp. salt
½ tsp. baking powder
½ c. cocoa
1¼ c. milk
2 tsp. vanilla

Cream sugar, shortening and margarine. Add eggs, one at a time, mixing well. Sift dry ingredients together 3 times. Alternately add milk and dry ingredients to sugar mixture. Add vanilla. Bake in greased tube pan at 325 degrees for 1 hour and 20 to 30 minutes. Remove from pan immediately. Stays moist for days.

Hershey Cake

1 lb. can chocolate syrup
2 c. sugar
1 c. butter
4 eggs
1 c. buttermilk
1 c. pecans (optional)
7 5¢ chocolate bars
2½ c. flour
2 tsp. salt
2 tsp. vanilla
½ tsp. soda

Cream sugar and butter well; add eggs one at a time, beating well. Add syrup and chocolate bars, melted. Add flour, salt, vanilla and the soda that has been dissolved in a cup of buttermilk. Bake in a floured and greased tube pan at 350 degrees for 1 hour or until done. Don't be surprised if it falls slightly.

Buttermilk Pound Cake
(Make by hand, best made in cold weather.)

1 c. Crisco
3 c. sugar
½ tsp. salt
½ tsp. soda
5 eggs, separated
3 c. flour (Sauer's all-purpose
    in 5 lb. box)
1 c. buttermilk
1 tsp. vanilla

Cream Crisco and sugar, add egg yolks one at a time. Scald soda with one tablespoon boiling water. Add to ½ cup buttermilk; then add this to creamed mixture. Add ½ cup buttermilk alternately with flour. Add vanilla and fold in beaten egg whites. Bake in tube pan at 375 degrees to start; after 30 minutes turn oven down to 300 degrees. Bake until done, (about another hour). Test with toothpick or straw and be sure it is well done.

76

Original Kentucky Whiskey Cake
(From Bess Mount)

5 c. flour sifted before measuring
1 lb. white sugar
1 c. brown sugar
¾ lb. butter
1 lb. shelled pecans
¾ lb. golden raisins cut in half
  or use ½ lb. chopped dates
6 eggs, beat separately
1 pt. whiskey
1 lb. red candied cherries
  (cut in pieces)
2 tsp. nutmeg
1 tsp. baking powder

Soak cherries and raisins in whiskey overnight. Cream butter and sugar until fluffy. Add egg yolks and beat well. Add soaked fruit, remaining liquid and the flour, reserving a small amount of flour for the nuts. Add to butter, sugar and egg yolk mixture. Add nutmeg and baking powder. Fold in beaten egg whites; add the lightly floured pecans last. Bake in a large greased tube pan (lined with greased paper) for 3 or 4 hours in a slow oven 250 to 275 degrees. Watch baking time. Store when cold, wrapped in cheese cloth. Bess said this cake is much better to let mellow about a week before serving.

Slainte—To Your Health

This ancient gaelic toast sounds around the world wherever there's the wearing of the green on St. Patrick's Day; for the Irish, at home or abroad, have a keen appreciation of fine food and drink and a generous habit of doubling their pleasure by sharing it with good friends. Tipsy Irish Cake, a blend of cake, custard and preserves, is a favorite Irish dessert. A spirited lacing of whiskey enhances the delicate flavor of the custard and the fruitfulness of the jam; and adds a lilting note of its own. So why not toast St. Patrick with a Tipsy Cake and Irish Coffee.

Irish Tipsy Cake

6 eggs, separated
½ tsp. salt
1 c. sugar
1 tsp. grated lemon rind
Juice ½ lemon
1 c. cake flour

Beat egg whites frothy; add salt; beat stiff; gradually beat in sugar, 2 tablespoons at a time and continue to beat until meringue is stiff and glossy. Beat egg yolks separately until light. Add lemon rind and juice, and beat until very thick. Very gently fold the yolk mixture into the meringue. Sift the flour over the mixture, ¼ cup at a time, and fold in gently, using as few strokes as possible. Grease and flour the bottom of 3-9 inch layer pans. Divide batter into the pans. Bake in a 350 degree oven about 25 or 30 minutes or until the cakes are browned and spring back when lightly pressed with a finger tip. Cool.

Custard

4 egg yolks
¼ c. sugar
¼ c. whiskey
Pinch salt
1¾ c. scalded milk
½ tsp. vanilla

Beat egg yolks, sugar and salt together. Stir in milk and cook over low heat, stirring constantly until mixture begins to thicken and coats the spoon. Stir in vanilla and whiskey. Cool.

Garnish

¾ c. whiskey
1 c. slivered almonds
½ c. raspberry jam

Assemble the cake. Sprinkle the layers with whiskey and spread with jam between them. Put the cake into a glass dessert bowl. Sprinkle with remaining whiskey and let soak 1 hour in ice box. Pour the cooled custard over cake; stud with almonds, porcupine style and garnish with candied cherries and mint. This one is my pride and joy. It is worth the trouble. You will agree afterwards. I am not from Ireland—so I think it is wonderful for company and Christmas.

78

Prune Cake

1 c. Wesson oil
2 c. sugar
2 c. self rising flour
1 tsp. cinnamon
1 tsp. nutmeg
1 tsp. allspice (sift together)
3 eggs, all at once
2 jars baby food (prunes)
1 c. chopped nuts

Mix together real well and pour into a tube pan that has been greased and floured. Bake at 300 degrees for 1½ hours.

I Cheese Cake

Crust:

2 c. graham cracker crumbs
⅓ c. sugar
1⅓ sticks margarine, melted

Thoroughly mix all ingredients together and line cheese cake pan (spring bottom). This is done by patting the mixture with finger tips to spread it evenly. Chill in ice box.

Filling:

3 eggs
3 8-oz. pkgs. cream cheese, softened
1½ c. sugar
⅛ tsp. salt
1 tsp. vanilla

Place all ingredients in mixing bowl and beat with electric beater until smooth. Pour into crust. Place the pan on a cookie sheet and bake for 1 hour at 350 degrees. Remove from oven, cool 10 minutes.

Topping:

2 c. sour cream
¼ c. sugar
2 tsp. vanilla

Mix together and pour over cake. Place in 450 degree oven for 10 minutes. Cool completely before cutting. It is better if left in ice box overnight

79

II Cheese Cake

Most delicious! I have used this for years. Serves 12. This recipe fills a large 10" spring pan. Will keep under refrigeration for a week or two.

Filling:

3 8-oz. pkgs. Philadelphia
  cream cheese
1½ c. sugar
2 Tbsp. sweet cream
1 Tbsp. vanilla
4 eggs

Cream the cream cheese, sugar, eggs, sweet cream and vanilla until light and creamy. Pour into crust which has been put into spring pan.

Crust:

38 graham crackers, crushed
1 stick butter
½ c. sugar

Mix thoroughly and press in pan. Bake at 350 degrees for 5 minutes. Cool; then pour filling in and bake at 350 degrees for 20 to 30 minutes. When cool put cherry pie filling on top. Cool completely before serving.

Vanilla Wafer Cake

Cream together real well
  until light and fluffy.
2 c. sugar
2 sticks oleo

Add 6 eggs, one at a time; beat well after each addition. Crush 1 lb. box vanilla wafers. Add 1 cup chopped pecans, 1 cup flaked coconut, 1 teaspoon salt and ⅔ cup milk. Mix together well. Put into a greased and floured tube pan. Bake at 250 degrees for 1½ hours.

I Louise's Apricot Nectar Pound Cake

1 box yellow cake mix
¾ c. Wesson oil
¾ c. apricot nectar
4 eggs

Combine the cake mix, Wesson oil, apricot nectar and 4 egg yolks. Fold into this mixture 4 stiffly beaten egg whites. Pour the mixture into an ungreased tube pan. Bake 45 minutes at 350 degrees. When done run a knife around the stem and sides to remove.

While cake is baking mix:
1½ cups confectioners sugar, juice and rind of 2 large lemons. Remove cake from pan; let cool slightly. Then punch holes in top of cake. Pour icing over the cake so that it will drip through it and down the sides.

II Apricot Nectar Pound Cake

1 pkg. lemon supreme cake mix
1 c. apricot nectar
½ c. Crisco oil
4 eggs
½ c. sugar

Mix cake mix, sugar, oil and nectar together and beat for 2 minutes. Add 1 egg at a time and beat until well blended. Bake in tube pan, that has been greased and floured, for 1 hour at 325 degrees. When done, and it has slightly cooled, pour the glaze over cake. Glaze: 1½ cup powdered sugar, juice and rind of 2 lemons. (Well blended.)

Applesauce Cake

1 c. butter
2 c. sugar
2 c. applesauce
2 eggs unbeaten
2 tsp. soda
4 c. sifted flour with
  1 Tbsp. cinnamon
  1 Tbsp. allspice
  2 Tbsp. vanilla

Cream butter and sugar. Add eggs. Heat applesauce and stir in soda. Add alternately with sifted flour and space. Bake in greased pan, square or round, or muffin tins at 350 degrees for 45 to 50 minutes. Roll or sprinkle powdered sugar on top. delicious on a cold day.

Sock-It-To-Me-Cake

1 pkg. butter recipe golden
   cake mix
1 c. (8-oz.) dairy sour cream
4 eggs
½ c. Crisco oil
¼ c. sugar
¼ c. water
Filling:
   1 c. chopped pecans
   2 Tbsp. brown sugar
   2 tsp. cinnamon

Preheat oven to 375 degrees. In a large mixing bowl blend together the cake mix, sour cream, oil, the ¼ cup sugar, water and eggs. Beat at high speed for 2 minutes. Pour ⅔ of the batter in a greased and floured 10 inch tube pan. Combine filling ingredients and sprinkle over batter in pan. Spread remaining batter evenly over filling mixture. Bake at 375 degrees for 45 to 55 minutes, until cake springs back when touched lightly. Cool right side up for about 25 minutes then remove from pan.

Glaze: Blend 1 cup powdered sugar and 2 tablespoons milk. Drizzle over cake.

Mahogany Cake

1 scant c. butter
1½ c. sugar
4 eggs, separated
1 tsp. soda
1 c. buttermilk
2 c. cake flour
3 Tbsp. cocoa
1 tsp. vanilla

Cream butter and sugar; add beaten yolks. Sift flour and cocoa and add to mixture. Add buttermilk to which soda has been added. Fold in stiffly beaten egg whites. Add vanilla. Bake in layers at 325 degrees for 30 minutes.

Filling:
   1 stick butter
   1 egg
   5 Tbsp. strong coffee
   1 c. pecans
   1 Tbsp. grated orange rind
   3 c. confectioners sugar
   1 Tbsp. cream
   2 squares chocolate
   1 tsp. vanilla

Cream butter and add sifted confectioners sugar. Beat in egg and add chocolate, coffee and tablespoon cream. Add chopped pecans, vanilla and orange rind. Sprinkle top of cake with grated pecans.

Doris' Chocolate Sheet Cake

Sift in large bowl and set aside:
- 2 c. sugar
- 2 c. flour

Bring to a boil:
- 1 stick oleo
- ¼ c. Crisco
- 4 Tbsp. cocoa
- 1 c. water

When this boils, pour over sugar and flour mixture. Then add ½ cup buttermilk, 1 teaspoon cinnamon, ½ teaspoon salt, 2 eggs and 1 teaspoon soda. Mix and bake in sheet pan 20 minutes at 400 degrees.

Icing:
- 1 stick oleo
- 4 Tbsp. cocoa
- 6 Tbsp. milk

Bring to a boil; then beat in box of powdered sugar. Add 1 cup chopped nuts and 1 teaspoon vanilla. Spread over sheet cake and when cool cut into squares. Good icing for other cakes.

Mary's Cherry Whipped Cream Cake

- 1 angel food cake (slice in 2 horizontal layers)
- 1 can prepared cherry pie filling
- 1 large or 2 small pkgs. whipped cream topping
- 1 8-oz. pkg. cream cheese
- 1 tsp. vanilla
- ½ c. granulated sugar
- ½ c. powdered sugar

Cream together cheese, granulated sugar, powdered sugar and extract. Prepare whipped topping as directed on pkg. and blend into cheese mixture. Spread frosting mixture between layers, on sides and top. Spoon cherry pie filling over frosted cake allowing it to drizzle down sides. Slice at serving time.

Strawberry Cake

1 box cake mix (yellow)
1 box strawberry jello
⅔ c. oil
4 eggs
2 Tbsp. sugar
½ c. water
½ c. strawberries
Makes 3 layers.
Icing:
   1 box sugar (powdered)
   3 Tbsp. butter
   ½ c. strawberries
Try this. It is delicious.

"Mississippi Mud"

2 c. sugar
1 c. shortening
4 eggs
1½ c. flour
⅓ c. cocoa
1¼ tsp. salt
3 Tbsp. chopped nuts
1 tsp. vanilla
1 pkg. small marshmallows

Cream sugar and shortening. Add eggs and beat well. Sift flour, cocoa and salt; add to other mixture. Bake in 13 X 9 pan. Bake 30 minutes at 300 degrees. Remove from oven and put on marshmallows. Let stand 10 minutes before spreading on icing.

Icing:
1½ sticks oleo, melted
1 box powdered sugar
⅓ c. cocoa
½ c. evaporated milk
1 tsp. vanilla
1 c. nuts

Sift cocoa and sugar together; add oleo. Next add milk, vanilla and nuts. Mix real well and spread on cake over marshmallows.

Cookies
Desserts

Cookies
Desserts

Pfeffernusse (Peppernuts)

3 c. brown sugar
2 whole eggs
1 c. shortening
Sprinkle of salt
1 tsp. cinnamon
1 tsp. anise oil (or less)
Flour for stiff dough
   (about 7-8 cups)
3 c. white sugar
1½ c. hot water
1 tsp. baking powder
1 tsp. ginger
1 tsp. cloves
1 tsp. black pepper

Chill dough overnight. Take up about a cup of dough and roll by hand into long snake-like form, size of little finger or smaller. Cut into pieces. Bake in 400 degree oven about 8 minutes. (Watch carefully).

Margaret's Lemon Bars

¼ c. confectioners sugar
1 c. flour
⅛ tsp. salt
1 stick real butter

Glaze:
   2 Tbsp. lemon juice
   ¾ c. confectioners sugar
   1 Tbsp. real butter

Mix together and put in 9 X 9" pan. Bake at 350 degrees for 15 minutes. Do not cool. Have ready: 1 cup sugar (plain), ½ teaspoon baking powder, ⅛ teaspoon salt, 2 eggs slightly beaten and 3 tablespoons lemon juice. Pour on crust and bake 20 minutes longer. Glaze while hot.

Pour on top and cool. Cut in squares.

Rocks

2 c. sugar
3 eggs
3 c. flour
3 lbs. dates chopped
1 tsp. cinnamon, nutmeg and
   allspice
1 c. butter
1 tsp. soda dissolved in
¼ c. cold water
1½ lbs. nuts

Cream butter and sugar, add beaten eggs. Sift flour and dry ingredients and add. Then add soda dissolved in cold water, then dates and nuts. Mix well. Makes 4 dozen or more cookies.

87

Ice Box Cookies

1 c. butter or oleo
1 c. brown sugar
2 c. flour
1 egg yolk
1 tsp. vanilla
1 c. chopped nuts

Mix well and spread thin on greased floured pan — 11 X 17". Beat egg whites slightly and brush top of dough. Sprinkle with chopped nuts and bake until light brown in color at 275-300 degrees. Cut while warm. This is a little difficult to pat evenly in baking pan. Involves time. Makes 70-80 cookies.

Stuffed Date Muffins or Drop Cookies

2 pkgs. dates or at least 50 dates
6 oz. pecans
1¾ c. light brown sugar
2 eggs
¼ tsp. salt
2½ c. flour (cake flour)
1 tsp. baking powder
1 tsp. soda
1 c. sour cream
½ c. oleo or butter

Stuff dates with nut halves. Cream shortening and sugar well. Beat in eggs. Sift dry ingredients, add alternately with sour cream to creamed mixture. Stir in dates, then be sure to use a date in each muffin or cookie with small amount of butter, in small size muffin pan (buttered). Bake in hot oven 350 to 400 degrees for 8 to 10 minutes. Leave in pan a few minutes; then loosen and remove from pan. Cool and top with golden frosting.

Golden Frosting

Lightly brown 1 stick oleo, remove from heat. Gradually add 3 cups confectioners sugar and 1 teaspoon vanilla. Slowly add warm water (about 3 tablespoons) until spreading consistency. Makes about 50 muffins or 5½ dozen drop cookies.

Beep's Lemon Whippersnappers

1 pkg. lemon cake mix
1 4½-oz. carton cool whip,
   thawed
1 egg
Powdered sugar (about ½ cup)

Combine cake mix, egg and cool whip, until well mixed. Drop by teaspoon into powdered sugar, roll to coat. Place 1½ inches apart on greased cookie sheets. Bake at 350 degrees for 10-15 minutes. Remove from oven, let cool. Makes 4 dozen.

Francis's Cookies

1 c. butter
3 to 4 Tbsp. sugar
3½ c. sifted flour
1 c. chopped nuts

Mix all the ingredients except ½ cup flour. Roll this out on ½ cup flour, about ¼ inch thick or less. They do not rise. Cut with a cutter about the size of ½ dollar, put a dab of jelly (plum is good because it is tart and stiff) and ½ pecan on each cookie. Bake at 350 degrees for 20 or 25 minutes. Take out and let cool on platter and dust with powdered sugar. Makes about 100; will keep indefinitely.

Mud Hen (Butterscotch Squares)

½ c. oleo
2 eggs (save 1 white out)
1 tsp. baking powder
1 tsp. salt
1 c. chopped nuts
1 c. sugar
1½ tsp. vanilla
1½ c. flour

Cream oleo and sugar, add unbeaten egg yolks and the 1 white. Add flour, salt and baking powder and vanilla. Spread in a greased pan; sprinkle chopped nuts. Using 1 egg white make a meringue, adding 1 cup brown sugar. Spread on top of number one mixture. Bake at 325 degrees for 30 or 40 minutes. Let cool in pan and cut in squares.

Orange Pecans

2 c. granulated sugar
½ c. water
Juice and grated rind of
    1 orange
2 c. pecan meats
1 kitchen spoon white Karo

Boil to 230 degrees or until spins thread. Stir until it begins to sugar, add the pecans and pour into buttered pan. Break apart when thoroughly cold and hardened.

Bourbon Balls

1 lb. vanilla wafers
1 Tbsp. white Karo
1 Tbsp. cocoa
1 c. ground nuts
3 Tbsp. rum or whiskey
1 c. sugar

Grind wafers and nuts together. Then mix all ingredients and shape into balls or cakes.

89

Nut Goodies

½ c. butter
2 eggs
½ tsp. vanilla
1½ c. sifted cake flour
1 c. sugar
Chopped nuts
1 c. brown sugar

Cream butter and sugar. Add eggs that have been beaten. Add flour and vanilla; spread dough in pan, approximately 7 X 12" in size, that has been greased and floured. Beat one egg white stiff and add 1 cup of brown sugar. Mix well. Spread on top of dough and sprinkle with chopped nuts. Bake in 350 degree oven for about 40 minutes or until nice and brown. Makes 2 dozen.

Coconut Bars

Part I
½ c. butter
½ tsp. salt
½ c. brown sugar
1 c. flour

Cream above ingredients. Spread stiff dough in greased pan and bake at 325 degrees for 14 minutes.

Part II
1 c. brown sugar
1 tsp. vanilla
2 well beaten eggs
1½ c. shredded coconut
2 Tbsp. flour
½ tsp. baking powder
1 c. chopped nuts

Combine sugar, vanilla and eggs and beat until foamy. Then add flour, baking powder, chopped nuts and coconut. Mix well; then spread Part II mixture over the first mixture and bake in 325 degree oven for 20 minutes. Different! You'll serve this again and again!

Beep's Hello Dollys

Put ¼ lb. butter in pan and melt at 350 degrees. Remove from oven and sprinkle 1 cup graham cracker crumbs over melted butter.

Add in layers:

1 c. chocolate chips
1 c. shredded coconut
1 c. Eagle brand milk
1 c. chopped nuts

Bake 30 minutes at 350 degrees. Remove.

Party Coffee Cake

½ lb. butter
3 eggs
2½ c. sifted flour
1 tsp. baking soda
1 tsp. vanilla
1 c. sugar
1 c. sour cream
2 tsp. baking powder
Pinch salt
1 tsp. lemon extract

Mixture:
    1 tsp. cinnamon
    1 c. nuts chopped
    ½ c. sugar

Cream sugar and butter; add 1 egg at a time, beating constantly. Add sour cream; mix in gradually flour to which soda, salt and baking powder have been added. Add flavoring. Then use half of batter in a long narrow greased pan. Sprinkle half of mixture and then top with rest of batter. Sprinkle balance of mixture on top. Bake at 375 degrees for 30 minutes or until done.

Beep's Oh and Ah Cake

3 1-oz. squares unsweetened
    chocolate
1 c. boiling water
1 tsp. red food color
1½ tsp. baking soda
½ c. shortening
2 c. sugar
½ tsp. salt
3 eggs
1 c. sour cream
2½ c. sifted cake flour

Melt chocolate in boiling water. Cool. Add food coloring and baking soda. Cream shortening, sugar, salt, and eggs until fluffy. Add flour alternately with sour cream. Add chocolate mixture and beat at medium speed on electric mixer for one minute, or by hand for 150 strokes. Pour into greased and floured 13 X 9 X 2 inch pan. Bake at 350 degrees for 45 minutes.

Beep's Sour Cream Cake Frosting

1 6-oz. pkg. (1 cup) semi-sweet
    chocolate pieces
    (chocolate chips)
¼ c. butter or margarine
½ c. dairy sour cream
1 tsp. vanilla
2½ to 2¾ c. sifted
    confectioners sugar

Melt chocolate pieces and butter over hot (not boiling) water; remove from hot water and blend in sour cream, vanilla, and ¼ teaspoon salt. Gradually add enough confectioners sugar for spreading consistency; beat well. Frost top and sides of two 9-inch layer or 10-inch tube cake. (It is best if you double the recipe!)

Never Fail Boiled Icing

Whites of 2 eggs
2 c. sugar
½ c. water
8 large marshmallows
¾ tsp. vanilla flavoring
½ tsp. lemon flavoring

Beat whites until stiff and cover with marshmallows. When sugar and water first begin to boil dip out 2 tablespoons syrup and add to whites. Repeat twice, using 6 tablespoons in all. Beat. When remaining syrup spins a thread that will fly away from spoon, pour slowly over whites, beating constantly. Add vanilla and lemon flavoring or 2 tablespoons of lemon juice.

Caramel Pecan Frosting

2 c. sugar
1 c. buttermilk
1 tsp. soda
⅛ tsp. salt
2 Tbsp. butter
1 c. pecans, finely chopped

Combine sugar, buttermilk, soda and salt; cook for 5 minutes, stirring constantly. Add butter and pecans; cook until a soft ball forms in cold water, (about 8-10 minutes). Set aside to cool; beat well. As you frost cake, place frosting in pan of hot water for easy spreading. This will frost top and sides of layer cake.

Use large pan, as this really bubbles up.

Caramel Icing

3 c. sugar
½ c. sugar, carmelized
1 c. sweet milk
1 stick butter
2 egg yolks, beaten
Vanilla to taste

Mix milk, sugar, butter and egg yolks. Cook on low heat until butter melts. Add caramelized sugar to above mixture and cook to 230 degrees F. Cool and beat.

Chocolate cake will scorch more easily than a plain cake due to the high percentage of fat it contains. It is necessary, for that reason, to bake it in a very moderate oven.

*To make a good uncooked icing, thorough beating is necessary. Too much sugar and too little beating makes a brittle hard icing.

Million Dollar Fudge
(Mamie Eisenhower Favorite)

4½ c. sugar
Pinch of salt
2 Tbsp. butter
1 tall can evaporated milk

Boil 6 minutes. Put in large bowl:
12 oz. semi-sweet chocolate or
    bits
12 oz. German sweet chocolate
1 pt. marshmallow cream
    (Hypolite)
2 c. pecans

Pour boiling syrup over ingredients in bowl. Beat until chocolate is melted; pour in buttered pan and let set before cutting in squares. This keeps indefinitely and it stays creamy.

Easy Coconut Candy

6 Tbsp. cream cheese
2½ c. powdered sugar
½ c. shredded coconut
2 tsp. vanilla
Pinch of salt

Pack mixed ingredients in greased pan and pour ½ square of melted bitter chocolate over it. Cool and cut in squares.

Divinity

I did not leave out anything. It is different from other divinity recipes, but it will be perfect everytime. Try it!

2½ c. sugar
½ c. white Karo
¾ c. water
½ c. chopped nuts or candied
    cherries, if desired
1 egg white
¼ tsp. salt
1½ tsp. vanilla

In a large sauce pan combine sugar, Karo and water. Cover and bring to a slow boil. Remove cover and boil over medium heat without stirring until it forms a soft ball, or 235 degrees. Remove from heat. Let stand while you are beating egg white until quite stiff; gradually add hot syrup beating constantly. Add salt and vanilla; continue beating until it loses its gloss and it becomes thick (about 10 minutes). Quickly stir in nuts and drop by teaspoon on wax paper. 30 to 35 pieces.

Pralines

2½ c. white sugar
½ c. evaporated milk
¼ c. fresh milk
2 c. chopped nuts
2 tsp. Karo
2 Tbsp. butter
Dash salt
½ tsp. vanilla

Cook very slowly, stirring constantly; add nuts and cook until 245 degrees or soft ball stage. Beat until creamy and drop by teaspoon on wax paper.

Fondant

2 c. granulated sugar
¼ tsp. cream of tartar
1 c. cold water
    to dissolve sugar

Mix ingredients. Heat and stir until sugar is dissolved, cooking to soft ball stage and washing down sides of pan occasionally with wet cloth swab. Pour on a platter without scraping the pan and cool until hand can be held on bottom of platter. Beat the mixture until it "sugars" and knead for a few minutes or until creamy. It becomes more creamy still if allowed to stand 20-24 hours in a covered jar before it is used.

Uses of Fondant

Peppermint cream: Melt about 1 cup fondant in the top of double boiler. Flavor with 2 drops oil peppermint and stir until creamy. Drop from tip of teaspoon or from pastry bag in small patties on heavy waxed paper. Stuffed dates or prunes: Wash and dry the fruit. The prunes should be steamed for 20 minutes before used. Score the fruit and place in each cavity a nut and small lump of fondant kneaded and flavored with vanilla. Roll stuffed fruit in powdered sugar.

Fondant candies dipped in chocolate: Melt dipping chocolate very slowly over hot, but not boiling water. Beat chocolate until creamy and keep warm. Drop fondant centers and dip them out with a fork. Place on heavy waxed paper. Let harden in a cool, very dry place. When they are hard, pack them in boxes.

Uncooked Peanut Butter Roll

1 box powdered sugar
⅛ lb. butter
2 Tbsp. cream
1 tsp. vanilla

Cream with hands or mixer, until light consistency to roll (like biscuit dough). Roll on oiled paper; spread with peanut butter and roll like jelly roll. Cut in desired pieces.

Mexican Pecan Candy

Boil together:
1 c. milk
2 c. sugar
1 c. unchopped pecans
1 Tbsp. butter

Put 1 cup sugar in large iron skillet and brown, stirring constantly. Pour other mixture into this and cook to soft ball stage, stirring all the time. Remove from stove; beat until color changes; drop on waxed paper.

Mints

2 c. sugar
5 drops oil of mint
½ c. boiling water
2 Tbsp. white Karo

Put in pan with top on it. When it comes to a boil remove from heat and beat until creamy. Drop on wax paper, (enough for nine round mints). Tint color desired before it comes to a boil.

Never beat fudge as soon as it is taken from the fire. Set in pan of cold water until cool, then beat.

Keep brown sugar in a large jar with dried prunes. The prunes keep the sugar from turning hard; the sugar sweetens the prunes.

95

Chess Pie Cookies

2 sticks margarine or butter
1 lb. box brown sugar
1 c. white sugar
¼ tsp. salt
1½ tsp. vanilla
Powdered sugar
2 c. flour
4 egg yolks
2 tsp. baking powder
1 c. chopped nuts
4 egg whites

Melt margarine and add sugars. Blend well. Add egg yolks and beat well. Sift dry ingredients and add. Fold in nuts and vanilla. Beat egg whites stiff and fold into batter. Grease and flour a 9 X 13 inch pan. Spread batter evenly. Bake at 350 degrees for 30 to 45 minutes. When done, sprinkle top with powdered sugar and cut into squares.

I Oatmeal Cookies

1 c. shortening
1 c. brown sugar
2 c. oats (uncooked)
1 tsp. soda
2 eggs
2 c. raisins
1 c. white sugar
2 c. flour
1 tsp. baking powder
¼ tsp. salt
1 c. nuts
1 box coconut

Mix well. Drop by spoonful on greased cookie sheet. Can add crystallized cherries, pineapple and dates if desired.

II Oatmeal Cookies

1 c. brown sugar
2 eggs
2½ c. sifted flour
½ Tbsp. baking powder
1 c. coconut
1 c. white sugar
1 c. butter (oleo)
1 Tbsp. soda
1 c. oats
1 c. nuts

Mix real well. Drop by spoonful on cookie sheet. Bake at 300 degrees for 20 minutes. Then increase heat to 375 degrees for 15 minutes.

To keep cookies fresh and crisp in the jar, place a piece of crumpled tissue paper in the bottom.

Oatmeal Toll House Cookies

¾ c. sifted flour
⅜ c. granulated sugar
½ tsp. soda
½ c. chopped nuts
1 7-oz. semi-sweet chocolate bits
½ tsp. salt
1 egg, unbeaten
½ tsp. hot water
1 c. uncooked quick oats
½ tsp. vanilla

Sift flour once before measuring, then sift together with salt. Cream butter until soft; then add sugar, creaming until light and fluffy. Add eggs and beat. Dissolve soda in hot water and add to mixture alternately with sifted dry ingredients. Add nuts, chocolate bits and oats and mix thoroughly. Drop by half teaspoon on greased cookie sheet. Bake at 375 degrees about 10 to 12 minutes.

Old-Fashioned Oatmeal Cookies

¾ c. butter or margarine
2 eggs
2 tsp. baking powder
1 tsp. ground cinnamon
1 tsp. vanilla
3 c. rolled oats (old-fashioned or quick cooking)
1 c. sugar
1 c. plus 2 Tbsp. all purpose flour
¼ tsp. salt
⅓ c. milk
1 c. seedless raisins
1 egg

Cream butter and sugar together thoroughly. Add eggs, one at a time, beating well after each addition. Sift together dry ingredients; add to creamed mixture alternately with milk. Add other ingredients. Drop teaspoonfuls onto greased cookie sheet, keeping 1 inch apart. Bake at 350 degrees for 12 to 15 minutes. Yield: About 4 dozen.

Mincemeat-Oatmeal Cookies

1¼ c. sifted all-purpose flour
¾ tsp. soda
1 c. light brown sugar, firmly packed
1⅓ c. mincemeat
½ tsp. salt
½ c. shortening
1½ c. uncooked quick-cooking oats

Sift together flour, salt and soda. Cream shortening, gradually adding sugar and beating until fluffy. Beat in egg and stir in mincemeat, prepared according to package directions. Gradually add flour mixture, blending well. Stir in oats. Drop teaspoonfuls onto greased cookie sheet, keeping 2 inches apart. Bake at 350 degrees, 15 minutes or until browned. Yield: 3 to 4 dozen.

Oatmeal and Nut Cookies

1 c. shortening (butter)
1 c. brown sugar
1 c. white sugar
1 Tbsp. salt
1 Tbsp. soda
1 Tbsp. vanilla
1½ c. flour
2 well beaten eggs
3 c. oats
2 c. nuts

This makes very stiff dough. Mix as any cake dough and lastly put in oats and mix by hand; then shape in rolls the size of a 50¢ piece in wax paper. Slice after chilled very thin. Bake on ungreased cookie sheet 10 minutes at 350 degrees. Store in can to keep crisp.

Mary's Fudge Cookies

In large bowl mix:
  3 c. minute oats
  1 c. chopped pecans or coconut
  1 tsp. vanilla extract
In large saucepan bring to a boil:
  2 c. sugar
  ½ c. cocoa
  1 stick oleo
  ½ c. milk

Pour over the first mixture. After mixing well, drop by spoonful onto wax paper. Cool few minutes and ready to serve.

Snowball Cookies

½ c. powdered sugar
1 c. butter or oleo
1 c. nuts (chopped)
1 tsp. vanilla
2 c. flour

Mix with hands, shape in small balls, place on cookie sheet (well greased). Bake 25 minutes at 325 degrees. Remove from oven and roll in powdered sugar.

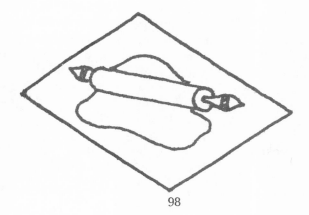

Date Squares

2 c. chopped dates
½ c. chopped pecans
Juice of 1 lemon
¾ c. butter
1½ c. rolled oats
1½ c. sifted flour
1 c. brown sugar
⅛ tsp. salt
½ tsp. soda

Cook dates and water until dates are tender, about 15 minutes. Add sugar, lemon juice and pecans. Cool. Combine rolled oats, flour, brown sugar, butter, soda and salt and mix until it resembles crumbs. Place ⅔ of mixture in a buttered square pan (an 8 or 9 inch pan is best). Cover with the date mixture and sprinkle the remaining crumbs over the top, pressing lightly. Bake in a moderate oven, 350 degrees 25 to 30 minutes. Cool and cut in squares.

Skillet Cookies

1 stick oleo, melted in large skillet
Beat together:
2 egg yolks
½ c. sugar
Then add to melted oleo. Add:
   1 c. chopped dates

Cook until dates are soft. Stir constantly.

Add:
   1 tsp. vanilla
   2 c. Rice Krispies
   1 c. nuts

Stir all together and make in a loaf. Chill firmly and slice or you can make into balls, size of a walnut and roll in powdered sugar.

Filled Jumbo Drops

Date filling (recipe below)
1 c. shortening
2 c. brown sugar (packed)
3 eggs
½ c. water
1 tsp. vanilla
3½ c. sifted Gold Medal flour
½ tsp. salt
1 tsp. soda
⅛ tsp. cinnamon

Heat oven to 375 degrees. Mix thoroughly shortening, brown sugar and eggs. Stir in water and vanilla. Sift together and stir in flour, soda, salt and cinnamon. Drop with teaspoon onto ungreased baking sheet. Place ½ teaspoon filling on dough, cover with ½ teaspoon dough. Bake 10 to 12 minutes. Makes 5 to 6 dozen.

Date Filling: Cook together until thick, (stirring constantly) 2 cups dates (cut small), ¾ cup sugar, ¾ cup water. Add ½ cup chopped nuts. Cool before storing.

Rum Balls

1 pkg. Swansdown white
    cake mix
2 boxes confectioners sugar
1 lb. butter
1 pint white rum
1 lb. ground pecans
Large box finely ground
    vanilla wafers

Cook cake in 2 pans so that when done it will not be more than ½ to ¾ inch thick. Place in refrigerator for a day or two so cake will not crumble. Mix sugar and butter in mixer and add rum slowly. This makes the icing. Cut cake into pieces about 1 inch square. Ice with the icing and then roll in vanilla wafer crumbs and pecans. Put into a tin box in a cool place. They will keep as long as three months in a cool place.

Doug's Fourth of July Ice Cream
(Makes 1 gallon)

Put on to scald ½ gal. sweet milk—do not boil. In a bowl add 8 whole eggs and beat real well with 2½ cups sugar and 2 tablespoons flour. Add to scalded milk and stir constantly until it is completely hot. Turn heat off and add 2 cans Carnation milk. When cool add vanilla flavoring.

Rum Duff

2 c. canned applesauce
¼ c. sugar
3 Tbsp. rum or 1 tsp.
    rum extract
1 Tbsp. grated orange rind
2 c. ginger snaps, broken
½ c. XX cream, whipped

Combine applesauce, sugar, rum, orange rind and ginger snaps. Stir until well mixed. Chill. Just before serving, fold in whipped cream. Pile into sherbet glasses. Serves 6.

100

Lemon Charlotte

1 pkg. lemon jello
1 c. boiling water
2 Tbsp. sugar
⅛ tsp. salt
2 Tbsp. lemon juice
1 Tbsp. grated lemon rind
2 c. heavy cream (whipped)

Combine jello, sugar, salt and hot water. Stir until jello dissolves. When cool, add lemon juice and chill. When it begins to congeal, whip until light and foamy. Fold in whipped cream and lemon peel. Pour into individual molds to set. Serve with pureed strawberries (fresh or frozen).

Frozen Chocolate Dessert

2 c. heavy cream, whipped
1 c. Fudge Sauce*
1 tsp. rum extract
½ c. Angel Flake coconut, toasted

Whip cream; fold in 1 cup chocolate sauce, then rum extract. Pour into freezer tray and sprinkle with toasted coconut. Freeze. 6 to 8 servings.

Fudge Sauce* :

1 6-oz. pkg. Semi-Sweet
    Chocolate Chips
¼ c. light cream
3 Tbsp. water

Bring cream and water to boil. Remove from heat; add chips and blend. 1 cup.

Rice Ambrosia

2 c. cooked rice
2 c. chopped apples, unpeeled
2 c. sm. marshmallows
1 c. crushed pineapple
½ c. sugar
⅛ tsp. salt
1 c. cream, whipped
8 maraschino cherries, cut

Combine as given and fold in whipped cream. Refrigerate a while before serving.

Macaroon Almond Ring

4 eggs (separated)
1 c. sugar
1 Tbsp. gelatin
1 pt. milk
1 doz. macaroons
½ tsp. each, vanilla and almond
    extract

Soak gelatin in cold water. Add sugar to egg yolks and stir well. Heat milk and pour over yolks. Cook until thick in double boiler. Add gelatin, extracts and let cool. Put macaroons in oven to dry and when cool, roll into crumbs and add to custard. Mix thoroughly. Add beaten egg whites. Pour into mold and let stand over night. After it has congealed, ice with whipped cream and sprinkle with grated coconut.

Cranberry Angel

1 baked and cooled 9-inch
   meringue shell*
1 pkg. strawberry gelatin
¼ c. sugar
1 c. boiling water
1 pkg. (10-oz.) frozen cranberry-
   orange relish, thawed
1 Tbsp. lemon juice
1 c. evaporated milk, chilled to
   icy cold

Mix gelatin and sugar, add boiling water and stir until completely dissolved. Stir in thawed cranberry-orange relish. Chill until thick but not set. Add lemon juice to chilled milk and beat until it holds a peak. Fold in gelatin mixture lightly, but thoroughly. Chill until mixture mounds when dropped from spoon, about 10 to 15 minutes. Turn into meringue shell which has been placed on serving plate. Chill until set, about 2 hours. 8 to 10 servings.

Meringue Shell* :
2 egg whites
⅔ c. sugar
½ Tbsp. vinegar or lemon juice

Add vinegar or lemon juice to egg whites. Beat until holds very stiff peak. Add sugar gradually, beating after each addition (1 Tablespoon at a time). Beat until meringue is very glossy and stiff. Draw a 9-inch circle on brown paper; place paper on baking sheet. Spread meringue over circle to a depth of about ¼ inch. With remaining meringue, form a wall around edge about 1 inch high. Bake in preheated very slow oven (275 degrees) until meringue is lightly browned, about 1 hour. Cool thoroughly before adding filling.

Orange Blossom Dessert

2 envelopes gelatin
1½ c. orange juice
1 c. boiling water
¾ c. sugar
½ tsp. salt
1½ c. heavy cream, whipped
½ c. shredded coconut
1½ tsp. grated orange rind
1 c. orange slices, drained
12 lady fingers, halved

Soften gelatin in ½ cup orange juice. Add boiling water and sugar; stir. Add remaining orange juice and salt. Chill until thickened. Then whip until fluffy; blend with cream. Fold in coconut, orange rind and orange slices. Line bottom of 7-inch spring mold with lady fingers, halved. Cover with about ⅓ of orange-cream mixture. Stand lady finger halves (rounded sides out) around side of pan. Add remaining orange filling. Chill overnight. Serve with whipped cream and garnish with orange slices. Makes 8 servings.

Pineapple-Macaroon Ice Box Dessert

1 c. butter
1 c. sugar
1 doz. macaroons broken into
   very small pieces
4 eggs
½ c. crushed pineapple
½ c. nuts, chopped fine
25 doz. lady fingers
   (split into halves)

Cream butter and sugar; add 1 of the eggs, beat five minutes; repeat until the 4 eggs are used. Add pineapple and nuts. Then cover the bottom of a casserole (square) with the split lady fingers, flat side down. Spread ½ of the butter mixture over lady fingers; add macaroons, then remainder of butter mixture. Cover with remaining lady fingers. Refrigerate 48 hours. Serve with whipped cream, sweetened to taste. Serves 16.

Coconut Party Torte

1 c. flour
1 Tbsp. baking powder
¾ tsp. salt
2 c. graham cracker crumbs
¾ c. shortening
1½ c. sugar
1½ c. shredded coconut
1¼ c. milk
1 tsp. vanilla
4 stiffly beaten egg whites
1½ c. heavy cream whipped

Sift together flour, baking powder, and salt; add crumbs. Cream well the shortening and sugar. Stir in coconut and vanilla. Add dry ingredients alternately with milk. Fold in egg whites. Pour into two 8 x 8 x 2-inch greased pans. Bake in moderate oven (375 degrees) 30 to 35 minutes. Cool. Spread whipped cream between layers and on top. Serves 12.

Peppermint Dessert

25 penny sticks peppermint
   candy
1 small pkg. miniature
   marshmallows
1 pt. whipping cream
2 c. chopped nuts
1 small box graham crackers,
   crushed
1 stick oleo, melted

Crush candy. Whip cream, but not stiff. Fold in nuts, candy and marshmallows. Make a crust of crushed cracker crumbs and oleo. Press crumbs into a buttered 15 x 10 2 inch pan. Pour peppermint mixture into pan and chill. Make the day before.

Five Layer Dessert

½ lb. vanilla wafers, crushed
¾ c. butter
1 c. powdered sugar
2 egg yolks
2 egg whites, beaten stiffly
No. 2 can crushed pineapple, drained
3 large bananas (sliced in pineapple juice)
½ pt. cream, whipped

Cover buttered pan with ½ of wafers. Cream butter, sugar and egg yolks well. Beat egg whites and fold into above mixture and spread over the crumbs. Top this with pineapple, then over this the bananas sliced. Spread with whipped cream and crumbs. Refrigerate several hours before serving.

Strawberry Foam Dessert

4 egg yolks
⅓ c. sugar
½ tsp. salt
⅔ c. milk
2 envelopes gelatin
8 Tbsp. cold water
1 tsp. vanilla
2 pkgs. frozen strawberries (whole)
4 egg whites
⅓ c. sugar
½ pt. XX cream whipped for topping

Beat egg yolks until lemon colored. Add ⅓ cup sugar, salt and milk. Cook over hot water until custard coats the spoon. Remove from heat and stir in gelatin which has been dissolved in cold water. Then add vanilla; cool and fold in the strawberries. Beat egg whites until stiff, gradually add other ⅓ cup sugar; fold into custard mixture and pour into crumb shell (vanilla or graham). (Pan 13 x 9 2") Chill. Top with whipped cream and garnish with pistachio nuts. Serves 20.

Marshmallow Date Loaf Dessert

16 small marshmallows
¼ c. light cream
1 c. (½ lb.) sliced dates
1 c. graham cracker crumbs
½ c. coarsely chopped walnuts
3 slices pineapple
½ c. XX cream, whipped

Cut marshmallows in small pieces or use double amount in small ones. Soak in light cream for 30 minutes. Add dates, crumbs, nuts and pineapple which has been cut into small pieces. Form into a roll about 3 inches in diameter on waxed paper. Roll up and chill several hours or overnight until firm. Slice and serve with whipped cream. Serves 6 to 8.

Mandarin Orange Cornucopias

2 11-oz. cans mandarin oranges
½ pkg. tiny marshmallows
1½ c. heavy cream or 1 pkg.
  whipped topping mix
½ tsp. almond flavoring
1 pkg. pie crust or
  1 pastry recipe
Dash of ginger

Drain oranges; cut marshmallows in half, combine with cream in large bowl and chill. Make pie crust, adding ginger. Divide in half. Roll each half into a 12 x 8 inch rectangle. Cut into 6-4 inch squares. Shape into a cone around brown paper. Moisten overlapping edge of dough and seal. Brush with cream; place on ungreased baking sheet. Bake in 425 degree oven for 15 to 20 minutes. Cool slightly; remove paper and cool completely. Beat chilled cream mixture until thick. Fold in flavoring and most of the oranges. Pile into cornucopias. Place remaining segments at open end as garnish. Makes 12.

Hot Fruit Bisque

12 macaroons, crumbled
1 can peaches, drained
  (#303 size)
1 can pears, drained
  (#303 size)
1 can apricots, drained
  (#303 size)
1 can pineapple, drained
  (#303 size)
½ c. cooking sherry
¼ c. brown sugar
¼ c. melted butter
½ c. slivered almonds

Mix fruits with sugar, sherry, and butter. Butter a 2½ qt. casserole and cover bottom with macaroon crumbs; alternate with fruit and crumbs, in layers, finishing with crumbs; sprinkle with almonds. Bake at 325 degrees until bubbly hot.

Mallow Pecan Torte

1 c. pecans
1 c. sugar
3 eggs
1 c. fine zwieback crumbs
1 tsp. baking powder
¼ tsp. salt
½ tsp. cinnamon

Chop nuts fine. Beat eggs in sugar, a little at a time. Combine crumbs, pecans, baking powder, salt and cinnamon; fold into egg mixture. Turn into greased 8-inch square pan. Bake in moderate oven 325 degrees for 40 to 45 minutes.

105

Topping:

1½ tsp. gelatin
1 c. milk
1 egg (separated)
¼ c. sugar
1 square (1-oz.) unsweetened
   chocolate
¼ tsp. salt
6 marshmallows (cut in pieces)
¼ c. whipped cream
½ c. chopped pecans

Soften gelatin in ¼ cup of the milk. Beat egg yolk lightly and combine with ¾ cup milk, finely chopped chocolate, sugar and salt. Stir over hot water until mixture thickens slightly. Blend in softened gelatin; stir until dissolved. Cool until mixture thickens. Fold in marshmallows, stiffly beaten egg white, whipped cream and pecans. Spoon over cooled torte and chill until firm. Cut in squares to serve. Makes 9 servings.

Angel Kiss Pie

3 egg whites
1 tsp. baking powder
12 graham crackers,
   finely crushed
⅛ tsp. salt
¾ c. sugar
1 c. pecans, finely chopped

Beat egg whites, baking powder, salt and sugar until stiff. Fold in crackers and nuts. Pour into well buttered pie pan and bake 20 minutes at 350 degrees. Serve with ice cream or whipped cream.

Pineapple Icebox Cake

Make cream filling:
   1 Tbsp. flour or cornstarch
   ⅓ c. sugar
   1 c. milk
   2 egg yolks, beaten
   Dash of salt
   1 tsp. butter
   1 tsp. vanilla
Add to this:
   1 small can crushed
      pineapple

Cream: ½ cup Crisco or other shortening and add gradually 1½ cups sifted powdered sugar. Mix well. Add 2 egg whites stiffly beaten and ¼ teaspoon vanilla.

Line dish or pan with waxed paper; then with slices of Angel Food Cake. Pour ½ of the cream filling and pineapple mixture over cake, then smooth over the first layer ½ of powdered sugar-egg white mixture. Sprinkle with chopped pecans.

Begin the next layer with the cake, then last of cream filling and pineapple mixture; then sugar-egg white mixture, last the pecans. Place in refrigerator for 12 or more hours. Slice in two-inch squares. Keeps well in refrigerator.

106

Cherry Whipped Cream Dessert

6 egg whites
¾ tsp. cream of tartar
2 c. sugar
2 c. soda crackers
¾ c. coarsely chopped nuts
2 tsp. vanilla

Beat egg whites until foamy, add cream of tartar. Gradually add sugar and beat until stiff. Fold in soda crackers (broken into size of dime), nuts, and vanilla. Bake in ungreased 13 x 9 x 2 inch pan for 35 minutes at 350 degrees. It will be toasty brown. Cool at room temperature. Refrigerate 3-4 hours, before filling.

Filling:

1 pint cream, whipped; add 1 tablespoon powdered sugar and spread over top of baked meringue. Spread 1 can of cherry pie filling on top of this. Refrigerate until ready to serve. Fix filling 2 hours before serving.

Molded Ambrosia

1 c. graham cracker crumbs
¼ c. butter or oleo, melted
1 can (9-oz.) crushed pineapple
1 pkg. orange flavored gelatin
⅓ c. sugar
1 c. hot water
1 c. sour cream
¼ tsp. vanilla
1 c. diced orange sections (may use mandarin orange sections)
½ c. flaked coconut

Combine crumbs and butter; reserve ⅓ cup for topping. Press remaining crumb mixture into an 8 x 8 x 2 inch dish. Drain pineapple, reserving syrup. Dissolve gelatin and sugar in hot water. Stir in reserved syrup. Chill until partially set. Add sour cream and vanilla; whip until fluffy. Fold in the pineapple, oranges, and coconut; pour over crumbs. Chill until firm. Cut in squares. Trim with maraschino cherries. Makes about 9 servings.

Orange-Apricot Cream Fluff

2 pkgs. orange flavored gelatin
1 c. boiling water
1 can (16 oz.) apricots
1 c. apricot syrup (drained from fruit)
½ c. orange juice
1 can (12 oz.) apricot nectar
2 egg whites
¼ tsp. salt
¼ c. sugar
1 c. whipped cream

Dissolve gelatin in boiling water. Drain apricots. Add 1 cup apricot syrup, orange juice and apricot nectar to gelatin mixture. Chop apricots; drain well, cover and set aside. Chill gelatin until almost firm. Beat in egg white and salt until mixture is light and fluffy. Fold sugar into whipped cream. Fold whipped cream and apricots into gelatin mixture. Rinse a 7 cup mold in cold water. Pile mixture lightly into mold. Chill until firm. Unmold, garnish with whipped cream and candied fruit. Serves 12 to 15.

Party Dessert

4 tsp. plain gelatin
2¼ c. pineapple juice
¼ c. sugar
Dash of salt
1 tsp. grated lemon peel
2 Tbsp. lemon juice
1 c. heavy cream, whipped
½ c. shredded coconut
1 pkg. frozen strawberries
  thawed
  or 2 c. fresh strawberries
  (in season) sliced in
  halves and lightly sugared

Dissolve gelatin in ½ cup pineapple juice; let stand 5 minutes, then set in hot water to dissolve. Remove from heat and add rest of pineapple juice, sugar, salt, lemon peel and juice; stir until sugar is dissolved. Cool until partially thickened, then beat until fluffy. Whip cream and fold quickly into whipped gelatin along with most of coconut. Pour into 1 qt. or 1½ qt. mold or bowl. Chill. To serve, unmold on plate, sprinkle with coconut; arrange a few berries around the base and over each serving. Makes 6 to 8 servings.

Quick Dessert

Dice or crumble 12 fig-filled cookies. Add 1 cup drained tidbits or crushed pineapple, and 1 cup small marshmallows. Chill several hours or overnight. About an hour before serving whip ½ cup heavy cream and fold in. Heap in dessert glasses, sprinkle with chopped nuts, and chill again. Makes 4 servings.

Variations: Macaroons or other cookies in place of fig bars may be used; add diced bananas with cream, and so on.

Lillian's Lemon Dessert

1 pkg. lemon jello
1 c. boiling water
2 Tbsp. flour
1 Tbsp. sugar
1 8-oz. pkg. cream cheese
1 c. sugar
1 tsp. vanilla
1 large can evaporated milk

Mix jello and boiling water and let cool. Mix flour and 1 tablespoon sugar with jello. Cream the cheese with the 1 cup sugar in mixer. Add vanilla and mix in the cooled jello. Chill and whip the evaporated milk and fold into mixture. Put in a vanilla wafer or graham cracker crust and sprinkle some crumbs on top.

108

Cherries On Snow

1½ c. graham cracker crumbs
1 Tbsp. sugar
¼ c. butter or oleo, melted
1 pkg. unflavored gelatin
¼ c. cold water
¼ c. cold milk
1 8-oz. pkg. cream cheese
½ c. sifted confectioners sugar
2 tsp. grated lemon rind
2 pkgs. whipped topping mix
1 can (1 lb. 5 oz.) cherry
  pie filling

Line sides with wax paper. Mix crumbs with sugar and melted butter and press into bottom of an 8 inch spring form pan. Soften gelatin in cold water. Heat milk and stir in gelatin and heat until gelatin melts. Set aside. Beat cream cheese and confectioners sugar until smooth. Add gelatin mixture and lemon peel; beat until well blended. Prepare topping mix according to pkg. directions and fold into the cream cheese mixture. Pour this filling into pan and refrigerate until firm. Gently spread cherry pie filling on top and refrigerate till serving time, preferably overnight. Cut in wedges to serve. Serves 9. Other sweetened fresh fruits may be substituted.

Strawberry Parfait Ring

1 c. sugar
⅓ c. boiling water
Red food coloring
4 egg whites
1 tsp. vanilla
¼ tsp. salt
2 c. heavy cream, whipped
1½ qts. fresh or frozen
  strawberries
Grated coconut
1 c. heavy cream whipped
  for garnish
2 qts. strawberry ice cream
  (about)

Cook sugar and water until syrup spins a thread (235 degrees F.) Add a few drops of red food coloring if you wish a pink mold.

Beat egg whites until stiff, gradually add hot syrup, beating until cool and light. Add vanilla and salt and fold in whipped cream. Pour into ring mold and freeze. Soften ice cream just enough to spoon over meringue, then freeze. At serving time unmold on your prettiest platter; fill center with strawberries and sprinkle coconut over top. Border ring with puffs of whipped cream, one for each serving. Makes 12 to 14 servings.

Trifle

1 white cake layer
1 large can fruit cocktail, drained
1 pkg. vanilla pudding mix, prepared
½ pt. whipping cream

Line bottom of medium bowl with cake that has been broken in pieces. Pour fruit over cake. Pour hot pudding over fruit. Set in refrigerator until pudding is cooled and firm, about 2 hours. Whip cream and spread over pudding. May be decorated with cherries and chopped nuts. This would be very pretty served in parfait glasses.

Persimmon Chiffon Pie

½ c. brown sugar
⅔ c. milk
1 envelope unflavored gelatin
3 eggs
1 c. persimmon pulp
¼ tsp. salt

Mix sugar, milk, beaten egg yolks and salt. Cook over low heat until hot. Add gelatin which has been dissolved in ¼ cup cold water. Add persimmon pulp and refrigerate for 1 hour. Beat egg whites until soft peaks form. Gradually beat in ¼ cup sugar. Fold into chilled mixture. Pour into baked pastry shells. Chill thoroughly.

Apricot Cake

1 lb. crushed vanilla wafers
2 c. chopped pecans
1 large can (#2¼ size) apricots, peeled and mashed
2 c. powdered sugar
2 sticks butter
4 whole eggs, well beaten
2 c. whipped cream (sweet)

Cream sugar and butter, add eggs, cook in double boiler until thick. Cool. Butter large oblong glass dish, spread ⅔ of crushed vanilla crumbs on bottom of pan, pour custard over crumbs. Add 1 cup nuts, ½ cup whipped cream, all of the apricots, other part whipped cream, remainder of nuts, then balance of wafers. Let set in refrigerator for 24 hours, slice and serve.

110

Applesauce Refrigerator Cake

1 15-oz. can sweetened
  condensed milk
½ c. plus 2 Tbsp. lemon juice
2 egg whites, (at room
  temperature)
2 c. applesauce
Vanilla wafers, about
  44 or 5¾ oz.
Whipped cream, if desired

In large-sized mixing bowl blend together condensed milk and ½ cup of lemon juice until thickened. Whip egg whites until stiff but not dry. Fold into milk mixture. Combine applesauce with the 2 tablespoons lemon juice. Line an 8 x 8 2 inch pan with waxed paper or metal foil. Place layer of wafers in bottom of pan; cover with half the milk mixture; spread half the applesauce on top. Repeat. Top with layer of wafers. Refrigerate 12 or more hours. Just before serving, unmold onto serving plate and peel off lining. Cut into 2 x 4 inch pieces. Garnish with whipped cream, if desired. Makes 9 servings.

Strawberry Angel Cake

2 small pkgs. strawberry gelatin
1 qt. vanilla ice cream
2 pkgs. 10 oz. strawberries
Angel food cake

Add 2 cups boiling water to gelatin and dissolve. Add 1 cup cold water to gelatin. Add ice cream and stir until melted; add strawberries. Break cake into bite size pieces. Alternate gelatin mixture and cake into mold. Chill until set. Freeze well; allow to partially thaw to serve.

Apple Dumplings

1¼ c. water
1¼ c. sugar
½ tsp. cinnamon
1 can biscuits (10)
4 or 5 apples, according to size

Mix water, sugar and cinnamon and boil together for 5 minutes. Set aside. Peel and slice apples. Flatten biscuits with rolling pin. Put 3 or 4 slices of apples in each biscuit. Dot with butter. Pull biscuit up over apples. Rub outside of biscuit with butter. Place in a 10 x 6 x 1½ inch pan and pour sugar mixture in pan. Bake in a 425 degree oven for 25 minutes. Serve with cream.

111

Pineapple Delight

1 3-oz. pkg. lemon flavored
  gelatin
½ c. boiling water
¾ c. sugar
1 #303 can crushed pineapple,
  drained a little
1 pt. whipping cream, whipped
1 c. chopped nuts
1 pkg. vanilla wafers

Dissolve gelatin and sugar in boiling water. Add pineapple and cool. Add whipped cream and nuts. Put a layer of vanilla wafers on bottom then a layer of mixture. Alternate layers with mixture on top. Refrigerate until firm.

Chocolate Ice Box Cake

1 lb. butter
1 lb. sugar
1 doz. eggs
1 tsp. vanilla
4 doz. almond macaroons
1 doz. lady fingers
½ c. bourbon
4 squares chocolate

Cream butter and sugar with an electric mixer for 20 minutes. Beat egg yolks with an electric mixer for 6 minutes. Beat egg whites until stiff, but not dry. Melt chocolate in double boiler. Cool, then add butter and sugar mixture and egg yolks. Add vanilla, then fold in egg whites. Soak macaroons in bourbon. Line tube pan with lady fingers and place along the side. (Split the lady fingers.) Place soaked macaroons on bottom on top of lady fingers. Pour chocolate mixture over macaroons. Repeat layers until ingredients reach the top. Refrigerate for at least 6 hours before serving. Serve with a dab of whipped cream and cherry on top. This can also be put into a long glass pan and cut into squares and served with whipped cream and a cherry.

To remove ring when finger is swollen, place hand in ice cold soap suds for a minute.

To remove rust from sink, use a soft cloth dipped in kerosene.

Use vinegar to remove rust stains from leaky faucets.

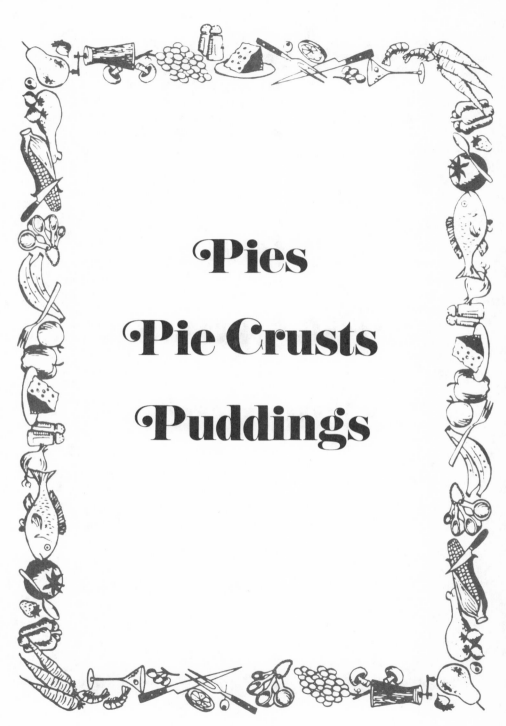

Pies

Pie Crusts

Puddings

Pies

Pie Crusts

Puddings

I Pineapple Pie

1 large can evaporated milk,
  chilled
1 large can crushed pineapple
  (not drained)
2 eggs
1 c. sugar
1 pkg. lemon jello
2 baked pie shells or cracker
  crumb crusts (9 inch)

Combine eggs, sugar, pineapple and bring to a boil. Add lemon jello and cool. Chill thoroughly. Fold whipped evaporated milk into pineapple-jello mixture. Pour into two baked pie shells. Chill before serving.

II Pineapple Pie

1 #2 can crushed pineapple
2 Tbsp. sugar
3 Tbsp. flour
1 egg
1 c. cream, whipped
18-20 regular marshmallows
⅛ tsp. salt

Drain pineapple; cook juice, sugar and flour slowly until it thickens. Beat egg well and add to mixture. Cook until thick. Add marshmallows and stir until melted. Add pineapple and chill. Fold in whipped cream and pour into baked shell. Refrigerate until ready to serve.

III Pineapple Pie

Scald:
  2 c. milk with 1 stick oleo
Add:
  4 egg yolks, beaten
  1 c. sugar with 4 Tbsp.
    cornstarch

Add egg mixture to hot milk and cook until thickened. Cool and add 1 can drained crushed pineapple. Pour custard into baked pie shell and top with meringue made from 4 egg whites, stiffly beaten with 8 tablespoons sugar. Bake in slow oven until brown.

Pineapple Coconut Pie

9-inch pie shell (unbaked)
3 eggs
¼ c. sugar
¼ tsp. salt
1 can (8½-oz.) crushed
  pineapple
1 c. white corn syrup
1 c. flaked coconut
2 Tbsp. melted butter
1 tsp. vanilla

Beat eggs. Beat in sugar and salt. Stir in undrained pineapple, syrup, coconut, vanilla and butter. Pour into shell. Bake in 400 degree F. oven for 45 minutes until set in center. Cool before cutting. Garnish with whipped cream.

115

Pineapple Cheese Chiffon Pie

1 can (9-oz.) crushed pineapple
1 3-oz. pkg. lemon gelatin
1 8-oz. pkg. cream cheese,
   softened
¾ c. sugar
1 c. evap. milk
2 Tbsp. lemon juice

Have baked pie shell ready. Drain pineapple, saving syrup. Add water to syrup to make 1 cup. Heat to boiling. Remove from heat; stir in gelatin until dissolved. Beat cream cheese, sugar and pineapple in a 3 qt. bowl at medium speed until creamy. Add gelatin mixture gradually at low speed and blend well. Chill until mixture is very thick, but not firm. Chill milk in ice tray until almost frozen at edges. Put ice cold milk in cold 1½ qt. bowl and whip until fluffy. Add lemon juice and whip until stiff. Add to chilled mixture and mix at low speed. Chill 15 minutes or until mixture is firm enough to mound well. Heap high into pie shell. If any is left, spoon into dessert dishes. Chill until firm, 2 to 3 hours.

Transparent Pie

½ c. butter
2 c. brown sugar
1 lb. citron, chopped
5 eggs
1 c. cream, whipped and
   unsweetened

Melt butter; add sugar and citron. Beat eggs, one at a time. Mix all together and cook in double boiler, stirring until thick. Pour into 12 small baked tart shells or 1 large shell. Chill. Serve with whipped cream.

Peppermint Chiffon Pie

10 inch baked graham cracker
   crust (recipe on box)
½ c. crushed peppermint
   stick candy
½ c. sugar
1 envelope unflavored gelatin
12 c. milk
3 egg yolks, slightly beaten
¼ tsp. salt
Red food coloring
3 egg whites
½ c. heavy cream, whipped

Prepare crust. Mix candy, ¼ cup sugar, gelatin, milk, egg yolks and salt. Cook and stir over low heat until gelatin dissolves and candy melts. Tint mixture with a few drops of coloring. Chill until partially set. Beat egg whites until soft peaks form; then gradually add remaining ¼ cup sugar, beating to stiff peaks. Fold into gelatin mixture. Fold in whipped cream. Chill until mixture mounds slightly when spooned. Pile into crust. Top with whipped cream and/or crushed peppermint candy when served if desired. Keep cold.

Raisin-Pecan Pies

Pastry

1 small pkg. cream cheese
1 stick oleo
1 c. flour
Muffin tins

Cream oleo and cheese. Add 1 cup flour and roll thin. Cut to fit into the muffin tins; prick with a fork.

Filling

1 stick oleo
1 c. sugar
2 egg yolks, well beaten
1 c. chopped nuts
1 c. raisins
2 egg whites, stiffly beaten

Cream oleo and sugar. Add well beaten egg yolks, then the nuts and raisins. Fold the beaten egg whites into the mixture. Fill unbaked pastry shells and bake at 250 degrees F. until brown and crisp, about 1 hour. Good at ball games.

Coconut Pie

½ c. sugar
2 c. sweet milk, scalded
1 c. coconut
2 egg yolks, beaten
1 Tbsp. cornstarch mixed with sugar

Beat egg yolks with sugar; add scalded milk and cook to consistency of custard. Add coconut and pour into a cooled, baked pie crust. Top with stiffly beaten egg whites, beaten with 4 tablespoons sugar. Brown in 400 degree F. oven.

Coconut Cream Pie

3 eggs, separated
2½ c. milk
1 c. plus 2 Tbsp. sugar
¼ tsp. salt
2 heaping Tbsp. cornstarch
2 Tbsp. butter or margarine
1 tsp. vanilla
1 c. coconut
1 baked 9-inch pie shell

In a 2-quart saucepan combine beaten egg yolks and milk. Combine ¾ cup sugar, salt and cornstarch; stir into milk. Cook, stirring constantly, over medium-high heat until smooth and thickened. Remove from heat; beat in butter, vanilla and ¾ cup coconut. Pour into baked pie shell. Beat egg whites with remaining sugar and dash of salt; spread on pie. Sprinkle remaining coconut over meringue. Bake at 425 degrees until golden brown.

Fudge Pie

3 Tbsp. cocoa
1 c. sugar
2 large or 3 small eggs
¼ c. sifted flour
2 Tbsp. water
¼ c. melted butter
1 tsp. vanilla
Dash salt

Mix and beat all ingredients, except butter. Melt butter and add last. Pour into an unbaked pie crust. Bake 10 minutes at 400 degrees then lower oven to 350 degrees and bake for 20 minutes or until pie is almost set. (Don't bake until firm.) The top is crisp.

Super Fudge Pie

1 stick butter
3 sq. unsweetened chocolate
4 eggs
1½ c. sugar
3 Tbsp. white Karo syrup
¼ tsp. salt
1 tsp. vanilla
1 9-inch unbaked pastry shell

Melt butter and chocolate in double boiler over low heat. Beat eggs until light; into the eggs beat the syrup, sugar, salt and vanilla. Add chocolate mixture, slightly cooled; mix well. Pour into pastry lined pan. Bake 25 to 30 minutes at 350 degrees F. or until top is crusty and filling set, but still somewhat soft inside. Do not overbake. Pie should shake like custard so it will not be too stiff when cool. May be served plain, but best served with topping of thin spade of vanilla ice cream.

Raisin Nut Pie

1 unbaked pie shell
2 Tbsp. vinegar
1 c. sugar
1 tsp. vanilla flavoring
½ c. raisins
2 egg yolks
2 Tbsp. butter
½ c. chopped nuts
2 egg whites, beaten

Mix sugar, butter, vinegar and egg yolks. Beat well. Add raisins, nuts, and vanilla. Beat egg whites until stiff and fold into above mixture. Pour into unbaked pie shell. Bake about 40 minutes at 350 degrees.

Fruit Custard Pie

3 egg yolks
¾ c. sugar
1 c. milk
1 c. cooked dried fruit
  (sweetened)
3 egg whites

Beat egg yolks; add sugar and beat until light. Add milk, and stir well. Spread dried fruit on pastry-lined pie pan. Add egg mixture, and bake at 325 degrees F. until firm. Then put meringue on top and bake at 350 degrees F. until brown. Serves 6.

I Chocolate Pie

1 c. sugar
6 Tbsp. cocoa
4 Tbsp. plain flour
3 egg yolks
½ stick oleo or butter
1 tsp. vanilla
2 c. milk (use 1 large can of
  evaporated milk and
  add water
  to make 2 c. of liquid)

Mix sugar, cocoa, and flour. To the slightly beaten egg yolks, add ½ cup of milk and mix thoroughly; add the rest of the milk to the egg yolks and stir well. Mix with dry ingredients, stirring constantly until mixture is free from lumps. Add oleo or butter in small pieces and cook until thick, stirring constantly. Cook this mixture in a heavy pan or double boiler. Pour into a cool, baked pie shell and top with meringue.

II Chocolate Pie

3 eggs
3 Tbsp. cornstarch
¾ c. sugar
½ c. "Nestles Quick" cocoa
¼ stick butter
1 small can evaporated milk
2 c. sweet milk
¼ tsp. salt
1 tsp. vanilla
1 baked pie crust

Mix sugar, 3 T. cornstarch, Nestles and salt together. Put milk in double boiler and bring to boiling point. Separate 2 whites from eggs and save for meringue. Add dry ingredients and egg yolks to milk and cook until thick. Remove from heat, add butter and vanilla. Pour into baked pie crust and top with meringue made from 2 egg whites stiffly beaten with 4 tablespoons sugar mixed with 1 tablespoon cornstarch, pinch salt. Brown in slow oven.

Chocolate Bar Pie

1 large chocolate bar with
  almonds, (7¼-oz. size)
1 large pkg. cool whip
Baked pie crust

Pick almonds out of chocolate bar and grind. Melt chocolate bar over hot water. Mix chocolate, almonds and cool whip. Pour into a prepared crust. Cool in refrigerator about 30 minutes or until set.

119

French Coconut Pie

3 beaten eggs
1½ c. sugar
½ tsp. coconut flavoring
½ tsp. vanilla flavoring
1 c. grated coconut
1 stick margarine
¼ tsp. salt
1 Tbsp. vinegar

Cream margarine, sugar and eggs well. Add other ingredients, mixing well. Pour into an unbaked pie shell. Bake at 350 degrees for 40-45 minutes.

Macaroon Pie

14 Ritz crackers, crumbled
14 dates, chopped
½ c. chopped nuts
¾ c. sugar
3 egg whites, beaten stiffly
½ tsp. salt
¼ tsp. baking powder
1 tsp. almond flavoring

Combine crackers, dates, nuts and sugar. Fold in stiffly beaten egg whites. Add salt, baking powder and flavoring. Mix well. Pour into 10" X 10" pan. Bake 20 to 25 minutes at 325 degrees F. Cool in pan. Cut in squares and serve with whipped or ice cream.

Jelly Pie

3 eggs
1 c. sugar
2 Tbsp. flour
2 Tbsp. tart jelly
½ stick oleo
½ c. water
1 tsp. vanilla
Pinch of salt

Bake in uncooked pie shell at 350 degrees F. for 30 minutes. Remove from oven just before pie reaches firm stage. You may make meringue of egg whites.

Orange Pie

⅓ c. butter
2 c. sugar
⅓ c. flour
6 egg yolks
2 egg whites (4 for meringue)
1½ c. fresh orange juice
¼ tsp. salt
¼ tsp. nutmeg

Cream butter. Sift flour and sugar together; beat egg yolks and 2 egg whites lightly. Stir all ingredients together lightly and pour into unbaked 10-inch pie shell. Bake 10 minutes at 450 degrees F., then at 300 degrees F. until firm. Top with meringue made of 4 egg whites, ½ cup sugar, ¼ teaspoon cream of tartar and pinch of salt. Cook 10 minutes at 400 degrees F.

Orange Dream Pie

⅓ c. butter
4 Tbsp. sugar
1¾ c. sifted flour
¼ tsp. salt

Soften butter with sugar and add flour and salt. Mix until dough will form. (An electric mixer on low speed may be used.) Place ⅔ cup of mixture in a small pan for crumb topping. Press remaining mixture evenly over bottom and sides of a 10-inch pie pan. Flute. Bake at 375 degrees F. until light golden brown. Also brown the ⅔ cup of crumb mixture for topping.

Orange Cheese Filling:
 ¼ c. undiluted frozen orange
  juice
 1 envelope unflavored gelatin
 ½ c. sugar
 ¼ tsp. cream of tartar
 3 eggs separated
 ¼ c. undiluted orange juice
 ½ c. sugar
 1 tsp. vanilla
 ¼ tsp. salt
 1 c. cream cheese
 1 c. whipping cream

Combine orange juice and gelatin in top of double boiler. Add egg whites, ½ cup sugar and cream of tartar. Cook over boiling water, beating constantly with electric mixer or rotary beater until stiff peaks form. Set aside. Combine in medium saucepan, ¼ cup undiluted orange juice, egg yolks, ½ cup sugar, vanilla and salt. Beat until light. Cook, stirring constantly, until smooth and thick. Remove from heat. Add 1 cup cream cheese; beat until smooth. Fold into gelatin-egg white mixture. Chill until thickened but not set, about 30 minutes. Beat 1 cup whipping cream until thick; fold into gelatin mixture. Spoon into baked shell. Sprinkle with reserved crumbs. Chill about 2 hours.

121

Buttermilk Chess Pie

1 9-inch pie shell (unbaked)
1½ c. sugar
1 stick butter
1 Tbsp. flour or cornstarch
3 eggs, well beaten
⅛ tsp. salt
¾ c. buttermilk
1½ tsp. vanilla

Preheat oven for 10 minutes. Have all ingredients at room temperature. Blend sugar, butter, flour and salt until creamy. Add well-beaten eggs and vanilla. Add buttermilk last. Bake at 400 degrees F. for 10 minutes. Reduce heat to 325 degrees F. and continue baking 45 minutes.

Never Fail Chess Pie

10-inch pie shell, unbaked
4 eggs, beaten
1½ c. sugar
2 tsp. cornmeal
Pinch of salt
4 Tbsp. cream
1 tsp. vanilla
¼ c. melted butter

Combine eggs, sugar, cornmeal, salt, butter, cream and vanilla. Beat well until blended. Pour into pie shell and bake for 30 minutes at 350 degrees F.

Magic Pumpkin Pie

1 unbaked pie shell (9-inch)
2 c. canned pumpkin
1 can sweetened condensed
    milk
1 egg
½ tsp. salt
½ tsp. nutmeg
½ tsp. ginger
¾ tsp. cinnamon

Blend all ingredients in a large mixing bowl, mixing well. Pour into an unbaked pie shell. Bake in a 375 degree oven until sharp-bladed knife inserted near the center comes out clean, about 50-55 minutes. Cool. Refrigerate at least 1 hour before serving. Top with whipped cream.

Apple Butter Pumpkin Pie

1 unbaked 9-inch pie shell
1 c. apple butter
1 c. cooked or canned pumpkin
½ c. firmly packed brown sugar
½ tsp. salt
¾ tsp. cinnamon
¾ tsp. nutmeg
⅛ tsp. ginger
3 slightly beaten eggs
¾ c. evaporated milk

Combine apple butter, pumpkin, sugar, salt and spices. Add eggs. Mix well; add milk gradually; mix, pour into pie shell and bake at 425 degrees F. about 40 minutes.

Cheese Pie

1½ c. grated cheese
1½ c. sugar
1 tsp. flour
½ tsp. salt
3 eggs
1 tsp. vanilla
1 tsp. grated orange rind
1 c. milk

Separate eggs and whip egg whites until stiff. Mix all other ingredients well. Fold in stiffly beaten egg whites. Pour into an unbaked pastry shell and bake in 300 degree oven for 35 minutes. For best results use sharp cheese.

Apple Cheese Pie

¾ c. sugar
3 Tbsp. flour
⅛ tsp. salt
1 c. grated medium sharp cheese
1 can #2 apple slices
3 tsp. lemon juice
3 Tbsp. light cream
½ tsp. cinnamon

Mix together sugar, flour, salt and ⅔ cup of cheese. Spoon half of this mixture into 8" unbaked pie shell. Combine apples, lemon juice, remaining sugar mixture and cheese. Turn into pie. Pour cream over entire filling. Bake in hot oven 425 degrees F. for 40 to 45 minutes.

Peanut Fudge Perfection Pie
(A different pie shell)

3 chocolate covered peanut
  candy bars, cut in pieces
⅓ c. peanut butter
1 c. finely crushed chocolate
  cookies
3 Tbsp. evap. milk
1 pkg. lemon-flavored instant
  pudding mix
1 envelope dessert topping mix

Combine candy bars and peanut butter in top of double boiler. Stir until candy is melted and blended with the peanut butter. Remove from heat and add cookie crumbs and milk. Mix until blended. Grease a 9-inch pie pan. With fingers press mixture into pie pan. Chill. Prepare pudding according to package directions. Pour into pie shell. Allow to set. When ready to serve, top with dessert topping mix prepared according to directions. Makes 8 servings.

Peanut Butter Pie

1 c. confectioners sugar
⅔ c. smooth peanut butter
Baked pastry shell

Mix together until mixture resembles corn meal.

Cream Filling:
2½ c. scaled milk
3 Tbsp. cornstarch
Pinch salt
3 egg yolks
¾ c. sugar
1 tsp. vanilla

Scald milk. Beat egg yolks and add to milk with sugar, cornstarch and salt. Cook in double boiler to consistency of custard. Add vanilla. Cool. Over bottom of baked pie crust, spread most of the peanut butter mixture. Then pour in the cold cream filling. Top with meringue (3 egg whites). Sprinkle remaining peanut butter mixture over meringue and bake at 350 degrees F. 10 to 12 minutes, or until golden brown.

Kitchen odors can be removed by placing an orange peel upon the top of the stove while in use.

To keep cauliflower or cabbage odorless while cooking, place a piece of bread on top of pan.

Cream Cheese Pie

1 small pkg. cream cheese
  (room temp.)
½ pt. whipping cream
½ c. sugar
½ tsp. almond extract
½ tsp. vanilla
Baked pastry shell

Have cheese very soft. Whip cream; add sugar slowly; then the flavoring. Add softened cheese and mix well. Pour into baked pie shell. Cover top with one can of Instant Pie Cherries. Chill.

Fruit Crown Cheese Cake

Fruit Mixture:

2 envelopes unflavored gelatin
½ c. water
1 can (8 oz.) fruit cocktail
1 Tbsp. sugar
1 Tbsp. lemon juice
1 tsp. rum flavoring or extract

Soften gelatin in water in top of double boiler; heat, stirring constantly, over boiling water until gelatin dissolves; remove from heat. Combine fruit cocktail and syrup, sugar, lemon juice, and rum flavoring or extract in small bowl; stir in 1 tablespoon of the dissolved gelatin. Pour into an 8 cup mold. Let stand at room temperature until cheese mixture is made.

Cheese Mixture:

2 eggs separated
½ c. milk
½ c. sugar
1 tsp. salt
2 c. cream-style cottage cheese
1 tsp. grated lemon rind
2 Tbsp. lemon juice
1 tsp. vanilla
1 c. cream for whipping

Stir egg yolks, milk, sugar and salt into remaining dissolved gelatin in top of double boiler. Heat, stirring constantly over simmering water, 10 minutes, or until mixture thickens slightly; cool. Press cottage cheese through sieve into large bowl. Stir in lemon rind, lemon juice, vanilla, and cooled gelatin mixture. Chill fruit layer in mold until sticky-firm; chill cheese mixture, stirring several times, until as thick as unbeaten egg white. Beat egg whites until they stand in firm peaks in medium size bowl. Beat cream until stiff in small bowl. Fold beaten egg whites, then whipped cream into cheese mixture; pour over sticky-firm fruit layer in mold; chill until firm. When ready to serve, loosen mold around edge with a thin blade knife, then dip very quickly in and out of pan of hot water. Invert onto serving plate; lift off mold. Peel and slice 1 banana; arrange slices, overlapping, in a ring around top; place a cluster of sugared grapes in center, if you wish. To make: Dip a small bunch of green grapes into a mixture of 1 egg white beaten slightly with ½ teaspoon water in small bowl, then into granulated sugar, turning to coat grapes well. Let dry on paper towels.

Joyce's Pineapple Cheese Cake

1 12-oz. can evaporated milk
1 c. hot water
1 c. sugar
1 box lemon gelatin
1 8-oz. pkg. cream cheese
1 c. crushed pineapple (drained)
  Optional
½ c. cherries (sliced) optional

Chill evaporated milk. Mix lemon gelatin and hot water; cool while milk is chilling. Cream the sugar and cream cheese. Mix with gelatin. Whip evaporated milk. Combine it and gelatin mixture. Add pineapple and cherries. Pour into vanilla wafer crust. Chill in refrigerator until it sets.

Vanilla Wafer Crust:
Mix together 3 cups vanilla wafer crumbs and 1 stick soft oleo or butter. Place in container, pressing together with spoon or fingers.

Variation:
Substitute strawberry gelatin for lemon and sliced strawberries for cherries.

Butterscotch Pie

3 eggs
6 Tbsp. flour
¼ tsp. salt
1 tsp. vanilla
1 c. brown sugar
2 c. milk
3 Tbsp. butter
2 Tbsp. caramel syrup

To make caramel syrup: Heat ½ cup white sugar in smooth, dry skillet until golden brown. Add ⅓ cup boiling water. Cook to a thick, smooth syrup.

Beat egg yolks with brown sugar; mix flour with a little water to make a paste. Add to first mixture; then add milk, salt and caramel syrup. Cook in top of double boiler until thick. Remove from heat, add butter and vanilla; cool. Pour into baked pie crust. May be topped with meringue, whipped cream or plain.

Mincemeat Ice Cream Pie

1 9-inch baked pie crust
1 qt. vanilla ice cream
1½ c. prepared mincemeat

Fold 1 cup of mincemeat into 1 quart of softened vanilla ice cream. Pour mixture into baked pie shell and place in freezer to set. Simmer the remaining mincemeat in sauce pan for 5 minutes. Chill. Spoon mincemeat around edge of filling. Serve in chilled plates.

Millionaire Pie

1½ c. sugar
2 eggs
2 Tbsp. vinegar
2 Tbsp. water
1 tsp. allspice
1 c. pecans
1 c. raisins

Beat eggs; add sugar and allspice. Stir in vinegar and water. Add pecans and raisins. Pour into uncooked pastry shell and bake in 350 degrees F. oven for 45 minutes. Spread with lemon frosting.

Lemon Frosting:

1 box confectioners sugar
1 orange, juice and grated rind
½ lemon (juice)
1 Tbsp. butter, melted

Sift sugar; gradually add rind, juice and melted butter. Spread on top of warm pie.

Heavenly Pie

1½ c. granulated sugar
1 tsp. cream of tartar
4 egg whites
4 egg yolks
3 Tbsp. lemon juice
1 Tbsp. grated lemon rind
⅛ tsp. salt
1 pt. heavy whipping cream
3 Tbsp. shredded coconut
  (optional)
Whole strawberries

Preheat oven to 275 degrees F. Sift sugar and cream of tartar. Separate eggs. Beat egg whites until stiff and glossy, slowly adding sugar, beating all the time. When meringue is glossy and stiff, spread over greased 10 inch pie plate, making bottom ¼ inch thick and the sides 1 inch thick. Sprinkle coconut around sides if desired. Bake 1 hour until light brown. Cool. Beat egg yolks slightly in double boiler. Stir in ½ cup sugar, 3 tablespoons lemon juice, 1 tablespoon grated lemon rind and ⅛ teaspoon salt. Stir over boiling water until thick, 8-10 minutes. When mixture cools, whip cream and fold custard into it. Spread custard over cooled pie shell, filling bottom well. Sprinkle coconut on top and chill for 12-24 hours. The longer it chills the better. Whip cream and dot on top of pie. Have 2 cups of strawberries washed, drained and sprinkled with sugar to dot over pie.
****

For a delicious pastry for apple pie, add ½ cup of grated sharp cheese to your favorite recipe.

To prevent the edge of pastry from browning too much, cover it with a collar made of aluminum foil.

Glazed Sweet Potato Pie

1 c. sugar
2 Tbsp. cornstarch
½ tsp. salt
¼ tsp. cinnamon
¼ tsp. nutmeg
⅛ tsp. cloves
¾ c. red Karo syrup
3 Tbsp. oleo
1 c. mashed sweet potatoes
3 eggs, slightly beaten
¼ c. chopped pecans, optional
1 unbaked 9 inch pastry shell

Mix sugar, cornstarch, salt and spices in heavy saucepan. Stir in syrup, butter and mashed potatoes. Bring to boil over medium heat, stirring occasionally. Boil 3 minutes until slightly thickened. Remove from heat and stir gradually into beaten eggs. Pour into unbaked pie shell. If desired sprinkle with chopped pecans. Bake in hot oven (400 degrees F.) 15 minutes, then reduce heat to 350 degrees and bake until filling is firm (about 40 minutes longer).

Old Fashioned Egg Custard Pie

1 Tbsp. flour
¾ c. sugar
3 eggs
1½ c. milk
½ stick butter or margarine
½ tsp. nutmeg or
   vanilla flavoring
1 unbaked pie shell

Mix together flour, sugar and eggs, beating until smooth. In a saucepan heat the milk and butter until butter is melted and milk is scalded. Add this to egg mixture. Beat well, until thoroughly mixed. Flavor with nutmeg or vanilla if desired. Pour into an unbaked pie shell. Bake at 400 degrees for 20-30 minutes. To test for doneness, shake pan gently. If the filling quivers instead of rippling and seems set, the pie is done.

Cracker Pie

3 egg whites
½ tsp. baking powder
1 c. sugar
12 crushed soda crackers
1 c. chopped nuts
12 chopped dates or ½ c.
   flaked coconut

Beat egg whites and when foamy sprinkle in baking powder. Beat until soft peaks form; add the sugar and beat until stiff. Add crushed crackers and rest of ingredients. Pour into a well greased 8 inch pie pan. Bake in a 275 degree oven for 30-45 minutes or until pie is firm and a nice brown. Serve with ice cream or whipped cream.

Strawberry Pie
(Ice Cream Pie)

Filling: Place 3 oz. pkg. strawberry flavored gelatin in a bowl.
Add:
1 c. hot water
½ c. cold water and mix well

Add: 1 pt. strawberry ice cream (cut up) to gelatin mixture. Place gelatin and strawberry mixture in refrigerator until it thickens and mounds when dropped from spoon, approximately 20 to 30 minutes. Gently fold in 1½ cups strawberries, fresh or frozen. Pour into a graham cracker or vanilla wafer crust and chill until firm, about 1 hour. This is a good freezer pie. Very good to eat frozen.

White Christmas Pie

Filling:
½ c. sugar
1 envelope unflavored gelatin
1¾ c. milk
3 egg whites
½ c. sugar
1 c. moist, shredded coconut
¼ c. flour
½ tsp. salt
¾ tsp. vanilla
¼ tsp. almond flavoring
¼ tsp. cream of tartar
½ pt. whipping cream

Make and bake a 9-inch pie shell with high fluted edge.

Blend thoroughly in a saucepan the sugar, flour, gelatin and salt. Gradually stir in the milk. Cook over medium heat until mixture boils, stirring constantly. Boil 1 minute. Place pan in cold water and cool until mixture mounds slightly when dropped from spoon. Blend in vanilla and almond flavoring. Carefully fold mixture into meringue made of cream of tartar, egg whites and ½ cup sugar. Gently fold in whipped cream and then the coconut. Pile into the cooled, baked pie shell. Chill several hours until set. Serve cold.

Black Bottom Eggnog Pie

1½ c. gingersnap crumbs
6 Tbsp. butter, melted
1 envelope unflavored gelatin
¼ c. cold water
2 c. dairy eggnog
⅓ c. sugar
2 Tbsp. cornstarch
¼ tsp. salt
2 squares unsweetened
  chocolate
1 tsp. vanilla
1 tsp. rum extract
2 c. heavy cream
¼ c. confectioners sugar

Combine gingersnap crumbs and butter thoroughly. Press firmly into a 9-inch pie pan. Bake in slow oven (300 degrees F.) 5 minutes. Cool. Soften gelatin in cold water 5 minutes. Heat eggnog to scalding, do not boil. Combine sugar, cornstarch and salt; mix with warm eggnog. Cook, stirring constantly, until mixture thickens. Remove from heat and stir in the softened gelatin until dissolved. Divide mixture in half. Melt 1½ squares of chocolate and stir into one half of the mixtures with vanilla. Pour mixture into gingersnap crust. Let remaining half cool, then add rum extract. Whip 1 cup of the heavy cream until stiff and fold into custard mixture. Spoon over chocolate layer. Chill. Whip remaining cup of cream until stiff; beat in confectioners sugar. Spread over pie. Grate remaining ½ square chocolate and sprinkle over top. Chill.

Molasses Pie

1 c. brown sugar
½ c. molasses
½ c. coconut
1 c. buttermilk
1 egg, beaten
¼ tsp. baking soda
½ tsp. ginger
½ tsp. cinnamon
1 Tbsp. flour
1 9 inch unbaked pie shell

Mix sugar, molasses, egg, coconut and buttermilk. Then add mixture of soda, ginger, cinnamon and flour. Mix well. Pour into unbaked pie shell. Bake in slow oven (300 degrees F.) for 1½ hours. To make attractive tarts for parties and teas, bake in pastry lined muffin tins.

Cherry Pie

1 graham cracker crust
1 can pie cherries, drained
1 3 oz. pkg. cherry gelatin
1 c. sugar
½ c. chopped nuts

Drain the cherries and save the juice. Add enough water to juice to make 1 cup of liquid. Add sugar to juice and bring to a rolling boil. Remove from heat and add the package of gelatin. Let cool. Add cherries and the nuts. Pour into pie shell and refrigerate for several hours. Top with whipped cream.

One Crust Cherry Pie

1 No. 2 can cherries
¾ c. sugar
3 Tbsp. cornstarch
¼ tsp. salt
Baked pie shell

Simmer cherries and half of sugar for 5 minutes. Combine rest of sugar with cornstarch, salt and little bit of cherry juice; add to cherries. Cook on low heat for 5 minutes. Pour into baked pie shell. Cool. Serve with ice cream or whipped cream. Red food color can be added to cherries to improve the color if desired.

Surprise Pie

1 c. sugar
¼ c. flour
1 3 oz. pkg. orange gelatin
1 small can crushed pineapple
   and juice
Red food coloring
1 can unsweetened cherries
   and juice
5 mashed bananas
1 c. chopped nuts
Graham cracker pie crust or
   baked pie shells

Mix sugar, flour, gelatin, pineapple and cherries and heat until thick. Cool. Add mashed bananas, chopped nuts and red food coloring. Pour into prepared pie shells and top with whipped cream. Let chill for 3-4 hours in refrigerator. This will make 3 8-inch pies. Good with plain pie crust or graham cracker crust.

I Pecan Pie

3 whole eggs
2 Tbsp. flour
1 tsp. salt
½ c. sugar
1 c. Karo (dark or light)
4 Tbsp. butter
½ c. water
1 c. chopped pecans

Mix ingredients together well. Bake in an 8 or 9-inch pie shell at 325 degrees, for 40 minutes. This is not so awfully sweet.

II Pecan Pie

Pastry:
  3 oz. cream cheese
    (cream well)
  1 stick oleo (cream)
  1 c. sifted flour
  ½ tsp. salt

Filling:
  1 egg (well beaten)
  ¾ c. brown sugar, packed
  1 Tbsp. soft oleo
  ⅔ c. chopped pecans
  ⅛ tsp. salt
  1 tsp. vanilla

Mix cheese and oleo; add flour and salt. Chill. Roll dough into 12 balls. Place in miniature muffin tins and press into shells. Add the following filling:

Mix and pour into miniature shells. Bake 25 minutes.

Creamy Pecan Pie

1 pkg. (3½ oz.) vanilla pudding
  and pie filling
1 c. dark corn syrup
¾ c. evaporated milk
1 egg, slightly beaten
1 c. chopped pecans
1 unbaked pie shell

Blend pie filling mix with corn syrup. Gradually stir in evaporated milk and egg. Add pecans. Pour into pie shell. Bake at 375 degrees until top is firm and just begins to crack, about 40 minutes. Cool at least 3 hours.

Caramel Pecan Pumpkin Pie

2 c. sugar
1 Tbsp. flour
5 c. cooked or canned pumpkin
4 eggs
1 Tbsp. vanilla
1 tsp. lemon extract
½ tsp. cinnamon
½ tsp. nutmeg
½ tsp. allspice
¼ c. corn syrup
½ c. milk

Blend sugar, flour, salt, cinnamon, nutmeg and allspice. Mix with pumpkin. Stir eggs very lightly (make no foam), add. Mix together the vanilla, lemon extract, corn syrup and milk. Add to the pumpkin mixture. Pour into unbaked pie shells. Bake 10 minutes at 425 degrees F.; then at 350 degrees F. for about 40 minutes. Makes 2 pies.

Topping:
  ¼ c. plus 2 Tbsp.
    brown sugar
  2 Tbsp. butter, melted
  ¼ tsp. salt
  ½ c. pecan halves (may be
    broken)

Combine the above ingredients and spread evenly over the pies just before they are done. Return to oven for about 5 minutes more.

Lemon Cake Pie

2 Tbsp. flour
¾ c. sugar
1 Tbsp. butter
2 egg yolks, beaten
¼ c. lemon juice
1 c. milk

Cream the flour, sugar and butter. Add egg yolks, lemon juice and milk, mixing well. Fold in 2 egg whites, stiffly beaten. Pour uncooked mixture into an 8-inch pie shell, which has been baked 5 minutes in a 475 degree oven. Finish by baking for 45 minutes at 325 degrees F. Will form a cake top with a layer of custard below.

Lemon Cloud Pie

2 eggs, separated
1 pkg. lemon pudding and
   pie filling mix
1 pkg. 3 oz. cream cheese
¼ c. sugar

Prepare pie filling according to package directions, using 2 egg yolks. Add softened cream cheese; beat well. Combine 2 whites and sugar. Beat until stiff peaks form. Fold into lemon mixture. Spoon into baked pie shell. Chill at least 2 hours.

Lemon Chiffon Pie

4 eggs, separated
½ c. sugar
½ c. lemon juice
Grated rind of 2 lemons
1 pkg. unflavored gelatin
¼ c. cold water
½ c. sugar
Whipped cream or
   whipped topping

Beat together egg yolks, ½ cup sugar, lemon juice and rind. Cook in top of double boiler until thick, stirring constantly. Soften gelatin in ¼ cup of cold water and stir into hot mixture and cool. Beat egg whites, adding ½ cup sugar gradually until very stiff and fold into egg yolk mixture. Pour into a baked pie shell or graham cracker crust and refrigerate for 2-3 hours, or overnight. Spread top with whipped cream or whipped topping when ready to serve. Serves 6-8.

I Lemon Pie

6 eggs, beaten separately
2 lemons
1 c. sugar
1 Tbsp. butter
Few grains salt
Baked pastry shell

Beat eggs separately and to the 6 yolks add the juice of 2 lemons, grated rind of 1 lemon, and the sugar. Cook in double boiler until thick. Remove from heat and add salt and butter. Pour over the beaten egg whites of 4 eggs and return to double boiler. Cook for 5 minutes, stirring all the time. Pour into baked pastry shell and add meringue made from 2 remaining egg whites. Bake in slow oven.

II Lemon Pie

1½ c. sugar
¼ tsp. salt
3 well beaten egg yolks
½ c. fresh lemon juice
7 level Tbsp. corn starch
1½ c. hot water
2 Tbsp. butter

Combine sugar, salt and cornstarch. Add water slowly; stir well and cook until clear and thick. Remove from stove, pour over beaten yolks. Return to stove and cook slowly for 6 minutes, stirring constantly. Remove from heat, add juice and butter. Allow to cool. Pour into cooled baked pie shell. Top with meringue: 3 stiffly beaten egg whites, 5 tablespoons sugar. Bake at 400 degrees until golden brown.

Lemon Pie Hawaiian

¾ c. crushed pineapple
    (drained)
¼ c. firmly packed
    brown sugar
¼ c. flaked coconut
4 Tbsp. softened oleo
1 pkg. lemon pie filling
¾ c. sugar
2 c. cold water
2 eggs separated
2 Tbsp. lemon juice
1 9-inch pie shell (unbaked)

Combine pineapple, brown sugar, coconut and 2 tablespoons oleo. Mix well; spread on bottom of unbaked pie shell. Bake in 425 degree F. oven for 15 minutes or until pastry is done. Cool. Combine lemon pie filling and ½ cup sugar. Gradually add water and 2 slightly beaten egg yolks. Cook over medium heat, stirring constantly until mixture comes to a full boil. Stir in remaining oleo and lemon juice. Cool. Beat 2 egg whites until foamy. Gradually add remaining ¼ cup sugar and continue beating until stiff peaks form. Fold into cooled lemon mixture; pour into prepared pie shell. Chill until firm.

Kentucky Lemon Pie

1 9-inch unbaked pie shell
5 eggs
1½ c. white corn syrup
1 c. sugar
3 lemons, juice
Grated rind of 1 lemon
¼ c. melted butter or oleo

Beat eggs well. Add syrup, sugar, lemon juice and grated rind. Add butter and beat until well mixed. Pour into 9-inch unbaked pie shell. Bake at 375 degrees F. for 10 minutes then reduce heat to 350 degrees F. and bake 30 to 40 minutes longer.

Hazel's Pie

1 c. Eagle Brand milk
¼ c. lemon juice
1 can pie cherries (well drained)
1 large carton Cool Whip
¾ c. pecans

Mix real well and pour into two 8-inch graham cracker crusts. Chill thoroughly.

Coconut Meringue

Combine in double boiler:
  2 egg whites, unbeaten
  ½ c. sugar
  ⅛ tsp. salt
  2 Tbsp. water

Beat with rotary beater until well blended. Cook 1 minute over boiling water; beat constantly. Remove from water and beat 2 minutes longer, or until mixture peaks. Pile lightly on filled pie. Sprinkle with toasted coconut. **To toast:** Spread ½ cup shredded coconut on cookie sheet, brown lightly in 400 degree F. oven. Watch closely; should be a golden brown. (Can be used without coconut).

Lemon Jelly Filling

2 egg yolks
1 c. sugar
2½ Tbsp. flour
2 lemons, juice (grated rind optional)
2 Tbsp. butter
½ c. boiling water

Mix in order given. Cook in double boiler until real thick and it shines.

Butter Crunch Pie Crust

½ c. butter or oleo
¼ c. brown sugar, packed
1 c. sifted flour
½ c. chopped pecans, walnuts or coconut

Heat oven to 400 degrees F. Mix all ingredients with hands. Spread in 9-inch pie pan and bake 15 minutes. Take from oven and stir with a spoon. Save ¾ cup for topping. Immediately press remainder of mixture in bottom and sides of pan. Cool. Pour in your favorite pie filling and sprinkle remainder of the crumbs on top. Chill for 1 hour. Delicious with Lemon Ice Box Pie.

Cream Cheese Pie Crust

1 pkg. (3 oz.) cream cheese
1 stick oleo or butter
1 c. flour

Mix all ingredients well, then pat out in pie pan and bake as usual.

No-Roll Pie Crust

1½ c. flour
1½ tsp. sugar
1 tsp. salt
2 Tbsp. sweet milk
½ c. cooking oil

Mix all ingredients in a 9-inch pie plate. With hand, mash and spread dough to sides and bottom to desired thickness. Bake in a very hot oven (450 degrees) for 15 minutes or until delicately browned.

South American Fruit Pudding

½ c. golden raisins (white)
¼ c. rum
1 pkg. vanilla pudding and
  pie filling mix
2 c. milk
1 tsp. vanilla
1⅓ c. flaked coconut
1 small jar maraschino cherries
  (halved)
¾ c. whipping cream, whipped
½ c. coarsely chopped pecans
½ c. sliced, pitted dates
¾ c. dry almond macaroon
  crumbs
Pecan halves

Soak raisins in rum overnight. Cook and stir pudding mix and milk over medium heat until mixtures comes to a boil. Remove from heat and add vanilla and coconut. Cool. Lightly oil a 1½ quart mold or loaf pan. Arrange cherry and pecan halves in a design on bottom of mold. Fold in chopped nuts, raisins, dates and macaroon crumbs into cooked pudding. Then fold in whipped cream. Spoon mixture carefully over design in pan. Freeze 8 hours or until firm. Unmold. Garnish with additional cherry and pecan halves. Serves 10 to 12.

Orange Marmalade Bread Pudding

2 c. stale bread (toasted and
  grated)
2 c. scalded milk
½ c. sugar
3 eggs, slightly beaten
2 Tbsp. melted butter
2 tsp. vanilla
Dash of salt
1 glass orange marmalade
1 tsp. nutmeg

Soak grated crumbs in hot milk. Cool. Add other ingredients, mixing well. Place in buttered casserole and bake in a 325 degree oven for 1 hour.

Apricot Pudding

1 c. dried apricots
4 eggs, separated
1 lemon
2½ Tbsp. flour
¼ c. melted butter
1¼ c. sugar
¼ tsp. salt
1¼ c. milk

Boil apricots in 2 cups water, reduce heat and simmer 20 minutes. Chop very fine or mash through sieve. Beat egg yolks well; add grated rind and juice of lemon. Add all other ingredients. Stir until well blended. Add stiffly beaten egg whites, folding in gently. Spoon into a greased 1½ quart casserole. Set casserole in pan of hot water. Bake in 350 degree oven for 40 minutes. Serve plain or with whipped cream. Serves 6.

Congealed Plum Pudding

1 pkg. lemon jello, dissolved in
  2 c. water (hot)
1 c. prunes (cooked & seeded)
1 cup raisins
1 c. grape nuts (cereal)
¼ c. citron
¼ tsp. cloves
½ tsp. cinnamon

Measure and sift dry ingredients. Add diluted milk and mincemeat. Mix and pour into baking dish. Combine ½ cup brown sugar, 1 cup boiling water, 1 teaspoon lemon juice and 1 teaspoon butter. Pour over uncooked pudding. Bake in moderate oven, 325 degrees for about 30 minutes. Serve hot.

Mincemeat Pudding

1¼ c. flour
2 tsp. baking powder
¼ tsp. salt
½ c. sugar
1 c. mincemeat
¼ c. water
¼ c. evaporated milk

Mix well. Let congeal in refrigerator after it has been placed in molds or in flat pan (to cut in squares). Serve with whipped cream.

Grape-Nuts Pudding

1 tsp. grated lemon rind
4 Tbsp. butter
1 c. sugar
2 egg yolks, beaten
3 Tbsp. lemon juice
2 Tbsp. cornstarch
4 Tbsp. grape-nuts (cereal)
1 c. milk
⅛ tsp. salt
2 egg whites, stiffly beaten

Add lemon rind to sugar and butter; cream well. Add egg yolks, beating well. Add lemon juice, cornstarch, grape-nuts, salt and milk, mixing well. Fold in egg whites. Pour in a buttered dish and place in a pan with 1-inch of hot water. Bake at 325 degrees for 1 hour. Serve hot or cold, with or without whipped topping.

Queen Elizabeth Pudding

1 c. chopped dates
1 c. water
¾ tsp. soda
¾ c. sugar
¼ c. butter
1 egg
2 tsp. vanilla
1½ c. flour
1 tsp. baking powder
¼ tsp. salt

Cook dates and water to a paste. Cool and add the soda, sugar, butter, egg and vanilla, creaming well. Sift flour, baking powder and salt together. Add to the above mixture, mixing well. Bake at 325 degrees in a greased 13½ x 8½ inch pan for approximately 30 minutes. Avoid overcooking. Leave in pan and pour the following Topping over the hot cake.

Topping:

1 stick plus 2 Tbsp. margarine
6 Tbsp. cream
1 c. brown sugar (packed)
1 c. chopped pecans

Mix topping and boil for 3 minutes. Pour over cake and broil until bubbles all over. Will burn quickly, so watch it.

Persimmon Pudding

1 c. flour
¾ c. sugar
½ tsp. salt
½ tsp. baking powder
½ tsp. cinnamon
½ c. chopped nuts
½ c. seedless raisins
1 c. fresh persimmon pulp
⅓ c. milk
1 tsp. vanilla

Sift dry ingredients; stir in raisins and nuts; combine remaining ingredients and stir into flour mixture. Turn into greased containers and fill containers ⅔ full. Cover and steam 1 hour.

Salads

Salad Dressings

Salads

Salad Dressings

Salad Hints

Before unmolding salad, moisten both the plate and the molded salad with wet fingers. The moist surface makes it easy to slide the mold into the center of the plate after unmolding.

Jello and gelatin are not the same, so watch your recipes and use whichever is called for.

Never boil gelatin and never add fresh pineapple to it.

Everything shows in a molded salad; so when adding fruit, bear in mind that these fruits sink: Canned apricots, Royal Anne Cherries, canned peaches and pears, whole strawberries, prunes, plums, fresh orange sections, grapes.

These fruits float: Fresh apple cubes, banana slices, grapefruit sections, fresh peach and pear slices, raspberries, strawberry halves, marshmallows and broken nut meats.

Important — Allow 3 hours for gelatin to "set." 6 hours is better.

When I can have my way, I add sour cream to any mayonnaise for any kind of salad mixing. It provides the "umph" that so many salads lack. If you are not "sourminded", use plain whipping cream.

Sesame seeds are here to stay! The use of toasted sesame seeds adds a delightful new flavor and texture to salad dressings, breads, cakes and cookies. (To toast sesame seeds, place on a shallow pan or baking sheet in 200-250 degree oven; watch closely and stir frequently.) They *must* be just golden brown.

Grease your salad molds with mayonnaise before pouring your molded salads; they come out more easily and the mayonnaise gives them an extra nice flavor.

To prevent a green salad from getting soggy, first put a saucer upside down in the bottom of the bowl then put the salad on top of it.

Eva's Tomato Cheese Salad

1 pt. tomato juice
1 can crushed pineapple
¼ pt. mayonnaise
¼ pt. cottage cheese
Dash of cayenne pepper
1 envelope gelatin
⅛ tsp. dry mustard
¼ tsp. ginger
1 tsp. onion juice
1½ tsp. salt
Tabasco to taste

Mix all together. Soak gelatin in cold water and dissolve in a little hot tomato juice. Add to salad and freeze. Serves 8. A tiny bit of red coloring can be added to give deeper pink color. The Club freezes this in hand freezer, but I usually do mine at home in my icebox.

Tomato Frozen Salad

1 large size can tomatoes
1 small size cream cheese
1 medium size chopped onion
1 c. mayonnaise
½ pkg. gelatin
3 medium size fresh tomatoes
    cut in wedges

Set aside 1 cup tomato juice. Mash remainder of tomatoes through a sieve. Mix the softened cheese, onion and mayonnaise together with the tomato puree. Heat the cup of tomato juice, and mix with the gelatin which has been softened in a small amount of cold water. Add this to the cheese mixture. Season with salt and cayenne pepper to taste; stir in the tomato wedges and freeze. Serve on lettuce leaf with mayonnaise.

Tomato Cottage Cheese Salad

1 can tomato soup
1 envelope gelatin
¼ c. cold water
1 c. cottage cheese
2 eggs, hard-boiled and chopped
½ c. olives, chopped
1 c. celery, diced
Dash onoin juice or
    1 tsp. chopped onion
1 c. mayonnaise

Soak gelatin in ¼ cup cold water. Heat tomato soup to boiling point, add gelatin and stir until dissolved. Set aside until cool but not hardened. Add remaining ingredients and chill until set. Serves about 6.

142

Avocado Ring

2 envelopes gelatin
1 c. grapefruit juice
⅔ c. sugar
1 c. celery, cut fine
⅛ c. onion, cut fine
¾ c. orange juice
⅓ c. lemon juice
¾ tsp. salt
3 avocados, mashed
¼ c. water

Bring juices to a boil, adding sugar and salt. Remove from heat and add gelatin which has been soaked in ¼ cup water. Cool. Add celery, onion and mashed avocados. Mix well and pour into ring mold which has been rinsed in cold water. Chicken, shrimp or lobster served in center of ring is delicious.

Avocado Shrimp Salad

5 large ripe avocados
Lemon juice to drizzle over
  avocados
3 lbs. shrimp, boiled and peeled
⅔ c. homemade mayonnaise
1 tsp. monosodium glutamate
1 c. finely cut celery
1½ tsp. sharply seasoned
  salad dressing
1 Tbsp. salt
1 Tbsp. minced green onions
1½ Tbsp. dill seed
1 tsp. white pepper

Peel and halve avocados and drizzle with lemon juice (seasons and keeps from turning dark). Refrigerate until ready to stuff. Combine shrimp with other ingredients. Mix well. Stuff avocado halves and place on salad greens. Garnish with mayonnaise and paprika. Serves 10.

Chicken Almond Mousse

4 to 5 lb. stewing chicken,
  cut up
4 c. hot water
1 Tbsp. salt
1 onion, sliced
2 Tbsp. gelatin
3 c. chicken broth
1 tsp. salt
½ tsp. pepper
1 tsp. onion, finely chopped
3 egg yolks, well beaten
¼ c. stuffed olives, sliced
¼ c. chopped blanched almonds
3 c. chopped cooked chicken
1 c. heavy cream, whipped

Simmer chicken in hot water, salt and onion until chicken is tender, (about 3½ hours). Cool chicken and broth separately. Remove chicken from bones and chop coarsely. Soften gelatin in ½ cup cold chicken broth. Heat remaining broth with salt, pepper and onion in top of double boiler. Stir a little of the hot mixture into egg yolks and then combine with rest of hot mixture. Cook and stir over boiling water until thickened and smooth. Add softened gelatin. Cool until the consistency of unbeaten egg white. Fold in olives, nuts, chopped chicken and cream. Pour into greased 1½ quart mold. Chill several hours before serving. Garnish with melon balls and strawberries if desired. Serves 6.

143

Fruit and Chicken Salad

1½ c. diced cooked chicken
2 c. diced apples
1 c. thinly diced celery
⅓ to ½ c. chopped nuts

Mix these ingredients with enough salad dressing to coat well. Store in refrigerator until well chilled. This is a good way to use leftover chicken or turkey.

I Hot Chicken Salad

3 c. diced, cooked chicken
  or turkey
2 c. thinly sliced celery
¼ c. pimento, in narrow strips
½ c. salted almonds, slivered
1¼ c. mayonnaise
3 Tbsp. lemon juice
2 Tbsp. grated onion
½ tsp. salt
¼ tsp. white pepper
1 c. crushed potato chips
½ c. grated American cheese

Add celery, almonds, pimento and mayonnaise (blended with lemon juice and grated onion) to the diced chicken. Toss lightly with a fork and add the seasonings. Pour into buttered casserole (shells or ramekins). Mix grated cheese with potato chips and sprinkle over chicken mixture. Bake about 30 minutes at 350 degrees F. or until heated through thoroughly. Serves 6 to 8. Serve with fruit salad and hot rolls any time of the year. It is delicious. It is also good as a late supper dish.

Combine cubed cooked chicken with pineapple chunks, avocado pieces and chopped celery. Blend with curry accented mayonnaise.

II Hot Chicken Salad

2 c. chopped, cooked chicken
  (2 whole breast will do)
¾ c. commercial mayonnaise
1 can cream of chicken soup
¼ c. water
2 Tbsp. grated onion
Salt and pepper to taste
¼ c. chopped green pepper or
  red pimento
Cayenne may be used
3 boiled eggs, sliced (quarter the
  slices)
1½ c. cooked rice
Crushed potato chips (for top)

Mix chicken with mayonnaise and soup. Add other ingredients, except potato chips. Pour into a greased casserole and top with crushed potato chips. Cook until bubbly hot in a 350 degree F. oven. May be made the day before for the seasonings to really set. Serves about 10.

144

Chicken Salad Hawaiian

2 c. diced cooked chicken
3 hard-boiled eggs, chopped
¼ tsp. salt
½ c. sliced celery
1 c. pineapple cubes, drained
¼ c. sliced stuffed olives
¼ c. diced sweet pickle
French dressing

Combine first 7 ingredients and mix with French dressing to taste. Chill and serve in lettuce cups. Serve with additional French dressing or mayonnaise. Serves 6.

Pimento Party Chicken

2 c. cooked chicken
  (cut in pieces)
4 oz. (½ c.) chopped pimento
3 hard-boiled eggs (chopped)
¾ c. chopped celery
¾ c. mayonnaise
1 envelope gelatin
½ c. cold water
1 c. hot chicken broth

Soak gelatin in cold water a few minutes; dissolve in hot broth and cool. Mix chicken, pimento, eggs, mayonnaise and celery. Spread in a rectangular or round mold. Pour cooled gelatin mixture over this, stirring slightly to mix in gelatin; chill. Do not freeze. Serve on lettuce and top with added mayonnaise.

I Cranberry Salad

1 pkg. orange jello
½ c. pineapple juice
¼ c. hot water
½ c. evaporated milk
⅓ c. salad dressing
¼ tsp. salt
2 c. ground, raw cranberries
⅔ c. drained crushed pineapple

Dissolve jello in hot water; stir in pineapple juice and cool until congealed. Whip milk; add salad dressing and salt. Fold into whipped jello. Add cranberries and pineapple. Pour into mold and chill. Serves 8.

II Cranberry Salad

1 pkg. pineapple-grapefruit
  gelatin
1 lb. can cranberry sauce
1 7 oz. bottle ginger ale
1 small can Bing Cherries

In saucepan combine gelatin and cranberry sauce. Heat and stir until almost boiling. Stir in ginger ale. After "fizzing" has stopped, add fruit. Pour into mold and chill until set.

145

III Cranberry Salad

1 qt. fresh cranberries
1½ c. sugar
2 Tbsp. plain gelatin
Pinch salt
½ c. orange juice
Grated rind of 1 orange
2 c. diced peeled apples
1 c. chopped nuts

Grind cranberries, using fine blade. Add sugar and mix. Let stand 15 minutes, stirring occasionally. Soften gelatin in orange juice for 5 minutes; stir over hot water until dissolved. Mix gelatin mixture with cranberries, apples and nuts. Place in mold which has been rinsed with cold water. Chill until set. Serves 8.

IV Cranberry Salad

1 lb. cranberries
1 c. sugar
1 small can crushed pineapple
1 orange, the juice
½ orange rind, ground
1 lb. marshmallows
2 large bananas, mashed
1 c. nuts, chopped
2 pkgs. raspberry or cherry jello
2 c. boiling water

Grind cranberries and ½ orange rind together. Dissolve jello in boiling water. Add sugar. Cool and then add remainder of ingredients. Pour into individual or one large mold.

Cranberry-Orange Salad

2 pkgs. orange gelatin
1 c. boiling water
2 cans (1 lb. each) jellied
   cranberry sauce, mashed
¾ c. orange juice
1 tsp. grated orange rind
   (optional)
1 c. chopped peeled apple
½ c. chopped celery

Dissolve gelatin in boiling water. Add cranberry sauce and orange juice. Mix well and cool until the consistency of uncooked egg whites. Stir in rind, apple, and celery. Pour into mold and chill until firm. Serves 8-10.

Cranberry Souffle Salad

1 pkg. lemon gelatin
1 c. hot water
½ c. mayonnaise
1 Tbsp. lemon juice
¼ tsp. salt
1 can (lb. size) whole cranberry
   sauce
½ c. chopped celery
1 (9 oz.) can crushed pineapple,
   drained

Dissolve gelatin in hot water; add mayonnaise, lemon juice and ½ cup of cranberry sauce. Blend thoroughly with rotary beater. Turn into freezing tray of refrigerator and chill for 15-20 minutes or until firm about 1-inch from edge, but soft in center. Turn into bowl and whip with rotary beater until fluffy. Fold in remaining sauce, celery and pineapple. Pour into 1 qt. mold; chill until firm, at least 1 hour. Unmold and garnish with salad greens. Serves 6.

Cranberry Chunk Salad

2 3 oz. pkgs. cream cheese,
   softened
¼ c. salad dressing
¼ c. lemon juice
⅛ tsp. salt
1 c. crushed pineapple
1 c. diced walnuts
1 c. diced bananas
1½ c. heavy cream
1 (lb.) can jellied cranberries,
   chilled and cut into chunks

Beat cream cheese with salad dressing, lemon juice and salt until smooth. Stir in pineapple, walnuts and bananas. Whip cream and fold into mixture. Lightly fold in cranberry chunks. Turn into a 9 x 5 x 3-inch pan that is lined on all sides with double thickness of waxed paper. Freeze. To unmold, place pan in hot water for count of 15. Turn onto chilled pan. Place in refrigerator about 30 minutes before serving. Slice to serve (12 servings). Ice with whipped cream topping. Garnish with cranberries. Delicious!

I Molded Cranberry Salad

1 can 8½-9 oz. crushed pineapple
1 lb. can whole cranberry sauce
Boiling water
1 3 oz. pkg. raspberry gelatin
1 c. mandarin orange sections
1 tsp. grated orange peel

Drain syrup from pineapple. Measure syrup and add boiling water to make 1¼ cups. Dissolve gelatin in hot liquid. Chill until partially set. Fold in cranberry sauce, drained orange sections, orange peel and crushed pineapple. Pour into molds and chill until set. Serve with a whipped cream dressing.

II Molded Cranberry Salad

2 c. cranberries, ground
2 c. apples, ground
2 c. sugar
1 c. seedless grapes
2 envelopes gelatin
½ c. cold water
2 c. pineapple or orange juice
½ c. lemon juice

Mix together the cranberries, apples, sugar and seedless grapes. Let stand to absorb sugar. Sprinkle gelatin in cold water to soften it. Mix with juices. When partially set, mix in ground fruit. Pour into molds and chill until firm. Serves 12.

Congealed Fruit Salad

1 3-oz. pkg. lime gelatin
1 c. boiling water
12 marshmallows
1 c. chopped grapefruit
1 c. chopped nuts
1 c. chopped celery
1 c. chopped apples
1 c. whipped cream

Dissolve gelatin in hot water. Add marshmallows and allow to melt. When cool, add grapefruit, nuts, celery and apples. When mixture begins to congeal add the whipped cream. If a little color is desired, a few maraschino cherries, chopped, may be added.

Custard Fruit Salad

1 large can fruit cocktail
1 medium size can pineapple
  chunks
1 small jar maraschino cherries
1 c. whole seedless green grapes
  or 1 c. halved seedless
  red grapes
1 c. miniature marshmallows
1 Tbsp. sugar
1 Tbsp. cornstarch
1 egg, beaten
Pinch salt

Drain fruits; reserve juice (except cherry). Add grapes and marshmallows. Mix sugar and cornstarch; add fruit juice and bring to a boil. Cook to the consistency of medium sauce. Remove from heat and add well beaten egg. Return to heat and bring to a quick boil. Pour over fruit mixture while hot. Chill overnight.

Frozen Fruit-Cheese Salad

2 c. small curd cottage cheese,
  sieved
1 c. dairy sour cream
3 Tbsp. confectioners sugar
¾ tsp. salt
1 c. pineapple tidbits, drained
1 c. chopped cooked prunes
1 c. diced orange
1 large banana, sliced
½ c. maraschino cherries, sliced
½ c. blanched almonds, chopped

Blend cottage cheese lightly with sour cream, sugar, salt, pineapple, prunes, orange, banana, cherries and almonds. Pour into two refrigerator trays and freeze until firm. Serve with Creamy Pink Dressing and garnish with cherries and orange sections. 12 servings. See salad dressing section.

Frozen Fruit Salad

1 pt. sour cream
2 Tbsp. lemon juice
½ tsp. salt
¾ c. sugar
1 can (9 oz.) crushed pineapple
¼ c. chopped maraschino cherries
¼ c. chopped pecans

Mix cream, lemon juice, sugar and salt. Add other ingredients and blend. Pour into muffin tins lined with paper cups. Freeze. Serves 10.

Fruit-Marshmallow Salad

1 medium can crushed pineapple
1 c. white cherries, pitted
1 c. chopped pears, bite size
1 c. chopped peaches
1 c. white grapes
2 c. miniature marshmallows
1 c. grated coconut
½ c. mayonnaise
1 small bottle maraschino cherries
Pecan halves (for garnish)

Drain fruits. Mix the fruits and marshmallows with ½ cup mayonnaise. Add ½ cup coconut; save ½ cup to sprinkle over individual servings. Top with 4 or 5 pecan halves and 3 cherries. Can be made the day before. (Save coconut, nuts and cherries until ready to serve).

I Fruit Salad

1 large can fruit for salad,
   drained
1 large can pineapple chunks,
   drained
1 c. grated coconut
1 c. pecans
1 c. small marshmallows
1 c. sour cream
2 Tbsp. sugar

Mix all ingredients together and let stand overnight in refrigerator. Serve on lettuce.

II Fruit Salad

½ pt. jar of favorite salad
   dressing
3 medium ripe mellow apples,
   chopped
1 can (#2) drained pineapple,
   cubed
3 large orange, peeled, seeded,
   cubed
1 lb. red grapes, seeded
1 c. chopped pecans
1 coconut, grated
½ pt. whipping cream

In a large mixing bowl combine all ingredients except cream. Mix well. Whip the cream and fold into mixture, mixing well. Chill before serving. Serves 30.

149

Sour Cream Fruit Salad

2 c. sour cream
2 Tbsp. lemon juice
½ c. sugar
⅛ tsp. salt
1 8 oz. can crushed pineapple
  well drained
1 banana, diced
4 drops red food coloring
¼ c. chopped pecans
1 (lb. size) can Bing cherries,
  drained

Combine sour cream, lemon juice, sugar, salt, pineapple, banana and enough food coloring to give pink tint. Lightly fold in nuts and cherries. Spoon into fluted paper muffin containers. Freeze. Remove from freezer about 15 minutes before serving to loosen cups. Peel off paper cups and place on salad greens. Makes 12 large cups.

Mandarin Salad

1 pkg. peach-flavored gelatin
1 c. boiling water
1 11 oz. can mandarin orange
  segments, drained
1 5-oz. can water chestnuts

Dissolve gelatin in boiling water. Drain orange segments. To the juice, add enough cold water to make 1 cup; stir into gelatin. Chill gelatin until thickened, but not set. Dice drained water chestnuts finely and fold, with orange segments, into thickened gelatin. Pour mixture into a 3-cup mold and chill until set. Serve with French Dressing. 6 servings.

Congealed Mandarin Salad

3 cans mandarin oranges
1 large and 1 small can crushed
  pineapple
1 pkg. orange jello
1 pkg. lemon jello

Drain fruit. Use juice and add enough water to make 4 cups liquid. Use 2 cups of the juice (hot) to dissolve jello. Add remainder of liquid. Let thicken to consistency of egg whites then add fruit. Let this thicken until the top is just firm, then spread the following topping over entire surface:

Topping:
Mix 1 medium size package miniature marshmallows into 1 cup mayonnaise. Fold 1 pint of whipped cream into this mixture. Spread over jello, fruit layer. Sprinkle with grated cheese just before serving.

150

Frozen Orange-Pecan Molds

1 8 oz. pkg. cream cheese,
  softened
¼ c. orange juice
½ c. chopped pecans
¼ c. maraschino cherries,
  chopped
½ c. pitted dates, cut up
1 c. crushed pineapple, drained
½ tsp. grated orange peel
1 c. whipping cream, whipped

Combine cheese and orange juice, beating till fluffy. Stir in pecans and fruits. Fold in whipped cream. Pack into individual molds or into 8½ X 4½ X 2½-inch loaf pan. Freeze firm. Let stand at room temperature about 15 minutes before serving. For a boost in height, unmold on orange slices. Serves 8.

Orange Pineapple Mold

2 Tbsp. unflavored gelatin
½ c. cold water
1 can (1 lb. 4½-oz.) crushed
  pineapple, drained
⅔ c. orange juice
⅓ c. lemon juice
⅓ c. sugar
2 c. dairy sour cream
2 c. sliced strawberries
½ c. chopped pecans

In saucepan sprinkle gelatin over water. Heat over low heat, stirring constantly until gelatin dissolves. Stir in pineapple, juices and sugar. Stir until sugar dissolves. Chill until jelly-like consistency. Stir in sour cream. Fold in strawberries and nuts. Turn into a 7-cup mold. Chill until set. Serves 8.

Pineapple Salad

1 #2 can crushed pineapple and
  juice
½ c. sugar
Juice of 1 lemon
2 Tbsp. unflavored gelatin
2 pkgs. 8-oz. cream cheese
1 small bottle maraschino
  cherries
½ pt. cream, whipped

Heat but do not boil, the pineapple, sugar and lemon juice. Add gelatin, which has been dissolved in a little cold water. Mash cream cheese and add to pineapple gelatin mixture. After it begins to become firm, add cherries (cut in small pieces) and cream. Add enough of the cherry juice to color the salad a delicate pink. Serve with mayonnaise on lettuce.

Pineapple Party Salad

2 envelopes unflavored gelatin
2 (no. 2) cans crushed pineapple
3 Tbsp. sugar
Dash salt
2 Tbsp. chopped chives
2 c. finely chopped celery
4 (3 oz.) pkgs. cream cheese
1½ Tbsp. lemon juice
½ c. diced canned pimento, drained
1 c. coarsely chopped pecans
¾ c. heavy cream, whipped

Drain pineapple and heat syrup to boiling. Mix gelatin, sugar and salt thoroughly. Dissolve in hot syrup. Chill until thickened but not set. Blend in pineapple, chives and celery. Soften cream cheese with lemon juice. Add a small portion at a time to the gelatin. Stir each time until mixture is smooth and well blended. Fold into pimento, pecans and whipped cream. Pour into lightly oiled 2 quart mold. Chill until firm. Garnish with tiny pimento diamonds, crisp greens, pineapple rings and ripe olives. 12 to 16 servings.

Lime Gelatin Salad

1 pkg. lime gelatin
1 c. boiling water
½ c. cottage cheese
½ c. chopped celery
½ c. crushed pineapple
½ c. chopped pimento
½ c. chopped pecans

Dissolve gelatin in boiling water. Cool and fold in remaining ingredients. Refrigerate until firm. May be cut into squares and served on lettuce leaves.

Mary's Lime Jello Cottage Cheese Salad

1 small can crushed pineapple
1 pkg. lime jello (no water)
1 pkg. Dream Whip (whipped)
1 lb. cream cottage cheese
1 c. chopped nuts

Place pineapple and jello in sauce pan, dissolve and bring to boil for 3 minutes. Set aside to cool. When cool add other ingredients, mix well and set in refrigerator for while.

Lime Salad

1 pkg. lime flavored jello
1 small can crushed pineapple
1 8 oz. box creamed cottage cheese
½ pt. whipping cream (whipped)
1 c. chopped celery
1 c. chopped pecans

Heat pineapple and juice from a boil for 2 minutes. Add jello and heat 3 more minutes. Mix whipped cream, cottage cheese, celery and pecans. Combine with cooled jello mixture. Pour into greased mold and chill.

152

Coca Cola Salad

1 large can crushed pineapple, drained
1 can black Bing cherries, drained
2 3-oz. pkgs. cherry gelatin
2 small cokes
1 c. chopped nuts

Drain juice from pineapple and cherries and add enough water to make 2 cups of liquid. Bring liquid to boil and pour over gelatin to dissolve. Add cokes and refrigerate until it begins to congeal. Add fruit and nuts. Pour in mold and chill until set.

Bing Cherry Congealed Salad

1 can sweetened pitted Bing cherries
1 flat can crushed pineapple (Drain and save juices — need 2 cups, add water to make 2 cups)
1 pkg. cherry gelatin
1 small pkg. cream cheese
1 c. chopped pecans

Heat 1 cup of the juice and dissolve in it the cherry gelatin. Pour a little of the hot mixture over cream cheese to soften; blend until very smooth. Add other 1 cup juice and continue creaming and beating. Add remaining hot mixture and chill until nearly set; then fold in cherries, pineapple and pecans. Pour into mold rinsed with water or lightly rubbed with salad oil. Chill. Serves 8.

Cherry Cups

1 lb. can pitted Bing Cherries
1 can (9 oz.) seedless grapes
½ c. sliced, stuffed olives
½ c. chopped pecans
⅓ c. lemon juice
1 pkg. (3 oz.) orange jello
1 envelope Knox gelatin

Drain cherries and grapes. Measure 2 cups of syrup from fruit. Heat; add to jello and softened gelatin; stir to dissolve. Add lemon juice. Chill until partially set. Add cherries, grapes, olives and pecans. Chill in 8 to 10 individual molds until firm.

Apricot Salad

1 pkg. lemon gelatin
1 can (#2½) apricots, drained, chopped
1 pkg. (3 oz.) cream cheese
½ to 1 c. chopped nuts

Save apricot syrup and add enough water to make 2 cups liquid. Heat to boiling and dissolve gelatin in it. Mix cheese into gelatin mixture. Refrigerate until begins to thicken, then add chopped apricots and nuts. Pour into mold. Congeal. Good with ham and green bean casserole. Serves 8.

Apricot Cheese Delight

1 large can apricots, drained
1 c. crushed pineapple, drained
2 pkgs. orange gelatin
2 c. hot water
¾ c. miniature marshmallows
1 c. fruit juices

Dissolve gelatin in hot water. Add 1 cup fruit juices. Fold in chopped fruit and marshmallows. Chill until firm. Spread with topping.

Topping:
½ cup sugar, 3 tablespoons flour, 1 egg (slightly beaten), 1 cup pineapple and apricot juice mixed. Combine and cook until thick, stirring constantly. Add 2 tablespoons butter. Cool. Fold in 1 cup whipped cream. Spread on top of congealed mixture. Cover with grated cheese. Chill. Serves 12 or more.

Congealed Apricot Salad

1 pkg. lemon gelatin
1 pkg. plain gelatin (1 Tbsp.)
1 c. apricot juice
½ c. orange juice
½ c. lemon juice
A little orange and lemon rind, grated
1 No. 2½ can apricots drained and sieved to pulp stage
2 3 oz. pkg. cream cheese or
1 c. mashed cottage cheese (thin cream cheese with cream)
1 c. chopped almonds or pecans
Pinch of salt

Heat fruit juices and dissolve gelatin in them. Let cool and when mixture begins to jell add other ingredients and chill until firm.

Anne Wilson's Strawberry Jello Salad

2 3 oz. pkgs. strawberry jello
2 c. boiling water
2 10 oz. pkgs. frozen strawberries
1 13½ oz. can crushed pineapple
2 large ripe bananas, sliced
1 c. sour cream

Dissolve jello in boiling water. Add berries, stirring occasionally to thaw. Add drained pineapple and bananas. Pour ½ mixture into 8 X 8 X 2 pan; chill. Spoon sour cream over chilled jello in even layer. Pour remaining jello over and chill until firm.

Sue's Strawberry Salad

2 pkgs. cherry jello
2 c. boiling water
1 small pkg. frozen strawberries
2 bananas, mashed
½ pt. sour cream
1 No. 2 can crushed pineapple

Dissolve jello in boiling water. Cool and add strawberries, bananas and pineapple. Pour half of mixture into mold and let congeal. Cover with sour cream and add remainder of jello mixture, partially set, and let congeal. Serve on salad greens. Serves 12.

Strawberry Salad

2 pkgs. strawberry gelatin
1 c. boiling water
2 10 oz. pkg. strawberries and juice
1 large can crushed pineapple, drained
1 pt. sour cream
3 bananas, mashed
1 c. chopped nuts

Dissolve gelatin in hot water and add all other ingredients except sour cream. Pour half of mixture in 12 X 8 X 2-inch pan. Chill until firm. Spread sour cream over congealed salad and spoon last half of salad on top of cream. Congeal. Serves 16-20.

Ida Mae's Frozen Cheese Salad

1 small can crushed pineapple (undrained)
1 small pkg. Philadelphia cream cheese
4 Tbsp. sugar
1 small bottle red cherries (undrained)
½ pt. whipping cream (or 1 pkg. dream whip)
½ c. mayonnaise

Cream cheese until smooth with sugar and mayonnaise. Cut up cherries; add pineapple and cherries to cream cheese mixture. Fold in whipped cream; freeze. Cut into squares, serve without mayonnaise on lettuce. Serves 10. If kept frozen and well wrapped will be good for weeks. Delicious!

Lois' Lemon Jello Salad

2 pkgs. lemon jello or 1 pkg. each
    lemon and lime
2 c. boiling water
2 c. clear crabonated beverage,
    7-Up or Ginger Ale
1 large can crushed pineapple
4 sliced bananas (not too ripe)
Miniature marshmallows, enough
    to cover solid top of salad

Dissolve jello in water. Cool a bit, and add cold beverage. Chill slightly. Drain pineapple and save juice for topping. Add to jello with bananas and marshmallows. Pour into large pyrex dish and chill.

Topping:

Combine and cook until thick, the
    following:
    ½ c. sugar
    2 Tbsp. flour
    1 c. pineapple juice
    1 beaten egg
    2 Tbsp. butter

Cool and fold in 1 package Dream Whip, prepared according to directions. Spread over top of salad.

Finely shred 1 cup longhorn cheese and sprinkle over topping.

3 tablespoons Parmesan cheese may be added if stronger flavor is desired.

Beet Salad

1 c. canned, diced beets
1 pkg. lemon gelatin
1 c. diced celery
1 Tbsp. horseradish
½ tsp. onion juice

Drain beets. Reserve liquid; add water to make 2 cups; heat. Add beet liquid to gelatin and dissolve. Add beets and remaining ingredients; mix. Chill until firm. Cut into squares; serve on lettuce.

Holly Ring Mold

1 pkg. lemon gelatin
1 envelope unflavored gelatin
¼ c. cold water
1¼ c. hot water
2 Tbsp. sugar
1 tsp. salt
2 Tbsp. prepared horseradish
2 Tbsp. vinegar or lemon juice
½ c. diced celery
½ c. diced cooked beets
½ c. finely chopped cabbage
3 Tbsp. minced onion

Soften gelatin in cold water. Dissolve lemon gelatin in hot water and add softened gelatin to lemon gelatin. Add sugar, salt, horseradish and vinegar. Cool. When it begins to thicken, fold in vegetables. Pour into ring mold. Put sprigs of holly around salad.

Merry Christmas Salad

1 pkg. lime flavored gelatin
1 c. boiling water
1 No. 2 can crushed pineapple
1 c. small curd cottage cheese
1 c. finely chopped celery
1 Tbsp. chopped pimento
½ c. chopped walnuts or pecans
Frost with:
1 3 oz. pkg. cream cheese
1 Tbsp. mayonnaise
1 tsp. lemon juice
Blend and beat until smooth

Dissolve gelatin in boiling water. Cool until syrupy, then stir in remaining ingredients. Turn into round 8 or 9 X 1½" cake pan. Chill.

Cut 6 wedges like Christmas Trees. Cut cranberry sauce into squares for base of trees and top each with walnut half. Decorate tree with cherries. Serves 6.

Decoration: Jellied Cranberry Sauce — 6 walnut halves — maraschino cherries.

Banana Salad

1 pkg. lemon gelatin
1 c. hot water
1 c. cold water
1 c. crushed pineapple, drained
2 bananas, cut in small pieces

Dissolve gelatin in hot water; then add cold water and refrigerate until it begins to set. Then add the drained pineapple and bananas. Congeal.

Topping:
1 c. pineapple juice
½ c. sugar
2 Tbsp. flour
1 egg, well beaten
2 Tbsp. butter
1 pkg. whipped topping mix

Cook first 5 ingredients until thick, stirring constantly. Cool and add 1 pkg. topping mix, mixed according to pkg. directions. Fold whipped topping into the cooled topping; spread on top of congealed salad. Garnish with chopped nuts.

Congealed Salad

1 pkg. lemon gelatin
1 c. hot water
1 c. small curd cottage cheese
1 c. undiluted evaporated milk
½ c. mayonnaise
½ c. chopped nuts
1 can (#303) fruit cocktail, drained

Dissolve gelatin in hot water and refrigerate until syrupy. Add cheese, milk and mayonnaise, mixing well. Add nuts and fruit cocktail. Congeal overnight and serve cut in squares on lettuce. Will go in an 8 or 9-inch casserole.

Créme de Menthe Salad

1 pkg. lemon jello
1 pkg. lime jello
2 c. boiling water
1 lb. drained cottage cheese
1 large can crushed pineapple
4 Tbsp. créme de menthe
1 small can evaporated milk

Mix jello in boiling water. Let cool. Stir together cottage cheese, pineapple, créme de menthe and evaporated milk. Add to jello and let jell.

Dressing:

¼ lb. sour cream
3 Tbsp. salad dressing
1 to 3 Tbsp. créme de menthe
1 Tbsp. sugar
1 tsp. poppy seeds

Mix together and serve over créme de menthe salads.

Turkey and Aspic Salad

Aspic Layer:

2 tsp. lemon juice
⅛ tsp. celery salt
¼ tsp. garlic powder
¼ c. cold water
1 envelope unflavored gelatin
½ c. boiling water
1 can (8 oz.) tomato sauce

Mix lemon juice, celery salt, garlic powder and cold water in a bowl. Sprinkle gelatin over and let soften 5 minutes. Add the boiling water; stir until gelatin is dissolved. Stir in tomato sauce. Cool, then pour into a mold. Chill until almost set before adding turkey layer.

Turkey Layer:

¼ c. lemon juice
¼ c. water
2 envelopes unflavored gelatin
1 tsp. salt
1 c. finely chopped celery
2 c. finely diced cooked turkey
⅔ c. mayonnaise
1 tall can evaporated milk

Place lemon juice and water in a medium size saucepan. Sprinkle gelatin over and let soften 5 minutes. Place pan over very low heat and stir until gelatin is dissolved. Remove from heat and cool slightly. Then add salt, turkey, celery and mayonnaise, stirring to mix well. Stir in milk. Chill until almost set. Ladle over aspic layer. Chill until set. Makes 6 to 8 servings.

Marinated Salad

2 stalks celery, chopped
1 bell pepper, chopped
1 onion, chopped
1 can French style string beans, chopped
1 can English peas (tiny) drained
1 small jar pimento, chopped
¾ c. vinegar
1 c. sugar
½ c. cooking oil
1 tsp. salt

Drain beans, peas and pimento and chop all vegetables. Mix all ingredients and let set 24 hours in refrigerator before serving.

Cucumber Salad

1 pkg. lime-flavored gelatin
¾ c. boiling water
4 Tbsp. lemon juice
1 tsp. finely chopped onion
½ c. sour cream
½ c. mayonnaise
1 c. chopped cucumber
¼ tsp. Tabasco sauce
½ tsp. salt

Dissolve gelatin in boiling water. Add lemon juice and chopped onion. Cool until consistency of egg whites. Blend in cream, mayonnaise, cucumber, Tabasco and salt. Pour into mold and chill until set. Yields 6 to 8 servings.

Crisp Kraut Salad

1 lb. can sauerkraut
1 c. (2 oz.) pimento, drained
½ c. chopped sweet onion
¾ c. sliced celery
1 c. shredded carrots
1 green pepper, seeded and sliced
¼ c. vinegar
½ c. sugar
¾ tsp. salt
⅛ tsp. pepper
Iceberg lettuce (optional)
Chopped parsley (optional)

Turn the kraut into a wire strainer and drain, pressing out all the liquid. Put all the ingredients into bowl; then combine the vinegar, sugar, salt and pepper. Stir until dissolved. Pour over kraut mixture. Toss lightly, cover and refrigerate for several hours. Serves 8.

Angel Salad

2 Tbsp. vinegar
2 Tbsp. water
1 Tbsp. sugar
2 Tbsp. butter
2 eggs, well beaten
½ pt. cream, whipped
20 marshmallows, chopped
6 slices pineapple, chopped
1 c. chopped nuts
Pinch salt

Combine vinegar, water, sugar, butter, salt and beaten eggs. Cook in top of double boiler, stirring constantly. Cook until thick. When cold, fold in whipped cream, marshmallows, pineapple and nuts. Refrigerate 24 hours before serving.

Happy Holiday Layers

1 pkg. lime-flavored gelatin
2 c. hot water
1 c. (9 oz. can) seedless white
   grapes, drained
½ c. chopped celery
1 Tbsp. unflavored gelatin
¼ c. cold water
1 c. boiling water
½ c. lemonade, frozen
   concentrate
½ c. mayonnaise or salad
   dressing
2 c. fruit cocktail (lb. can)
1 pkg. cherry-flavored gelatin
1 c. hot water

First layer: Dissolve lime gelatin in 2 cups hot water. Chill until partially set. Add grapes and celery; pour over lime layer and chill until firm.

Second layer: Soften unflavored gelatin in ¼ cup cold water; dissolve in 1 cup boiling water. Add lemon concentrate; blend in mayonnaise. Chill until partially set; then pour over lime layer and chill until firm.

Third layer: Drain fruit cocktail; reserve syrup, adding water to make 1 cup. Dissolve cherry gelatin in 1 cup hot water. Add fruit cocktail syrup. Chill until partially set. Then add fruit cocktail; pour over the layers in the mold. Chill until firm. Unmold on salad greens and serve with mayonnaise.

Cora's Raspberry Salad

1 10 oz. pkg. marshmallows
1 pkg. frozen raspberries
2 3 oz. pkgs. cream cheese
½ c. mayonnaise
½ pt. whipping cream

Melt marshmallows with raspberries over low heat. Let cool. Add cream cheese blended with mayonnaise. Add whipped cream and freeze in desired mold.

Broccoli Congealed Salad

1 10 oz. pkg. frozen chopped
 broccoli
1 envelope unflavored gelatin
¼ c. water
1 10 oz. can chicken broth
¾ c. real mayonnaise
2 Tbsp. lemon juice
Dash Worcestershire sauce
4 hard-boiled eggs, chopped
1 small onion, finely chopped
Lettuce

Cook broccoli according to package directions; drain. Soften gelatin water. Heat chicken broth in small saucepan; add gelatin and stir until dissolved. Cool. Gradually add cooled chicken broth mixture to real mayonnaise; stir in lemon juice and Worcestershire sauce. Chill until mixture is consistency of unbeaten egg whites. Fold in broccoli, egg and onion. Place in 1 quart ring mold and refrigerate until set. Serve with crisp lettuce. Serves 6.

Mariner's Salad

4 Tbsp. unflavored gelatin
⅔ c. lemon juice
½ c. horseradish
2 c. celery, thinly sliced crosswise
2 tsp. salt
½ c. sliced ripe olives
2 tsp. pepper
4 7-oz. cans tuna
5 c. warm tomato juice

Soften gelatin with lemon juice. Mix together remaining ingredients with the exception of tomato juice. Heat tomato juice and add to gelatin mixture. Combine with other mixed ingredients and pour into mold. Chill until set; unmold on salad greens. Makes 10 servings. Serve with Mariner's Spicy Sauce.

Mariner's Spicy Sauce:

1 c. mayonnaise
2 tsp. horseradish
2 tsp. prepared mustard
2 Tbsp. pickle relish
1 Tbsp. chopped parsley
2 tsp. grated lemon peel
¼ c. lemon juice

Combine all ingredients and mix well. Delicious on any fish or meat salad. Makes 1½ cups salad dressing.

Crab Meat Salad

½ c. cold water
2 Tbsp. plain gelatin
1 can tomato soup
1 small pkg. cream cheese
1 c. chopped celery
1 medium green pepper, chopped
1 tsp. minced onion
¼ tsp. salt
1 6½-oz. can crab meat flaked

Dissolve gelatin in cold water. Heat soup (don't boil) and stir in gelatin until thoroughly dissolved. Add softened cream cheese (room temp.) and beat mixture until smooth. Chill until partially set; then add remaining ingredients. Pour into 1½ qt. mold or individual molds. Serves 8.

Sweetheart's Marinated Beans

1 can French Style Beans
1 can English Peas (Giant)
1 stalk celery, chopped
2 medium size onions, cut into rings
1 small can pimentos, sliced

Blend together; pour over the above bean mixture and refrigerate overnight:

1 c. vinegar
1 c. sugar
½ c. corn oil
Salt and pepper

Applesauce Mold

1 can applesauce
1 pkg. raspberry gelatin
1 small can crushed pineapple
4 Tbsp. sugar
2 Tbsp. grated orange rind
1 small 7-Up drink

Dissolve gelatin in heated applesauce. Add other ingredients in order given. Stir till 7-Up stops fizzing. Pour in mold and chill. Real good!

Dessert Salad

1 No. 2 can crushed pineapple
1 5 oz. jar maraschino cherries, sliced
1 3 oz. jar stuffed olives, sliced
½ c. chopped pecans
2 pkgs. orange jello
1 envelope gelatin

Drain fruit and olives. Use all of pineapple juice and ½ cup olive juice (do not use cherry juice). Add enough water to make 4 cups. Soften gelatin in ¼ cup water (part of above 4 cups liquid). When partially congealed, add fruits, nuts and olives.

Dressing: Grated rind of 1 orange and 1 lemon. Mix juice of orange and lemon with one beaten egg, 1 tablespoon flour and ½ cup sugar. Cook in double boiler until thick. Then add grated rind and let cool. Before serving fold in 1 cup XX cream, whipped. Chill and serve over salad.

When unmolding a large salad on a tray, dampen the tray with cold water so that the salad will slide into place.

To prevent congealed salads from weeping, add ½ envelope of unflavored gelatin to your salad recipe.

162

Golden Winter Salad

1 pkg. orange jello
2 c. water
1 apple
2 Tbsp. lemon juice
1½ c. diced grapefruit sections
  (membrane free)
¼ c. chopped walnuts or pecans
Few grains of salt

Dissolve gelatin in 2 cups water according to directions on package. Chill until syrupy. Core, peel and cube apple; sprinkle with lemon juice and salt. Combine with grapefruit and nutmeats; fold into gelatin. Mold. Serve with mayonnaise, salad dressing or celery seed dressing. Serves 4-6.

Green and Red Salad

Mix and let cool:
  1 lb. marshmallows
  1 box lime jello
  2 c. hot water
Add and chill until firm:
  1 c. grated cheese
  1 small can crushed pineapple
  1 c. whipped cream

Dissolve 1 package raspberry jello in 2 cups hot water. Cool and add 1 cup chopped nuts. Pour over top of the Lime Jello mixture and let set until firm. Serve on lettuce with fruit salad dressing or sour cream dressing.

Sour Cream Dressing

½ c. thick sour cream
2 Tbsp. vinegar or lemon juice
1 tsp. to 1 Tbsp. sugar
¼ tsp. salt
⅛ tsp. paprika

Beat cream with wire whisk or fork and add other ingredients slowly. (1 tablespoon minced onion may be added for vegetable salad.)

Hollands' Request Salad

½ c. dry raisins
¼ c. mayonnaise
¼ c. crushed pineapple
⅓ tsp. salt
2 c. carrots, shredded
½ c. celery, chopped
¼ c. pineapple, diced
Lettuce

Soak raisins overnight. Drain. Combine mayonnaise, crushed pineapple and salt. Add remaining ingredients and blend well. Serve on lettuce. Serves 10.

Corned Beef Loaf

1 Tbsp. unflavored gelatin
¼ c. cold water
1½ c. tomato juice
1 tsp. lemon juice
½ tsp. salt
1 can (12 oz.) corned beef,
  shredded
3 hard-boiled eggs, chopped
½ c. chopped cucumber
2 c. diced celery
1 Tbsp. grated onion
1 c. salad dressing

Sprinkle the gelatin over the cold water to soften. Heat tomato juice and add gelatin to this, cool. Add lemon juice and salt; mix well. In another bowl mix the shredded corn beef, chopped eggs, cucumber, celery, onion and salad dressing. Add to gelatin mixture and mold. Serve as a main dish on lettuce. Serves 8-10.

Angel Fluff Salad

1 3 oz. pkg. black raspberry
  gelatin
1 c. boiling water
1 c. miniature marshmallows
1 small can crushed pineapple
¼ c. sugar
¼ c. chopped nuts
1 c. cottage cheese
1 c. heavy cream, whipped or
  1 pkg. dessert topping mix,
  prepared

Dissolve gelatin and marshmallows in boiling water. Add all remaining ingredients except cream. Refrigerate until thick. Fold whipped cream into gelatin mixture. Pour in mold or pan. Refrigerate until set. Serves 16.

3-Layer Congealed Salad

2 pkgs. celery gelatin
1 pkg. seasoned tomato gelatin
1 3 oz. pkg. cream cheese
2 Tbsp. mayonnaise
½ c. finely shredded cabbage
¼ c. finely shredded carrots
½ c. diced cucumber
1 tsp. chopped parsley
1 tsp. grated onion, optional

Mix 1 pkg. celery gelatin according to pkg. directions. When starts to congeal add the finely shredded cabbage and carrots. Pour the first layer and let congeal. Next, mix tomato gelatin according to pkg. directions and when it begins to congeal, add the cucumber, parsley and onion. Pour over the first congealed layer. After second layer congeals, fix the other celery gelatin by pkg. directions and whip in the cream cheese and mayonnaise. Pour over the second layer. When this last layer is congealed and ready to serve, sprinkle with paprika. **NOTE:** Finely diced radishes and finely chopped green bell pepper may be substituted for the other vegetables.

Ripe Olive Sombrero Salad

2 (3 oz.) pkg. lemon gelatin
2 c. hot water
1¼ c. cold water
2 Tbsp. vinegar
2 Tbsp. lemon juice
1 c. pitted ripe olives
Dash Tabasco sauce
2 Tbsp. chopped pimento
¼ c. mayonnaise
¼ tsp. salt
½ c. thinly sliced celery
½ c. shredded carrot
¼ c. chopped green pepper
1 (8½ oz.) can crushed pineapple,
  drained

Dissolve gelatin in hot water. Stir in cold water, vinegar, lemon juice, and Tabasco. Cool until slightly thickened. Slice olives into rings. Combine 1¼ cups of gelatin mixture with olives and pimento. Set aside for middle layer but do not chill. Blend mayonnaise and salt into remaining gelatin mixture. Add celery, carrots, pepper and pineapple well drained. Pour 1¼ cups vegetable mixture into 8½" ring mold; chill until set. Cover with olive mixture and chill again. Top with remaining vegetable mixture. Chill. Serves 8.

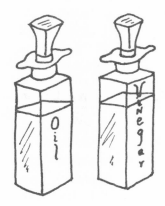

Harlequin Salad

1 8-oz. pkg. cream cheese
1 Tbsp. lemon juice
2 Tbsp. mayonnaise
½ tsp. salt
½ c. drained crushed pineapple
¼ c. maraschino cherries,
  quartered
½ c. finely chopped nuts
1 c. whipping cream
3 apples, unpeeled and diced

Soften cream cheese and blend in mayonnaise, lemon juice and salt. Stir in nuts, pineapple, and cherries. Whip cream and fold in diced apples; add to mixture. Turn into 1½ quart mold and chill for 4 hours or overnight. To serve, unmold on a platter and garnish with watercress. Serves 10-12.

Cream Cheese Dressing

3 Tbsp. chopped green onions
1 Tbsp. chopped parsley
1 can Ancovy filets, chopped
1 lemon (juice)
1 c. mayonnaise
3 oz. pkg. cream cheese
3 Tbsp. tarragon vinegar

Put onions, parsley, anchovy filets in the vinegar and lemon juice. Cream the cheese to the consistency of mayonnaise by adding cream or milk. Add mayonnaise and other ingredients and mix well. Paprika or pimento may be added for color, and a little brown sugar if you like. Serve with chopped salad, etc.

Creamy Pink Dressing

1 c. dairy sour cream
2 Tbsp. cherry juice
2 Tbsp. mayonnaise

Blend sour cream with cherry juice and mayonnaise. Refrigerate until needed. Makes 1 cup.

Fruit Dressing

½ c. sugar
1 Tbsp. flour
1 egg yolk
Juice of 1 lemon
½ c. unsweetened pineapple juice
1 c. heavy cream, whipped

Combine sugar, flour, and egg yolk in top of double boiler. Add lemon juice and pineapple juice. Cook until thick. Add whipped cream, and serve over fruit salad. Will keep 3 days in refrigerator.

Fruit Confetti Dressing

½ c. real mayonnaise
½ c. dairy sour cream
1 Tbsp. wine vinegar
½ tsp. salt
1 c. fruit cocktail, drained

Blend mayonnaise, cream, vinegar and salt. Fold in fruit cocktail. Makes 1¾ cups.

Joyce's Cheese Dressing

½ c. mayonnaise
½ c. dairy sour cream
3 Tbsp. milk
2 Tbsp. lemon juice
⅔ c. crumbled Roquefort or
   Blue Cheese

Combine ingredients, mixing well. Makes 1⅓ cups

Low Calorie Salad Dressing

1 pkg. salad dressing mix
2 Tbsp. powdered pectin
3 Tbsp. lemon juice
¾ c. cold water

Mix all ingredients and shake well. This has all the body and flavor of the conventional dressing.

Salad Dressing

3 Tbsp. vinegar
2 Tbsp. sugar
1 Tbsp. butter
2 tsp. dry mustard
1 tsp. salt
2 egg yolks
Evaporated milk or sour cream

Mix all ingredients except milk into a paste and heat over low heat until it becomes very thick, stirring well all the time. When cold, thin with evaporated milk or sour cream. Makes quite a lot.

Seafood
Poultry
Eggs

Seafood

Poultry

Eggs

Chicken and Asparagus

9 chicken breasts
3 cans mushroom soup
2 small cans asparagus
1 can pimento
1 can almonds
3 cans French fried onions

Boil chicken with stalk of celery, salt and pepper. Remove bones. Thin soup with stock from boiling chicken. Mix all ingredients. Bake 35 minutes in 350 degree F. oven. Remove from oven. Sprinkle French fried onions and almonds over top. Return to oven for 10 to 15 minutes to heat onions.

Chicken Balls

½ c. bread crumbs
1 c. milk
2 c. raw white meat of chicken
  ground
1 Tbsp. melted butter
½ tsp. chopped parsley
1 egg, slightly beaten
1 tsp. salt
Dash of nutmeg
1 c. blanched almonds, slivered

Soak bread crumbs in milk with ground chicken. Mix with butter, parsley, egg, salt and nutmeg. Chill thoroughly and shape into about 1 inch balls. Roll in slightly beaten egg then in blanched almonds. Place in a skillet or baking dish with ¼ cup chicken broth. Cover and cook at low heat for 20 minutes. *Just before serving, mix:* 1 tablespoon cornstarch with 1 cup cream and pour over the chicken balls. Add ½ teaspoon grated lemon rind and cook until thick. Serve balls with sauce topped with slivered almonds. (An elegant luncheon dish).

Lois's Chicken-Beef Casserole

4 oz. dried beef
6 chicken breasts (boned)
1 pkg. sour cream
1 can cream of mushroom soup
1 small can mushrooms
2 or 3 strips bacon

Line 1½ or 3 quart shallow dish with dried beef. Place chicken on beef. Mix sour cream, soup and mushrooms; spoon around and over chicken. Lay bacon on top and bake in 250 degree oven for 4 hours.

Baked Chicken Breast

6 chicken breasts or 1 three
   pound fryer cut up
1 c. flour
3 tsp. paprika
3 tsp. salt
2 c. chopped celery
Mix:
   1 c. cream of chicken soup
   1 c. grated cheese
   ½ c. half and half (or milk)
   2 chopped pimentos
   1 c. buttered bread crumbs

Mix well in sack and shake chicken pieces in flour. Brown chicken in ½ cup salad oil in skillet. Spread celery in bottom of baking dish; then add chicken pieces on top.

Pour over chicken and celery Sprinkle bread crumbs on top. Bake 45 minutes at 350 degrees. Sprinkle ½ cup sliced almonds on top last 10 minutes.

Stuffed Chicken Breasts

2 Tbsp. chopped onion
2 Tbsp. chopped celery
⅔ c. canned mushroom pieces
¾ c. butter, melted
¼ tsp. pepper
¾ tsp. salt
4 Tbsp. lemon juice
½ c. chopped toasted almonds
6 fryer breasts, boned
1½ c. potato chips, finely crushed
6 strips bacon

Sauté onion, celery and mushrooms in ¼ cup of butter. Add pepper, ¼ teaspoon salt, lemon juice and almonds. Fill cavities of boned chicken breasts with stuffing. Close and fasten with skewers. Roll chicken in ¼ cup melted butter, then in potato chips. Place in pan, skewer side down. Salt and place bacon strip on each breast. Bake at 350 degrees F. for 1½ hours or until done.

I Chicken Casserole

3 or 4 chicken breasts, cooked
   and chopped
1 can cut asparagus (small)
1 can cream of mushroom soup
½ c. sharp cheese, grated
(thin soup with asparagus liquid)
1 pimento, chopped
3 hard-boiled eggs, chopped
1 8-oz. pkg. tiny noodles, cooked
   in chicken broth

Mix all ingredients together. Place in buttered casserole dish; cover with grated sharp cheese; sprinkle with paprika. Bake 30 to 40 minutes at 350 degrees F.

II Chicken Casserole

1 frying chicken
1 envelope chicken noodle soup
  mix
1 c. minute rice
1 can mushroom soup
1 can water

Place cut up chicken in buttered casserole. Pour both soup mixes over chicken. Add rice, and pour canned soup and water over this. Cover with foil and bake 3 or 4 hours at 300 degrees F.

Chicken Chartreuse

1 fat hen (3-5 pounds)
2 cans mushroom soup
1 heaping Tbsp. minced onion
2 c. rice
1 can mushroom caps
1 heaping Tbsp. minced celery

Cook hen in water (seasoned with salt, pepper, celery salt and bay leaf) until very tender. Let cool in broth and skim off fat. Remove chicken from bones and cut in small pieces. Wash rice and cook in chicken broth, (stirring occasionally) until almost done (still firm). While chicken is cooking, sauté onions and celery in small amount of butter. Mix all ingredients, pour into greased casserole and bake in moderate oven (350 degrees) 1½ to 2 hours. Just before removing, stir well, sprinkle with paprika and top with mushroom caps. Will serve about 12. Also good after freezing.

Easy Chicken Delight

1 stick oleo
1 pkg. dry onion soup mix
2 c. water
1 c. rice, uncooked
Fryer parts
Salt and pepper to taste

Melt oleo in skillet; add other ingredients in order given. Cover and bake for 1 hour at 350 degrees. Serve with bread, salad and dessert.

Chicken Divine

4 chicken breasts, whole
1 large onion, quartered
2 carrots
2 stalks celery
1 can chicken broth
1 tsp. salt
4 Tbsp. butter
4 Tbsp. flour
2 c. broth
¾ c. cream (half and half)
3 Tbsp. sherry
½ c. whipping cream
½ c. Parmesan cheese

Boil first six ingredients until chicken is tender, about 45 minutes. Remove bone and skin. Place chicken in baking dish. Sprinkle with sherry (about 1 tablespoon in all). Strain broth for sauce. Make a white sauce cooking butter, flour, broth, cream and sherry until slightly thick. Save ⅔ cup of sauce and pour remaining sauce over chicken. Whip the cream and add to the ⅔ cup of sauce and pour over top of chicken. Sprinkle with Parmesan cheese. Cover and refrigerate overnight. Let stand out of refrigerator about 30 minutes. Place uncovered baking dish in pan of water. Bake at 325 degrees F. for 35 minutes.

Chicken Enchiladas

1 large chicken,
   (cooked and cubed)
2 cans cream of chicken soup
1 large carton sour cream
1 small can diced green chilies
1 pkg. corn tortillas
Grated Cheddar cheese

Mix soup, sour cream and chilies. Fry tortillas until crisp. Spread soup mixture over bottom of casserole dish. Roll soup mixture and diced chicken up inside tortillas and place side by side in dish. Cover with remaining mixture and sprinkle with cheese. Bake at 400 degrees for 20 to 25 minutes.

Chicken Eugenie

2 slices of ham ¼" thick
6 chicken breasts, legs or thighs
2 cans cream of chicken soup
½ c. cream
½ tsp. grated onion
½ c. chopped celery

Lightly sauté ham and chicken. Mix soup and milk, heat only. Add onion and celery. Place ⅓ piece of ham on a large piece of aluminum foil; place one piece of chicken on ham; fold foil up (cup fashion); pour ½ cup sauce over chicken. Seal foil and place on cookie sheet. Bake at 375 degrees F. about 1 hour and 15 minutes. Place foil wrapped chicken on each plate. Fold foil back to give access for eating. Serves 6.

174

Chicken Liver Wraparounds

½ lb. chicken livers
½ c. French dressing
¼ tsp. garlic salt
10 slices bacon, cut in half
  crosswise

Cut chicken liver into about 20 pieces. Combine dressing and garlic salt. Marinate livers in dressing about 15 minutes. Wrap bacon slices around each piece of liver and fasten with wooden pick. Place on a rack in shallow baking pan. Bake at 350 degrees F. for 30-35 minutes, until bacon is crisp. Serve hot. Also good to wrap unmarinated liver in bacon and bake as directed. You can also use smoked or fresh lobsters in place of chicken liver and wrap in bacon. Bake as directed.

Chicken Loaf

1½ c. milk
1½ c. chicken broth
4 eggs, beaten
2 c. soft bread crumbs,
  firmly packed
4 c. cooked chicken, diced
1 c. cooked rice
¾ c. diced celery
2 Tbsp. chopped pimentos
1 tsp. salt

Combine the milk and broth in a bowl and blend in the eggs. Add bread crumbs. Let this mixture set for several minutes to give time for crumbs to soak up milk and broth. Then add diced chicken, rice, celery, pimentos and salt. Spread evenly in a buttered casserole 13 x 9 x 2. Cover and put in refrigerator to season overnight. Bake for 1 hour at 350 degrees F. and serve with sauce. Serves 12 generously. Cut in squares.

Sauce:
½ stock butter or oleo
6 Tbsp. flour
2 c. chicken broth
1 Tbsp. chopped parsley
1 tsp. salt
½ tsp. paprika
1 tsp. lemon juice
1 3-oz. can mushrooms, drained
1 c. light cream (evaporated
  can be used)

Blend well as for cream sauce and cook slowly until right consistency.

Joyce's Chicken Loaf

1 3-4 lb. hen
1½ c. chicken broth
1 c. cooked rice
4 well beaten eggs
1½ c. bread crumbs
1½ c. milk
1 pimento, chopped

Boil the hen until tender in enough lightly salted water to make 1½ cups broth. Bone the hen and cut the meat into bite size pieces. Save the broth to use later. If there is not enough broth to make 1½ cups, add a little hot water.

Mix all the ingredients well in the order given. Put in a 9 x 13 inch loaf pan. Bake in a 350 degree oven for 45 minutes. Allow to cool in the pan before turning out. This dish may be prepared the day before using. Serve with sauce. Serves 10.

Sauce for chicken loaf:
½ c. butter
2 Tbsp. flour
½ to 1 c. medium cream
¼ c. chopped pimento
1 small can mushrooms
   (sautéed in butter)

Make white sauce of butter, flour and cream. Add mushrooms, pimento and parsley. Serve warm over chicken loaf.

Chicken "Meal-In-A-Mold"

2 envelopes unflavored gelatin
1½ c. cold water
1 c. salad dressing
1 can condensed beef broth
1 tsp. salt
2 c. diced cooked chicken
1 c. sliced celery
2 Tbsp. chopped onion
2 Tbsp. chopped pimento strips
   (green pepper strips, pimento strips)

Sprinkle gelatin on water in small pan to soften. Place over moderate heat, stirring constantly, until gelatin is dissolved (about 3 minutes). Combine salad dressing with beef broth, gelatin and salt. Chill. Stir occasionally until mixture mounds when dropped from spoon. Add chicken, celery, onion, and pimento; mix well. Chill until firm in 1 qt. mold. Garnish with green pepper and pimento strips. Serves 6.

Chicken-Mushroom Souffle

Sauce:

½ c. butter
½ c. flour
1 c. cream
3 c. milk
2 c. chicken stock
1 tsp. salt
2 c. or more diced, cooked
    chicken
1 c. mushrooms, sliced
1 c. water chestnuts, sliced
¼ c. pimento, chopped
¼ c. sherry

Make sauce of butter, flour, milk, cream, chicken stock and salt. Cook until thick. Then add chicken, mushrooms, water chestnuts, pimento and sherry. Blend well and serve hot over souffle.

Souffle:

5 slices bread, buttered on both sides. Cut each slice into four pieces and place in buttered casserole. Pour over bread slices:

2 c. milk
¼ lb. New York State cheese,
    grated
4 whole eggs
1 tsp. dry mustard (heaping)

Beat eggs, add milk, cheese and mustard. Pour over bread slices in casserole and cook 50 to 60 minutes in a pan of water at 350 degrees F. (It is better if it stands awhile before cooking). Serve hot chicken sauce over souffle topped with toasted almonds.

Chicken With Noodles

1 large hen
1 stick margarine
1 c. bell pepper, chopped
1 c. celery, chopped
1 c. onion, chopped
½ lb. processed cheese
1 6-oz. jar stuffed olives
1 6-oz. can sliced mushrooms
1 pkg. wide noodles
4 c. chicken stock
1 can mushroom soup

Boil hen in lightly salted water (enough water for about 5 cups stock). Save stock. Bone chicken and cut in large pieces. Sauté in margarine, the bell pepper, celery, and onion. Stir in cheese; add olives, mushrooms and chicken. Boil noodles in 4 cups stock; cook until all stock is absorbed. Add 1 can mushroom soup. Mix all ingredients and serve hot. 1 cup stock can be used to moisten the mixture if needed. Dish can be prepared a day ahead, and heated in casserole in a 300 degree oven about 45 minutes. Serves 8.

Chicken Pie With Cheese Crescents

2 fryers
1 c. celery
1⅔ c. milk
⅓ c. butter
4 eggs (hard-boiled)
2½ c. broth from cooked
  chickens
4 Tbsp. flour (scant)
salt
pepper

Boil fryers; remove bones, skin and vein from cooked meat. Put meat back into broth and let it set in refrigerator over night or for several hours. Layer meat and hard-boiled eggs. Cook celery in broth. Pour broth and celery mixture over the chicken. Make white sauce as follows: Melt butter; mix flour in and stir in milk. Cook on medium heat until sauce thickens. Add seasonings to white sauce. Pour sauce over chicken mixture. Put this dish in preheated oven and cook until it bubbles. Take out of oven and put uncooked *cheese crescents* on chicken pie. Cook at 400 degrees F. until crescents brown.

Cheese crescents:

2 c. flour
3 tsp. baking powder
1 tsp. salt
1 c. grated American cheese
⅓ c. cooking oil
⅔ c. milk

Sift dry ingredients together; mix in cheese. Pour oil and milk in 1 cup, but do not stir. Pour all at once into flour mixture. Stir with fork until mixture cleans side of bowl and rounds up into ball. Knead a few times on oil paper. Roll out between 2 pieces of oil paper. Peel off top paper; cut into pie wedges. Roll up, beginning at the widest end, rolling to the point. Bake at 425 degrees F. from 10 to 12 minutes, or until brown. This is a good casserole topping or can be used for serving with salads or cokes.

Chicken Strata

9 thin slices day old bread
3 c. diced cooked chicken
½ c. chopped onion
½ c. diced celery
½ c. mayonnaise
1 tsp. salt, dash pepper
2 eggs, well beaten
2 c. milk
1 can mushroom soup
½ c. shredded sharp cheese

Spread 2 slices bread with butter, set aside. Cut remaining bread into 1 inch cubes. Arrange half of bread in bottom of buttered 8 x 12 x 2 inch baking dish. Combine chicken, celery, onions, mayonnaise and seasonings; spoon over bread cubes in dish, sprinkle with remaining unbuttered crumbs. Beat eggs well; mix with milk and pour over casserole. Chill 1 hour or overnight in refrigerator. When ready to cook, spoon soup over top. Top with 2 buttered pieces of bread, cut in ½ inch cubes. Bake at 350 degrees F. for 50 minutes or until set. Just before taking from oven sprinkle with shredded cheese.

Chinese Chicken Almond

Sauté ½ cup sliced onion in 2 tablespoons butter till tender, not brown. Add the following and heat to boiling:

1 lb. can bean sprouts and liquid
1 8-oz. can sliced water chestnuts,
    drained
1 c. celery slices
2 c. diced cooked chicken
½ c. chicken broth
1 4-oz. can sliced mushrooms
    with liquid

Make sauce of following and add to chicken (boiling hot), stirring constantly:

3 Tbsp. cornstarch
¼ tsp. salt and ¼ tsp.
    monosodium glutamate
¼ c. water
2 Tbsp. soy sauce

Serve with 4 cups hot cooked rice. Sprinkle with ½ cup slivered toasted almonds. Soy sauce may be passed. Makes 4 to 6 servings.

179

Toppings for casseroles:

For one casserole mix together ¼ cup bread crumbs and 2 tablespoons melted butter. Or toss ½ cup small bread cubes in 2 tablespoons melted butter or margarine. Butter may be flavored with grated Parmesan cheese, grated lemon rind, minced garlic, onion juice, thyme, marjoram, or other herbs.

Other toppings:

Crumbled crackers, crumbled cheese Ritz crackers; crisp cereals; crushed potato chips.

Chinese Chicken Casserole

3 c. cold, cooked chicken cut into pieces
2 tsp. lemon juice
1 Tbsp. soy sauce
¼ c. finely cut green onions
1 c. finely cut celery
1 5-oz. can water chestnuts, drained and sliced thin
1 1-lb. can fancy bean sprouts, well drained
½ tsp. salt
Dash of pepper
1 c. mayonnaise
¼ c. chopped toasted almonds
1 6-oz. can chow mein noodles
1½ qt. casserole

Sprinkle chicken with lemon juice and soy sauce; chill 2 hours longer. Add remaining ingredients, except almonds and noodles. Mix well. Turn into greased 1½ quart casserole. Sprinkle almonds on top. Bake at 350 degrees F. for about 25 minutes. Serve on crisp noodles. 6 to 8 servings.

Ann's Chicken Tostadas

1 large chicken, cooked and cubed
1 c. chicken broth
1 onion, chopped
1 small can diced green chilies
1 large can tomatoes (cut up)
2 c. grated Cheddar cheese
1 dozen corn tortillas

Cook onions in small amount of oil until tender. Add chilies, tomatoes, chicken and broth. Simmer covered for 1 hour. Add cheese slowly and stir. Let simmer 15 minutes. Fry tortillas flat until crisp. Place layer of chicken mixture, sour cream, lettuce, chipped olives on top of flat tortillas and eat while warm and crisp.

Curried Olive-Chicken Mold

1 c. ripe olives
2 envelopes gelatin
½ c. cold water
1 can cream of chicken soup
⅓ c. lemon juice
½ tsp. salt
1 tsp. curry powder
1 c. mayonnaise
1½ c. diced, cooked chicken
1 c. diced celery
1 Tbsp. thinly sliced green onion
parsley

Cut olives into large wedges, reserving ¼ cup whole olives for garnish. Soften gelatin in cold water. Heat soup. Add gelatin; stir until gelatin is dissolved. Blend in lemon juice, salt and curry powder. Chill until firm. Unmold; garnish with whole in mayonnaise, chicken, celery, olives and onion. Turn into 1½ quart ring mold. Chill until form. Unmold; garnish with whole olives, parsley and, if you wish, cranberry relish. Makes 8-10 servings.

Curry Rice and Chicken

1 c. rice (cook and drain)
1 c. chopped celery
½ c. bell pepper
1 large chopped onion
1 stick butter
2 cans chicken broth or
  fresh broth
2 c. diced chicken
1 large can mushrooms
1 tsp. parsley (flaked)
1 tsp. curry powder
Salt and pepper to taste
Slivered almonds

Sauté celery, pepper and onions in melted butter. Add to the cooked rice. Add broth, chicken and other ingredients. Add almonds on top and cook in a covered dish in a 350 degree F. oven about 30 minutes. This can be made a day before using, then removed from refrigerator an hour before baking.

Kentucky Chicken

3 lbs. chicken breasts
2 c. bread crumbs
¾ c. Parmesan cheese
¼ c. parsley leaves (fresh)
1 clove garlic (crushed)
2 tsp. salt
⅛ tsp. pepper
1 c. melted butter

Mix bread crumbs with cheese, parsley, salt and pepper. Dip each piece of chicken into melted butter, then in crumb mixture (coat well). Arrange in an open shallow roasting pan. Pour remaining butter over all. Bake 1 hour or until tender, 350 degrees F. Do not turn chicken but baste frequently with pan drippings. Serves 10.

Mississippi Rice With Chicken

1 3-lb. chicken
½ envelope dry onion soup mix
1 can condensed cream of
    mushroom soup
2 Tbsp. chopped pimento
3 c. cooked rice
½ c. grated American cheese

Cook chicken until tender. Remove meat from bones, cut into bite-size pieces. Combine soup mix, soup and pimento. Alternate layers of rice, chicken and soup mixture in a casserole, ending with soup mixture. Sprinkle with cheese. Bake at 375 degrees until cheese is melted and golden brown. Serves 6.

One-Dish Chicken Dinner

1 qt. thinly sliced pared Irish
    potatoes
2 c. cubed, cooked chicken
1 10-oz. pkg. frozen green peas
1 can cream of chicken soup
½ soup can milk
2 Tbsp. instant minced onion
2 tsp. salt
1 tsp. Worcestershire sauce
½ tsp. dried marjoram
¼ tsp. dried mustard
⅛ tsp. pepper
Dash hot sauce, paprika

Layer half the potatoes in bottom of lightly greased 11 x 7 x 2 inch baking dish. Sprinkle with salt. Top with chicken. Let peas stand at room temperature for a few minutes, then break and scatter over chicken. Top with remaining potatoes. Again, sprinkle with salt. Combine other ingredients and heat, stirring occasionally until smooth. Pour evenly over potatoes. Sprinkle top with paprika. Cover and bake for 1 hour, or until potatoes are done, in a 350 degree oven. Serves 6.

Paella For 6

2½ lb. frying chicken or
    2 lbs. chicken breast and thighs
2½ lbs. fresh shrimp
2 dozen small clams
1 large onion
1 clove garlic
2 c. short grained rice
1 large tomato
1 pkg. (10-oz.) frozen peas
1 pkg. Italian style green peas
2½ tsp. salt
1½ tsp. saffron
1 tsp. paprika
2 oz. jar pimento
1½ c. olive oil

Tom's Paella

Paella is the famed dish of Spain, probably Spain's greatest culinary gift. Paella is supposed to have originated in Valencia, but there is a great rivalry among many Spanish cities as to which makes the best Paella. The dish was first cooked over an open fire as a noon meal by the farmers in the field. They used a shallow flat pan called a Paella that had as large a surface as possible in direct contact with the fire. The fire had to be hot enough to brown the meat and start the rice steaming.

Since no two Spanish cooks make Paella the exact same way, you can prepare it at home with your own variations as long as you follow a few simple rules.

The dish must include rice, the short grained variety as grown in Spain. The liquid should be water, not canned tomatoes, tomato sauce or tomato paste. All browning should be done in olive oil because olive oil browns evenly and coats the rice without being absorbed.

The chicken does not have to be boned. At least one kind of shell fish should be used but several kinds are better. It is customary to leave clams and mussels in their shell. If made with fish, choose a fish with a mild flavor. If you use meat, use veal, pork or ham. A sweet and spicy sausage can be used as well.

In addition to tomatoes, use at least one green vegetable. In Spain they precook the vegetables, but they can be added raw or partially cooked. Onions, garlic, paprika and salt should be added for seasoning. Saffron gives the dish a distinctive color and tang.

In a skillet, sauté the chicken in ½ cup olive oil until it is golden brown. Remove the chicken from the skillet and reserve it. Shell and devein 2½ lbs. large shrimp and sauté them in the remaining oil, in the skillet, stirring frequently, until they are pink; remove the shrimp from the skillet and reserve them.

Scrub 24 small clams and put them in a kettle with about ½ inch water. Steam them, covered for about 6 to 8 minutes, or until the shells are opened. Discard any clams that do not open. Drain the clams and reserve them and their liquid.

In the remaining oil in the skillet, sauté one large onion and one garlic clove (minced) until they are pale yellow. Add 2 cups short grained rice and cook it, stirring constantly until the grains are coated with oil. Transfer the rice to a Paella pan. Arrange over the rice as evenly as possible the chicken pieces and the shrimp, one large tomato, peeled and coarsely chopped and one package (10 oz.) each of frozen peas and Italian green beans, defrosted and drained. If desired, a package of frozen artichoke hearts, thawed and drained, can be substituted for either the peas or beans.

Measure the clam liquid and add enough water to make 4½ cups liquid. Bring it to a boil and stir in 2½ teaspoons salt, 1½ teaspoons ground saffron and 1 teaspoon paprika. Heat the rice mixture in a Paella pan or casserole and pour in the hot liquid. Cook it over moderately high heat for 10 minutes. Lower the heat to medium and cook it for 15 minutes longer or until the liquid is absorbed and the rice is tender. Or bake the Paella in a moderate oven, 350 degrees, for 25-30 minutes. Arrange the clams in their shells on top. Arrange a 2 oz. jar pimentos, drained and cut into strips, over the surface of the dish before removing it from the heat. Garnish the dish with lemon wedges or olives and serve immediately.

Goodby Turkey

5 Tbsp. flour, sifted
1 tsp. salt
¼ tsp. onion salt
¼ c. butter, melted
2½ c. milk or light cream
1⅓ c. minute rice
1½ c. turkey or chicken broth
1 c. grated American cheese
1½ c. cooked (cut) asparagus
2 c. turkey, cut in bite
  size pieces

Make cream sauce of butter, flour, salt and milk. Pour rice from box into a 2 quart buttered, shallow baking dish. Combine broth and ½ of the salt and pour over rice. Sprinkle half of cheese over rice. Top with asparagus and then the turkey. Pour on sauce, then the remaining cheese. Bake about 20 minutes at 375 degrees. Top with toasted slivered almonds before serving. Serves 6.

Favorite Turkey Casserole

1 8-oz. pkg. egg noodle
  dumplings
2 c. diced turkey
1 c. grated cheese
1 c. bread crumbs
1 can cream of mushroom soup
1 c. milk
½ c. thinly sliced blanched
  almonds
¼ tsp. onion powder
¼ tsp. celery salt

Cook noodle dumplings as directed on pkg., using less than ¼ teaspoon salt. Dilute soup with milk; bring barely to a boil. While hot, mix ½ cup grated cheese into the soup. Place a layer of noodle dumplings and a layer of diced turkey in a 2 quart buttered casserole. Sprinkle with half the onion powder, celery salt and thinly sliced almonds. Make the second layer same as the first. Now pour the soup mixture over contents. Dot with butter. Sprinkle with half cup of cheese and bread crumbs. Bake at 375 degrees F. about 25-30 minutes or until bubbly hot. Serves 8.

Macaroni Oyster Loaf

1 c. elbow macaroni
1½ c. milk
1 c. shredded Cheddar cheese
1 c. soft bread crumbs
¼ c. butter
2 Tbsp. each, minced chives, parsley, green pepper
1 tsp. lemon juice
1 tsp. Worcestershire sauce
½ tsp. salt
½ tsp. dry mustard
⅛ tsp. black pepper
⅛ tsp. nutmeg
3 eggs, well beaten
1 jar (12 oz.) fresh small oysters
Watercress for garnish

Cook macaroni in boiling salted water until tender; drain. Shred cheese and heat with milk until cheese melts; add crumbs, butter, chives, parsley, green pepper, lemon juice, Worcestershire sauce, salt, dry mustard, pepper and nutmeg. Stir in beaten eggs and macaroni. Turn half of mixture into a 9 x 5 inch buttered loaf pan and cover with oysters. Top with the remaining macaroni mixture. Bake in a 325 degree F. oven for 50 minutes or until set and golden brown. Unmold on a hot platter and garnish with sprigs of watercress. Serves 6.

Salmon Loaf

1 can salmon
2 eggs
1 can mushroom soup
1 small onion
⅛ lb. crackers

Mix together everything but cream soup. Put in baking dish, pour cream soup over it. Bake about 30 minutes in 300 degree oven or until brown. Top with pepper and pimento.

Marvel Seafood Casserole

1 can crab meat
1 large can mushrooms, stem and all
2 cans shrimp
½ tsp. dry mustard
Bit of onion, grated
1 tsp. chopped parsley
½ lb. pkg. Cheddar cheese, grated
Buttered bread crumbs
Paprika

Make sauce in double boiler of:
  ½ stick butter or oleo
  4 Tbsp. flour
  1 pt. sweet milk

Mix sauce and above ingredients together and top with buttered crumbs.

Bake in casserole 20 to 30 minutes at 350 degrees F. Serve hot!!

185

Barbecued Shrimp

1 dozen shrimp, jumbo size
1 qt. cooking oil
1 c. fine cracker crumbs
½ c. flour
1 egg
1 c. milk
Salt and pepper to taste
1 pt. smoke sauce

Peel and devein shrimp, leaving shells on tails. Wash and clean thoroughly. Dust shrimp with flour. Break egg in bowl; beat well; add milk, salt and pepper to taste. Dip shrimp in egg and milk, then roll in fine cracker crumbs. Pour oil in deep saucepan and heat to 350 degrees. Drop shrimp into fat and fry 4 minutes to seal moisture in shrimp. Remove from deep fat and saturate in the smoke sauce. Put in shallow pan and place under broiler or in the oven for 5 minutes; or until shell or tails become brown and crisp. Shrimp are ready to serve. Serve a mild tasty barbecue sauce with the shrimp.

Shrimp-Crabmeat Casserole

1 medium bell pepper, chopped
1 medium onion, chopped
1 c. chopped celery
1 16-oz. can crabmeat
2 cans shrimp
½ tsp. salt
⅛ tsp. pepper
1 tsp. Worcestershire sauce
1 c. mayonnaise
1 c. bread crumbs

Mix all ingredients and top with bread crumbs. Bake 30 minutes at 350 degrees F. Serves 8.

Shrimp Delicious

6 Tbsp. butter
1 c. finely chopped green onion
2 lbs. raw shrimp, shelled and
  deveined
Salt and pepper to taste
½ lb. thinly sliced mushrooms
1 Tbsp. flour
1 c. sour cream

Melt 4 tablespoons butter in a skillet. Add the green onions and shrimp. Cook, stirring the shrimp until they just turn pink, 3 to 5 minutes. Do not overcook. Sprinkle with salt and pepper and set aside. Melt the remaining butter in another skillet and cook the mushrooms until they give up their liquid. Continue cooking until most of this liquid has evaporated. Stir in flour, salt and pepper to taste. Add the shrimp mixture and carefully stir in the sour cream. Heat thoroughly, but do not boil or the cream may curdle. Serve hot with rice. Serves 4.

186

Shrimp Rice

1 c. diced bacon
1 c. uncooked rice
1 lb. shrimp, cooked
2 Tbsp. chopped onion
2½ c. cooked tomatoes

Fry bacon until crisp. Remove and cook onion in 2 tablespoons of bacon fat until a light yellow. Add tomatoes and rice. Mix well. Cover and heat to boiling point. Lower heat and simmer 20 minutes. Stir occasionally with fork. Set in warm place where there is no danger of scorching for another 20 minutes to allow rice to become fluffy. Add shrimp and bacon to above mixture. Pour in casserole and bake at 350 degrees for 15 minutes. Serves 6.

Tuna Casserole

1 6½ oz. can tuna
  (in small pieces)
3 Tbsp. chopped onion
3 Tbsp. chopped pimento
1 c. favorite grated cheese
1 c. water
1 10½-oz. can mushroom soup
Dash of Tabasco
3 c. hot, cooked rice
Dash of salt
1 c. evaporated milk

Mix well tuna, onion, pimento, rice and Tabasco. Pack jello molds or large mold ½ full. Unmold in shallow baking dish. Mix soup, milk and water. Pour around molds or lightly over. Top with cheese. Cook at 350 degrees F. 30 minutes or until cheese bubbles and browns. 6 servings. (Butter the molds and casserole.)

Aunt Ruth's Tuna Casserole

1 can tuna (for 4 people)
1 can cream mushroom soup
½ can water
½ tsp. salt
1 can Chinese noodles
1 small can cashew nuts
½ c. chopped celery
½ c. chopped bell peppers
½ c. chopped onions

Mix tuna, mushroom soup and ½ can water. Take chopped celery, bell peppers and onions and place in a small stew pan with just enough water to barely boil. Add ½ teaspoon salt and pour this into the tuna mixture. Add ¾ can Chinese noodles and 1 small can cashew nuts. Stir all together. Sprinkle the remaining Chinese noodles over top and place in oven just long enough to brown noodles and heat thru. Serve this with Waldorf salad and hot rolls. Makes a delightful meal.

Hot Deviled Eggs

1 Tbsp. butter
4 Tbsp. flour
¼ tsp. dry mustard
⅛ tsp. paprika
½ tsp. salt
¼ tsp. Worcestershire sauce
2 c. milk
6 hard-boiled eggs
½ c. chopped ripe olives
⅓ c. grated Parmesan cheese
Bit of bay leaf
Pepper to taste

Melt butter; blend in flour, mustard, paprika, salt and Worcestershire. Add milk and bay leaf. Cook and stir until thickened. Remove bay leaf.

Cut eggs into halves and remove yolks. Mash and blend with a little of the sauce. Season to taste. Heap into whites and arrange in shallow baking dish. Add olives and half of the cheese to remaining sauce and pour over and around the eggs. Top with remaining cheese and bake at 350 degrees F. for 15 to 20 minutes or until thoroughly heated. Serves 4.

Spanish Omelet

Sauce:
1 slice bacon (cut up and fried slowly), ⅓ cup green pepper (minced); add and sauté ½ cup green onion (chopped), 1 cup canned tomatoes, 3 stuffed green olives (sliced). Add and simmer about 10 minutes ¼ teaspoon salt and dash of cayenne pepper.

Omelet:
3 eggs (lightly beaten)
¼ tsp. salt
1 Tbsp. butter

Melt butter; add eggs and salt mixture. When eggs begin to "set" around the edge of pan, run spatula under edges so eggs will flow to the bottom of pan and cook. When eggs are almost done, flip the omelet over to cook the other side. Fold into a plate and put sauce inside the egg.

188

Meat Meat Casseroles

Meat

Meat

Casseroles

Barbecue Boston Butt Roast

3 lb. Boston butt roast or
  shoulder roast
Celery
Salt and pepper
1 large onion, chopped
1 large can tomato juice
1 large garlic bud
¾ c. vinegar
1 tsp. salt
1 tsp. pepper
½ tsp. celery seed
1 Tbsp. Worcestershire sauce
½ Tbsp. sugar

Make this the day before using it, as this recipe takes time. Better too, made the day before. Boil roast with celery, salt and pepper until tender—falls off bone. Remove all fat, gristle, etc.; cut in small pieces. After boiling together the rest of the ingredients a while, add the cut up roast, and cook until thick. Good! Serve on buns, along with potato chips, congealed salad and dessert.

Beef Stroganoff With Ground Beef

1 lb. ground beef
1 can cream of chicken soup
1 medium onion, chopped
¼ tsp. Accent
¼ tsp. paprika
¼ tsp. salt
¼ tsp. pepper
1 carton sour cream
2 Tbsp. flour
2 4-oz. cans mushroom stems
  and pieces

Brown onion in a little butter; then brown meat. Add 2 tablespoons flour. Cook about 5 minutes. Add seasonings. Add mushrooms and soup. Cook until meat is done. Add sour cream just before serving. Serve over noodles, with parsley, or minute rice.

Cheeseburger Meat Loaf

1½ lbs. lean ground beef
1 egg
½ c. fine bread crumbs
¼ c. finely chopped parsley
1 tsp. salt
1 8-oz. can tomato sauce with onions
½ c. sweet pickle relish
1 c. shredded Cheddar cheese
Pepper to taste

Place ground meat, egg, bread crumbs, parsley, salt and pepper in mixing bowl. Pour ½ can tomato sauce with onions; reserve remaining sauce. Mix meat loaf mixture thoroughly. Pack ½ of mixture firmly into loaf pan. Sprinkle evenly with cheese and pickle relish. Pack remaining meat loaf mixture firmly on top. Bake at 350 degrees for 1 hour. Carefully spoon off fat. Pour remaining tomato sauce on top. Bake 15 minutes more. Let stand about 5 minutes, then invert on heated serving platter. Serves 6.

Anne's Chili Beans

½ lb. pinto beans
2 1-lb. cans tomatoes
1 can diced green chilies
1 Tbsp. vegetable oil
2 chopped onions
1½ cloves garlic
¼ c. parsley flakes
2 lbs. ground beef
¼ c. or less chili powder
1 Tbsp. salt
¾ tsp. pepper
¾ tsp. cumin

Cook beans until tender; add tomatoes and remove from heat. Brown ground beef in oil; add onions, garlic, parsley, chili powder and cook 10 minutes. Add beef mixture to beans. Add salt, pepper and cumin; cook 1½ hours or more. Serves about 8.

Chilly Night Chili

1 lb. hamburger
1 large onion, chopped
1 or 2 cans kidney beans
1 can tomato soup, undiluted
1 tsp. salt
1 Tbsp. chili powder

Brown meat and onion in butter and cook until meat is brown—about 10 minutes. Add everything else. Simmer covered for 1½ hours. Use 1 or 2 cans kidney beans, depending on how many you are feeding. Taste it first, then add more chili powder if you like.

Chili Relieno Casserole

1½ lbs. ground beef
1 onion chopped
1 tsp. salt
2 8- or 10-oz. cans green chili
   peppers
2 c. grated sharp cheese
3 beaten eggs
1½ c. milk
½ c. flour
Hot sauce

Brown meat, onion and ½ teaspoon salt in shallow, greased casserole. Spread 1 can green chili peppers; add meat mixture, then other can chili peppers. Combine eggs, milk, flour, rest of salt and pepper. Pour on top. Bake at 350 degrees for 45 to 50 minutes.

For hiccups take 1 teaspoon white sugar.

Marinade for Chuck Roast Beef

4 to 6 lb. chuck roast
½ c. chopped green pepper
⅔ c. chopped onion
¾ c. chopped celery, including
   leaves
⅓ c. vinegar
2 envelopes garlic salad
   dressing mix or
   1 clove garlic
½ c. salad oil
1 c. grape juice
1 Tbsp. Worcestershire sauce

Combine all ingredients except meat and blend in electric blender or chop very fine. Pour over roast in a large shallow dish. Cover with foil or plastic wrap and allow to marinate 12 to 24 hours in refrigerator, turning meat occasionally. When ready to cook, place meat on rack in pan and roast in 325 degree F. oven for 2 to 2½ hours or until desired tenderness.

Cornburger Pie

Brown 1 lb. ground beef and ⅓ cup chopped onion in 1 tablespoon melted shortening. Add 2 teaspoons chili powder, 1 teaspoon salt, 1 teaspoon Worcestershire sauce and 1 cup canned tomatoes. Cover and simmer over low heat for 15 minutes. Add 1 cup drained kidney beans. Pour meat mixture into a greased 1 or 1½ quart casserole. Top with ½ of corn meal muffin recipe. Bake in a hot oven 425 degrees for 25 minutes.

Enchilada Casserole

1 can chili without beans
1 can enchilada sauce
1 pkg. corn tortillas
1 can ripe olives, diced
1 onion, diced
Lots of grated Cheddar cheese

Mix chili and enchilada sauce; heat slightly. Fry tortillas until limp. Dip limp tortillas in chili and sauce mixture. Fill with cheese, onions and olives. Roll. Place side by side in flat pan and cover with remaining sauce. Sprinkle cheese over top and bake at 350 degrees for 30-45 minutes.

193

Deviled-Egg-And-Ham-Casserole

6 hard-boiled eggs
2 Tbsp. mayonnaise
½ tsp. salt
½ tsp. dry mustard
Dash of pepper
¼ c. butter or oleo
¼ c. flour
2 c. milk
1 c. grated American cheese
1½ c. drained, cooked peas
1 c. diced cooked or canned ham
½ c. dry bread crumbs
2 Tbsp. butter or oleo, melted

Halve the eggs; remove yolks and mash with mayonnaise, salt, pepper and mustard; fill whites. Arrange eggs in buttered 10 x 6 x 1½ inch baking dish. Melt butter; blend in flour. Gradually stir in milk; cook, stirring constantly, till thick. Stir in cheese, peas and ham. Pour over eggs. Combine crumbs with butter and sprinkle over mixture. Bake 15 minutes at 375 degrees F. Makes 6 servings.

Ham Loaf

1½ lbs. cured ham
1½ lbs. fresh pork
  (cut away fat and grind
  together)
2 eggs, well beaten
1 c. bread crumbs
1 c. sweet milk
½ tsp. salt and pepper

Mix together and baste loaves
with:

  1½ c. light brown sugar, packed
  1 Tbsp. dry mustard
  ½ c. vinegar
  ½ c. water

Add the eggs, sweet milk, salt and pepper and bread crumbs to the ground meat; work in well until mixed. Shape into two loaves and place in baking dish. Cook about 30 minutes at 350 degrees to 375 degrees; then baste with sauce below and continue cooking for about an hour, or until done; baste during this time.

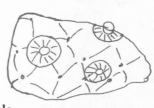

Ham and Rice Casserole

½ c. chopped onion
½ c. chopped bell pepper
⅓ c. chopped celery
½ c. cheese, cubed
2 c. cooked rice
Salt and pepper
2 Tbsp. butter
1 can mushroom soup
1 c. sweet milk
4 c. diced ham
1 can shoe string potatoes

Sauté onion, bell pepper, and celery in butter; then add soup. Add other ingredients, except shoe string potatoes, mixing well. Pour into a buttered casserole. Sprinkle top with shoe string potatoes. Bake in a 300 degree oven until bubble hot. Serves 8.

Hash Pizzare

1 can (1 lb.) corn beef hash
¼ lb. sharp American cheese,
  shredded
1 8 oz. can tomato sauce
½ tsp. garlic salt
1 2-oz. can mushrooms, drained
½ tsp. crushed oregano
2 Tbsp. grated Parmesan cheese

Chill hash; cut hash in 6 slices. Arrange in ungreased baking dish, 11 x 7 inches. Sprinkle American cheese over hash slices. Mix tomato sauce, mushrooms, garlic salt and oregano. Sprinkle with Parmesan cheese. Bake about 20 minutes at 375 degrees until hot. Serve hot with garlic bread and green salad.

Easy Lasagna

1 lb. ground beef
1 lb. Mozzarella cheese, grated
6 boiled eggs, sliced
¼ c. Parmesan cheese
1 small box lasagna noodles
  (I use regular egg noodles)
2 onions, chopped
2 cloves garlic, finely diced
1 #2½ size can tomatoes
1 6-oz. can tomato paste
2 basil leaves
1 tsp. dried parsley

Brown beef, onions and garlic in 2 tablespoons oil. Add tomatoes, parsley, tomato paste, ½ cup water, basil, salt and pepper. Simmer 15 minutes. Butter baking dish; layer cooked noodles, Mozzarella cheese, eggs and meat sauce; sprinkle cheese. Repeat. Serves 6 adults. Bake at 375 degrees for 20 minutes or until bubbly. Can be made early in the day or can be frozen. This is much easier than it looks and has a mild flavor that children like.

Meat Pie

2 lbs. ground beef
1 large onion, chopped fine
2 small pkgs. mixed vegetables
Salt and pepper
Dash Worcestershire sauce
1 can mushroom soup
Potato chips, crushed
Shredded cheese

Sauté meat and onion in little oil. Cook vegetables until tender and drain. Put a layer of meat and vegetables; then pour soup over this in a buttered dish. Crumble potato chips and cheese over top. Cook at 350 degrees F. until bubbly hot.

Rinktum Diddy

1 medium onion, chopped
1 can tomato soup
1 c. cheese, cut in small blocks
2 eggs
Salt and red pepper
Butter

Sauté onion in butter. Place in double boiler and add soup. Add cheese and stir until it melts. Salt and pepper to taste. Stir in lightly beaten eggs. Cook until thick. Serve hot over crackers. This is a nice supper dish.

Beep's Mexico Casserole

1 8-oz. can tomato sauce
1 can enchilada sauce
1 pkg. corn tortillas
1 lb. ground beef
1 c. grated cheese
½ c. sliced ripe olives (black)

Brown the ground beef. Combine the tomato sauce and enchilada sauce. Heat. In a casserole dish make layers of tortilla shells, browned meat, sauce, cheese and ripe olives—until all the ingredients are used. This should make three layers, ending with ripe olives on top. Cover and bake at 325 degrees for about 45 minutes. (If too hot, substitute another can of tomato sauce). Enchilada sauce you don't have to use.

Ravioli Casserole

1 lb. ground beef
1 medium onion, chopped (½ c.)
1 clove garlic, minced
1 Tbsp. salad oil
1 10-oz. pkg. frozen
  chopped spinach
1 can (1 lb.) spaghetti sauce
  with mushrooms
1 8-oz. can tomato sauce
1 6-oz. can tomato paste
½ tsp. salt
Dash of pepper
1 7-oz. pkg. shell or elbow
  macaroni, cooked (2 c.)
1 c. shredded sharp cheese
½ c. soft bread crumbs
2 well beaten eggs
¼ c. salad oil

Brown first three ingredients in the 1 tablespoon salad oil. Cook spinach according to package directions. Drain, reserving liquid; add water to make 1 cup. Stir spinach liquid and next five ingredients into meat mixture. Simmer 10 minutes. Combine spinach with remaining ingredients; spread in a 13 x 9 x 2 inch dish. Top with meat sauce. Bake at 350 degrees for 30 minutes. Let stand 10 minutes before serving. Makes 8-10 servings.

Rice and Hamburger Meat

1 c. chopped celery
1 c. chopped onion
1 Tbsp. butter or margarine
1 c. tomato juice
1 lb. ground beef
1 tsp. salt
1 can tomato paste
1 c. natural brown or long-
    grained rice
⅓ c. grated Parmesan cheese

Cook celery and onion in butter until golden brown. Cover, and cook until vegetables are tender. Add tomato juice, beef, salt and tomato paste. Simmer 10 minutes. Meanwhile, cook rice according to package directions. Place rice, while hot, in casserole dish. Put meat mixture over top of rice. Sprinkle with cheese. Broil for 2 or 3 minutes. Makes 8 servings.

Texas Hash

2 onions, chopped fine
2 green peppers, chopped fine
1 lb. ground beef
3 Tbsp. shortening
1 tsp. chili powder
2 c. canned tomatoes
½ c. uncooked rice
1 tsp. salt
¼ tsp. pepper

Sauté onions and pepper in shortening, add ground beef and cook until mixture falls apart. Add rice, tomatoes, juice and seasonings. Pour in a casserole and bake at 350 degrees for about 45 minutes or until rice is done.

Green Pepper Steak

3 bell peppers
2 Tbsp. shortening
2 c. beef stock (or water)
1½ lb. steak
2 Tbsp. soy sauce
1 Tbsp. monosodium glutamate
1 Tbsp. salt
1 Tbsp. sugar
1 Tbsp. cooking sherry
2 Tbsp. cornstarch

Cut bell peppers in 1 inch squares and boil 3 or 4 minutes. Heat shortening in 12 inch frying pan and sauté boiled peppers ½ minute. Remove shortening from pan. Add 2 cups beef stock and bring to boil. Add steak, soy sauce, monosodium glutamate, salt and sugar. Mix well. Add sherry and cornstarch (diluted with 1 tablespoon water). Stir until gravy thickens. Serve with rice. Serves 6 to 8.

Steak A La Creole

2 lbs. round steak
Salt and pepper
2 Tbsp. bacon drippings
2 Tbsp. flour
1 large onion, chopped
1 green pepper, chopped or
  chopped celery
1 c. water
2 c. tomatoes, fresh or canned
1 clove garlic, minced
1 bay leaf
½ tsp. dried thyme (optional)
¼ c. chopped parsley

Salt and pepper the meat and brown in fat. Brown flour, along with onion and green pepper, in the fat remaining in the skillet. Add water and tomatoes and other seasonings. Simmer 30 minutes. Add more water, if needed. Return meat to gravy and cook slowly until tender, about 1 hour. Serve over rice. Serves 6.

Fruit

Casseroles

Vegetables

Fruit

Casseroles

Vegetables

I Broccoli Casserole

2 pkgs. frozen chopped broccoli, cooked
3 eggs
1 c. grated Cheddar cheese
½ c. milk
½ stick butter (4 Tbsp.)
3 Tbsp. chopped onion (or dry minced onion)
1½ tsp. salt

Combine all ingredients with slightly beaten eggs. Pour into greased casserole and bake for 30 minutes at 350 degrees.

II Broccoli Casserole

3 pkgs. frozen broccoli
2 cans frozen shrimp soup
1 c. grated sharp cheese
1 c. dairy sour cream
Dash of Worcestershire and Tabasco sauces

Cook broccoli in salted water until tender. Drain. Thaw soup in top of double boiler. Fold in sour cream, ½ cup cheese and broccoli. Add Worcestershire and Tabasco. Pour into buttered 2-qt. casserole. Top with remaining cheese. Place in 350 degree F. oven until just hot. Serves 12.

III Broccoli Casserole

4 pkg. frozen broccoli
1 medium onion, chopped
½ stock margarine, melted
1 roll garlic cheese, chopped
1 can mushrooms, pieces and stems
1 can mushroom soup
Cornflake crumbs

Cook broccoli with onion in unsalted water until just tender. Drain thoroughly. While still hot add chopped cheese. Stir until melted. Add other ingredients except crumbs, mixing well. Pour in a buttered casserole 9 x 13 inches. Sprinkle with crumbs and bake 30 minutes at 350 degrees F. Serves 10-12.

Golden Broccoli

2 pkg. frozen broccoli
2 tsp. salt, pepper to taste
2 Tbsp. lemon juice
1 can cream of chicken soup
½ c. grated Cheddar cheese

Cook broccoli in salted water as directed on pkg. until tender. Drain. Place broccoli in shallow serving dish. Sprinkle with lemon juice and pepper. Cover with soup. Sprinkle cheese on top and place under broiler for 10 minutes or until cheese is melted and bubbly. Serves 8.

Rice and Broccoli Casserole

2 pkgs. frozen chopped
  broccoli
1 can cream of chicken soup
½ c. milk
1 c. rice
2 c. water
1 onion, chopped
1 stock margarine
1 c. grated cheese
2 tsp. salt
¼ tsp. pepper

Cook broccoli slightly (not done). Drain. Cook rice in 2 cups water. Sauté onion in margarine. Combine broccoli, soup, milk, onion, half the cheese, salt and pepper. Pour over rice and top with remaining cheese. Bake in moderate oven for 30 minutes.

Delta Rice Casserole

1½ c. rice
3 c. water
¾ c. chopped bell pepper
6 hard-boiled eggs
1 can mushroom soup
1 can cream of chicken soup
Pimento, cut into strips
Grated sharp cheese

Cook rice and bell pepper in water until done. Place layer of rice in a buttered casserole. Add 1 pimento cut into strips and three hard-boiled eggs (sliced in rounds). Mix together the 2 cans of soups and pour half of soups over rice. Add another layer of rice, three more hard-boiled eggs (cut into rounds) and more pimento strips, followed by remaining soups. Garnish with pimento and sprinkle grated sharp cheese over top. Cook in a 350 degree oven until hot and bubbly.

Dirty Rice

1 large onion, chopped
1 stick oleo
1 c. rice (uncooked)
2 cans beef consomme
1 tsp. salt
1 can mushroom stems and pieces

Sauté onion in oleo, and add to other ingredients. Pour into a casserole and bake for 1 hour at 325 degrees.

Rice Casserole

½ can cheese soup
1 c. rice
1 stock celery, finely chopped
1 can beef consomme
1 can mushroom soup
1½ cans water
1 medium onion, chopped
1 Tbsp. red bell pepper, chopped

Mix ingredients together and bake in uncovered baking dish for 1 hour in 375 degree F. oven.

Feathered Rice

1 c. uncooked rice
1 c. sliced, drained mushrooms
1 Tbsp. melted butter
2 c. boiling water
1 pkg. dehydrated onion
   soup mix

Put rice in shallow pan; toast in 400 degree F. oven, stirring occasionally until golden brown in color. Cook mushrooms in butter for 3 minutes. Combine rice, water and soup mix. Put in casserole with tight cover. Bake in 400 degree F. oven for 15 minutes.

Velma's Rice Casserole

1 c. rice
1 stick oleo
1 tsp. salt
1 tsp. vinegar
3 chicken boullion cubes
1 small can mushrooms
1 small can pimento, chopped fine
1 small bell pepper, chopped fine
1 small onion, chopped fine

Sauté pepper and onion in oleo. Add 2 cups water. Put all in casserole and bake for 1 hour at 375 degrees.

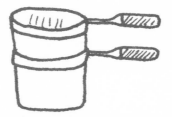

Scalloped Corn and Oyster Casserole

½ c. finely chopped celery
1 can frozen condensed oyster
   stew
1 can (2 c.) cream style corn
1½ c. medium fine cracker
   crumbs
1 c. sweet milk
1 slightly beaten egg
1 can Negro Head oysters
  (cut in halves)
¼ tsp. salt
Dash ground pepper
2 Tbsp. melted oleo
½ c. medium fine cracker crumbs

Combine first 9 ingredients; pour into greased 2-qt. casserole. Mix oleo with ½ cup cracker crumbs; sprinkle over top. Bake in moderate oven 350 degrees F. for 1 hour. Makes 6 servings.

I Squash Casserole

2 lb. yellow squash
1 large onion, chopped
2 eggs, beaten
3 Tbsp. butter
1½ c. grated Cheddar cheese
Small amount of parsley and
  pimento for color
Salt and pepper to taste

Cook squash with a little of the onion. Add some salt and pepper. Drain. Sauté onion in butter. Mash squash and add sautéed onion. Add well beaten eggs, parsley and pimento, more salt and pepper and 1 cup of cheese. Mix a little red pepper with black pepper. After all is mixed, drain off excess grease and oil. Put in casserole (9 x 13) and top generously with grated cheese. Sprinkle with paprika. Bake in 350 degree F. oven for 20 to 30 minutes. Serves 10.

II Squash Casserole

1½ lb. yellow squash
1 small onion, minced
1 Tbsp. parsley, minced
1 egg, slightly beaten
¼ c. milk
½ c. mashed cottage cheese
½ tsp. salt
½ tsp. pepper
1 tsp. sugar
¼ c. finely chopped pecans

Parboil squash, mash; add all other ingredients except nuts. Place in casserole; sprinkle pecans over the top. Bake in 350 degree F. oven until top is nicely browned, about 30 to 45 minutes. Yields 6 to 8 servings.

Spanish Squash Casserole

Cook squash with onions. Drain; add canned tomatoes, whole kernel corn and cheese. Season with salt and pepper. Simmer until cheese is melted. (You can judge the proper proportions according to the amount of squash.)

I Sweet Potato Casserole

4 c. sweet potatoes, cooked
  and mashed
1 c. butter or oleo, melted
2 c. sugar
4 eggs
2 c. evaporated milk
1 c. shredded coconut
½ tsp. cinnamon
½ tsp. nutmeg
½ tsp. cloves

Mix potatoes with melted oleo and sugar. Whip in the eggs; add spices, milk and part of the coconut, saving a little to sprinkle on top. Mix well and pour into baking dish; sprinkle with coconut and bake 35 minutes at 375 degrees F.

II Sweet Potato Casserole

4 large sweet potatoes
½ c. milk (more if needed)
1 Tbsp. butter
½ c. sugar
⅛ tsp. cinnamon
⅛ tsp. salt

Cook sweet potatoes. Cream well. Add other ingredients. (Should be consistency to hold a peak.) Pile potatoes roughly around edges of large, shallow buttered casserole, leaving center unfilled. Brown lightly. Then fill center with caramel sauce.

Caramel sauce:

1 c. sugar
½ c. butter
½ tsp. vanilla
½ c. cream (half and half)

Melt butter and sugar in iron skillet and cook until caramel color. Lower heat and add cream slowly, stirring constantly. Cook 2 minutes longer. Add vanilla. Pour into center of potatoes in casserole and serve hot. Finely chopped nuts may be sprinkled over potatoes. 8 servings.

Sweet Potatoes in Honey

Peel 4-6 sweet potatoes. Cut them in ¼ inch slices. Parboil 10 minutes. Drain and remove to casserole. Add a small jar of honey and juice of an orange. Finish baking in the oven until potatoes are tender and glazed.

Sweet Potato Balls

2 c. hot, mashed sweet
  potatoes
¼ c. pineapple juice
Crushed corn flakes

Add pineapple juice to potatoes and beat until smooth. Form into balls the size of small eggs. Roll these in crushed corn flakes. Place in a buttered shallow 2-qt. baking dish and bake at 325 degrees for 25 minutes. Serves 4-6.

Scalloped Sweet Potatoes and Apples

6 medium size sweet potatoes
1½ c. apple slices
½ c. firmly packed brown sugar
½ tsp. salt
1 tsp. mace
¼ c. butter

Wash and cook potatoes in boiling water to cover, until just tender. Peel and cut into crosswise slices ¼ inch thick. Butter a 2-qt. casserole and arrange half the potatoes in bottom; then ½ of the apple slices. Sprinkle with ½ of the brown sugar, salt and mace. Dot with 2 tablespoons butter. Repeat layers, ending with apples, seasoning and butter. Cook in 350 degree F. oven for about 50 minutes.

Banana-Sweet Potato Casserole

4 medium sweet potatoes
6 Tbsp. butter
½ c. nuts, chopped
1 c. brown sugar
½ c. coconut
4 bananas, mashed
Cream or orange juice
Corn flakes, crushed

Cook sweet potatoes until soft; drain and mash. Beat in 4 tablespoons butter, nuts, coconut and ¾ cup sugar. If mixture seems a little dry, add cream or orange juice. Place half of mixture in casserole; cover with mashed bananas. Add remaining potato mixture. Sprinkle top with corn flake crumbs. Add remaining 2 tablespoons butter and ¼ cup brown sugar. Cook at 350 degrees for 20 minutes.

Cheese Onion Pie

4 c. thinly sliced onions
1 Tbsp. butter
2 c. shredded Cheddar cheese
3 eggs
⅔ c. half and half milk
1 tsp. salt
¼ tsp. pepper
6 tomato slices

Have ready a 9-inch unbaked pastry shell with high fluted edges. Sauté onions in butter until onion is soft and golden color. Spread alternate layers of onion and cheese in shell, ending with cheese. Combine eggs, milk, salt and pepper, beating lightly. Pour over the cheese-onion filling. Bake at 400 degrees about 30 minutes; five minutes before end, arrange 6 tomato slices and finish baking.

Stuffed Potatoes

2 c. stiff mashed potatoes
1 egg
1 c. bread crumbs
Salt and pepper to taste
1 onion, chopped
1 clove garlic, crushed
1 small green pepper, chopped
2 Tbsp. olive oil
1 lb. ground beef
1 small can tomato paste
1 c. water
½ tsp. salt
½ tsp. sugar
1 8 oz. can tomato sauce

Sauté onion, garlic and green pepper in olive oil until tender. Stir in meat and cook until no longer red. Add tomato paste and ½ cup of the water with salt and sugar. Cook, stirring frequently, for 15 minutes. Add can of tomato sauce and rest of water. Cook for 15 minutes uncovered; then for ½ hour, covered. Cool. When ground meat filling is cool, scoop a mound of cooled mashed potatoes in hand and press to form an indentation. Fill scoop with 1 to 1½ tablespoons ground meat filling. Cover with another flattened mound of mashed potatoes. Form into a ball. Roll in beaten egg, then in bread crumbs, seasoned with salt and pepper. Fry in deep fat.

Celery Casserole

3 c. diced green celery, ¾ inch
½ c. toasted, slivered almonds
½ tsp. salt
⅛ tsp. white pepper
½ stick butter or oleo, melted
2 c. grated sharp Cheddar cheese
2 c. sauce (below)
1 c. cracker crumbs

Into a 2 qt. casserole, place ingredients in order listed. Bake about 50 to 60 minutes at 350 degrees F. 6 servings. Green celery has best flavor, is crisper and more tender.

Sauce:

2 c. sweet milk
¼ c. flour
½ tsp. salt
½ stick butter or oleo

In preparing fresh vegetables, add one to two tablespoons of sugar while cooking in order to bring back the natural flavor.

Minted Peas

2 pkgs. frozen green peas
  (10 oz.)
2 Tbsp. butter
½ tsp. salt
⅛ tsp. pepper
2 Tbsp. mint jelly

Cook peas as directed on package; drain well. Add remaining ingredients. Toss lightly and reheat.

Joyce's Cheese Loaf — Green Peas

1 c. whole milk
1 tsp. salt
1 Tbsp. butter or oleo
½ c. vinegar
1 small can chopped pimento
3 whole eggs
1 Tbsp. mustard
½ c. sugar
1 lb. grated sharp Cheddar
  cheese
1 c. cracker crumbs
Creamed green peas (use your
  favorite recipe to prepare
  these using a medium
  white sauce)

Make a sauce of the milk, eggs, salt, mustard, butter and sugar. Add vinegar and cook until thick. Pour over cheese, pimento and cracker crumbs. Pour into a greased ring mold which has been sprinkled with five cracker crumbs. Bake for 45 minutes in a 350 degree oven.

Cool slightly, at least 10 minutes, before removing from the mold. Unmold onto serving dish and fill the center with the creamed green peas. May be made the day before and refrigerated until needed.

To remove strings easily from beans, put in boiling water for five minutes after washing them.

Honey-Glazed Carrots

½ bunch carrots
½ tsp. salt
2 Tbsp. butter
2 Tbsp. honey
Dash nutmeg

Scrape carrots (3 or 4) and cut into sticks. Cook in small amount of salted water until tender. In small pan melt butter and honey. Spoon over drained carrots. Continue heating until carrots are well glazed. Add dash of nutmeg if desired. Serves 2 or 3.

208

Artichoke Hearts Elegante

1 pkg. frozen artichoke hearts
1 Tbsp. dried minced onion, dehydrated
1 clove garlic, crushed
1 Tbsp. chopped parsley or ½ Tbsp. dried parsley
½ c. dry bread crumbs
1 tsp. salt, pepper to taste
¼ c. olive oil
2 Tbsp. water
4 Tbsp. grated Parmesan or Romano cheese

Cook artichokes in boiling salted water for 5 minutes. Drain well. Place in buttered baking dish. Mix all remaining ingredients. Sprinkle over artichokes. Bake at 400 degrees for 20 minutes or until soft. Serves 4.

Green Noodle Casserole

2 pkgs. green noodles (6 oz. size)
4 lb. hen, cooked
1 stick oleo
1 c. chopped celery
1 c. chopped onion
1 c. chopped green pepper (optional)
½ lb. Velveeta cheese
1 small jar stuffed olives
1 large can sliced mushrooms
Almonds

Cook chicken in enough water to make stock. Reserve 1 cup to thin sauce if necessary. Cut chicken into bite size pieces. Boil noodles in remaining stock, letting all the liquid be absorbed.

Sauté celery, onions and pepper in the stick of oleo. Melt cheese and add to sautéed mixture. Add stuffed olives and mushrooms. Mix well and then add the chicken and noodles. Put in casserole; sprinkle almonds on top and bake at 350 degrees F. until hot through. This is a good luncheon dish, and colorful if made with green noodles. Others may be used. Serves 10 to 12.

Asparagus Casserole With Peanuts

2 medium size cans of green asparagus
¼ medium size onion, grated
4 hard-boiled eggs, sliced
1 Tbsp. Worcestershire sauce
3 c. milk
½ lb. sharp cheese, grated
3 Tbsp. flour
2 10¢ pkgs. shelled peanuts (crushed)
1 c. cracker crumbs
1 stick butter or oleo
Salt and red pepper to taste

Make cream sauce of butter, flour and milk in double boiler. Add onion and seasoning; stir until sauce is slightly thickened; then add cheese and blend well. Add eggs. (If sauce is too thick, then with asparagus liquid.) Drain asparagus and cover bottom of 2-qt. casserole. Cover with part of sauce and sprinkle with part of peanuts and crumbs. Bake 30 minutes in 350 degree F. oven until slightly browned. Serve hot. Serves 8 to 10.

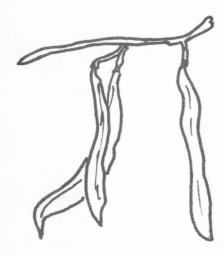

Green Bean Casserole

3 Tbsp. butter, melted
2 Tbsp. flour
1 tsp. salt
¼ tsp. pepper
1 tsp. sugar
1 c. sour cream
½ tsp. grated onion (more if
  desired)
2 cans French style green beans,
  drained
½ lb. grated Cheddar cheese
½ c. corn flake crumbs

Combine butter and flour; cook gently. Remove from heat. Stir in seasonings and cream. Fold in beans. Place in shallow 2 quart casserole. Cover with cheese, then crumbs mixed with 1 tablespoon butter. Bake 30 minutes at 350 degrees F. Serves 8.

Baked Grits

1 c. grits, cooked according to
  directions
1 stick butter or oleo
1 roll of Kraft garlic cheese
2 whole eggs, well beaten
  (Place in measuring cup and
  fill the rest of cup with milk.)

While grits are hot, melt the butter and cheese in it. Add milk and eggs. Bake in moderate oven about 30 minutes or until top is brown. Serves 6.

210

Mary's Kraut Casserole

1 lb. pork sausage
1 c. cooked rice
1 c. sour cream
Small can chopped kraut

Brown sausage and drain. Mix other ingredients well and add cooled sausage. Bake in covered casserole dish 30 minutes at 300 degrees.

Mushrooms and Almond Casserole

4 Tbsp. butter
4 Tbsp. flour
½ tsp. salt
2 c. milk
⅛ tsp. red pepper
6 hard-boiled eggs, chopped
1 large can mushrooms,
   chopped
¼ lb. slivered almonds

Melt butter in saucepan. Gradually stir in flour; when smooth remove from heat and slowly add milk. Return to low heat and cook until thick; then add salt and pepper. Add chopped mushrooms, eggs, and blanched slivered almonds to cream sauce. Pour in a buttered casserole and cover with buttered crumbs. Bake in a 350 degree oven until brown. Serves 10-12.

Creamed Spinach With Almonds

1 pkg. frozen chopped spinach
1 c. cream or 1 c. of cream of
   mushroom soup (undiluted)
4 Tbsp. almonds *or* sautéed
   mushrooms
Salt and pepper to taste
Dash of nutmeg

Cook spinach according to directions. drain well and season with salt and pepper. Add cream or soup and a dash of nutmeg. Heat only until hot. Arrange on serving platter and garnish with almonds or mushrooms. Serves 4.

Green and Gold Casserole
(Spinach)

1 pkg. frozen spinach
6 slices bread, buttered
3 eggs
½ tsp. salt
¼ tsp. prepared mustard
⅛ tsp. pepper
1½ c. milk
2 Tbsp. minced onion
1 c. grated cheese
1 Tbsp. lemon juice

Line casserole with ½ the buttered bread, with the buttered side down. Cut part of the bread in half and place around side of casserole. Put ½ thawed spinach, broken in pieces over bread. Sprinkle ½ grated cheese over spinach. Sprinkle ½ onion over this. Place second layer of bread, spinach, cheese and onion. Mix other ingredients and pour over top of casserole. Bake 1 hour at 350 degrees F. Serve hot.

Hominy Casserole

2 cans drained hominy
1 c. chopped pecans
1 can mushroom soup
½ c. milk
¼ tsp. red pepper
1 tsp. Worcestershire sauce
¼ tsp. celery seed
Buttered bread crumbs

Mix hominy and pecans. Place in casserole. Combine other ingredients and pour over hominy and pecans. Top with buttered crumbs and bake about 35 minutes in 350 degree F. oven.

Apricot Casserole

1 large can peeled apricots
½ pkg. light brown sugar
½ box cheese Ritz crackers
½ stick butter

Drain apricots 1 hour; add sugar and let stand over night. (I let this stand several hours.) Arrange apricots in bottom of pyrex dish. Crumble (lightly) cheese Ritz crackers with hand. Drizzle melted butter over crumbs; then spread over apricots. Bake for 30 to 40 minutes at 350 degrees.

Apricot Souffle

⅓ lb. dried apricots
3 egg whites
6 Tbsp. sugar

Steam dried apricots in water until well done. Pour off water and press through a sieve and sweeten to taste. Store in refrigerator until ready to use.

Beat the egg whites until stiff, adding the sugar. Fold apricot puree into the egg whites and pour into buttered casserole. Set the casserole in a pan of hot water and cook at 275 degrees F. until slightly brown on top, about 40 to 60 minutes. Serve hot with meat. Can be reheated by setting in pan of boiling water. Serves 8 to 10.

Cooked Pineapple Casserole

½ c. flour
½ c. sugar
Juice of large can pineapple
    chunks

Mix together and cook on medium heat until sauce thickens.

Grate 1 cup Cheddar cheese. Alternate layers of pineapple, cheese and sauce. Bake at 350 degrees F. in baking dish until hot and bubbly. Good with ham or chicken.

Curried Fruit

1 16-oz. can pear halves
1 16-oz. can peaches
1 lb. jar figs
1 can (1 lb. 4 oz.) pineapple
    slices
1 tsp. cinnamon
3 Tbsp. brown sugar
1 tsp. curry powder
½ tsp. nutmeg
½ stick oleo

Drain fruit and dry. Place pineapple slices on bottom of casserole. On each sliced stack one peach, pear and fig. Sprinkle with sugar and spices. Dot with oleo. Bake for 50 minutes at 325 degrees. Baste frequently. Serve warm.

Jellied Apples

10 apples, peel and core. Drop in cold water and let stand half an hour.

In saucepan let boil:

2 c. sugar
4 c. boiling water
Put apples in boiling syrup
Add 2 lemons, sliced

Cook on surface of stove until perfectly transparent and the syrup jellies. Do not use a very sour apple; Winesap is preferred. They should be whole when done.

Fruit Casserole

3 oranges, quartered and sliced. Do not peel. Just cover with water and cook over medium heat until tender. Cool.

1 No. 2½ can peaches
1 No. 2½ can pears
1 No. 2½ can sliced pineapple
1 small jar maraschino cherries
½ stick oleo
½ c. flour
⅔ c. sugar
½ tsp. salt
½ c. sherry (or more)
Brown sugar

Drain fruit well and cut into bite size pieces (except cherries).

Melt oleo; blend in flour, sugar and salt. Mix well with the fruit. Add the sherry and pour into buttered casserole; sprinkle generously with brown sugar. Heat thoroughly in 350 degree F. oven. Serves 10 to 12. Can be made the day before (leave off the sugar until ready to use).

Game

Game

Roast Duck

6 Ducks with broth and salt
Coarse ground black pepper
Red peppers crushed
2 lbs. real butter
3 onions
6 small cooking apples
3 small potatoes
Several dashes M.S.G.
3 cloves garlic
Garlic powder
Tabasco sauce
Season to taste
2 dozen lemons
1 10 oz. bottle Worcestershire
  sauce
Bay leaves

Rub ducks inside and out with salt, black pepper and red pepper. Place in roaster. Have butter soft and rub ducks inside and out. Fill the cavity of each duck with potato, apple, onion and garlic. Pour other ingredients over. Add ½ bay leaf to each duck. Cover roaster. Stuff ducks and let stand in marinade over night. Begin roasting at 150 degrees; increase temperature each hour to 300 degrees until ducks are tender.

Dressing for ducks:

Make cornbread and soften with broth. If you need additional liquid don't mind using water because the broth is real rich. Sauté onions, celery and sage (if desired) before adding to softened cornbread. Add 6 to 8 beaten eggs. Put in pan and bake at 300 degrees until done. (Golden brown).

Wild Duck
(1 Duck)

1 tsp. soda
1 potato, quartered
½ onion
Salt and pepper to taste
Crushed red peppers
½ onion
½ cooking apple
Celery leaves
Juice of ½ orange
Bacon strips

Soak duck 30 minutes to hour in salted water to cover, to which soda has been added. Rinse duck. Put it in pan of fresh water with potato and ½ onion. Boil for 30 to 45 minutes. Pour off water, wash duck thoroughly and start all over again. Season cavity of duck with salt, black pepper and red pepper. Insert ½ onion, apple, and sprigs of celery leaves. Place duck in roaster in 1 inch of water. Squeeze orange juice over duck, lay a strip of bacon over the breast and salt and pepper. Cover and cook in 275 degree oven for 3½ to 4 hours. Baste often. Remove cover the last ½ hour to brown duck. Allow ½ duck per person. This recipe should be used only on fish eating duck.

Orange Duck

1 Duck
Salt and pepper
½ c. soy sauce
2 oranges
1 Tbsp. Curacao
1 Tbsp. orange marmalade
2 livers, chicken or duck
1 Tbsp. flour

Rub duck inside and out with salt and pepper, then brush with melted butter and soy sauce. Grate peel from oranges and set aside. Slice oranges, remove seeds, and stuff duck with orange slices and orange marmalade. Place in roaster, sear at 450 degrees for 10 minutes. Cover and cook for 1½ hours basting occasionally. In the meantime, simmer finely chopped livers in enough salted water to cover, until tender. Pour off pan juice from duck. Discard excess fat. Simmer juices gently and add grated orange peel and chopped livers with their broth. Thicken with flour. Put Curacao in gravy boat; add gravy and serve with wild and brown rice. ½ duck per person.

218

Venison Roast
(This recipe is 50 years old)

1 5 lb. roast
2 tsp. salt
2 bay leaves
1 can cream of mushroom soup
2 Tbsp. sherry
1 tsp. black pepper

Cover roast in cold water and soak over night. Salt and pepper roast. Place roast and bay leaves in a large boiler on moderate heat and cook for 1½ hours in enough water to cover. When meat is tender remove top from boiler and cook the water down to 1½ cups. Add the mushroom soup and sherry. Simmer 15 minutes longer.

Baked Venison Roast

5 lb. venison roast
½ c. vinegar
Water to cover
Salt and pepper
5 slices beef suet or bacon slices

Soak venison roast in vinegar water for several hours. Take out and place in cool water for an hour. Drain; salt and pepper roast on all sides, rubbing in well. Place the suet or bacon on the roast, holding in place with tooth picks. Place on sheet of heavy duty foil; wrap well. Place in 325 degree oven. Bake 30 minutes per lb. or until done. Just before removing it from oven, uncover and let brown. The drippings make good gravy. Serves 10.

Smoked Venison

1 8-10 lb. venison roast
½ c. salt
4 Tbsp. black pepper
3 Tbsp. red pepper
¼ c. vinegar

Wash venison carefully and trim any fat or cartilage. Make small slits in meat with knife about 2 inches apart and 1 inch deep all over roast. Make a paste of remaining ingredients and stuff each slit with a demitasse spoon of seasoning paste. Rub remaining seasoning over side of roast. Seal tight in a container and keep in refrigerator for 24 to 48 hours, turning over 2 or 3 times. When ready to cook, place on spit over coals and smoke approximately 4 to 5 hours. When done, wrap in aluminum foil to hold juices and keep warm until serving. Serves 12 to 16 people.

Deer Steaks

4 round steaks
Meat tenderizer
MSG, dash
2 c. milk
½ tsp. salt
¼ tsp. black pepper
Flour

Sprinkle meat with MSG and tenderizer on both sides. Have your butcher run these through his tenderizer, like for round steak, or you can pound them with edge of saucer. Cover steaks with milk and let soak for 3 hours. Remove from milk and season with salt and pepper; dredge with flour. Fry in deep fat. Serve hot with brown rice and gravy.

Quail On Toast

Birds should be picked, not skinned, as the fat just under the skin is preserved by picking and lost by skinning. Use an iron or an electric skillet. Lay birds, breast up, on slices of bacon; use one stick of butter to four birds; lay another slice of bacon on top of each bird. Cover and cook slowly 20 minutes. Remove cover; turn birds breast side down, bacon protecting breast, for gentle browning. When done, pour butter gravy over French or salt rising bread, toasted. Place quail on toast with crisp bacon on top and under bird. Serve on plate garnished with a slice of orange and a spoonfull of grava jelly or muscadine jelly on top of each bird.

Southern Fried Quail

4 quail
¼ c. flour
Salt and pepper
1 stick butter

Roll quail in dry mixture flour, salt and pepper until they are completely covered. Melt butter and let heat, but not brown. Brown quail and cook slowly for 20 minutes, until tender. Don't overcook. Serves 2 to 4.

Smothered Quail

6 quail, dressed
6 Tbsp. butter
3 Tbsp. flour
2 c. chicken broth
½ c. sherry (optional)
Salt and pepper
Cooked rice

Prepare quail; brown in heavy skillet or dutch oven in butter. Remove quail to baking dish. Add flour to butter in skillet and stir well. Slowly add chicken broth, sherry, salt and pepper. Blend well and pour over quail. Cover baking dish and bake at 350 degrees for about 1 hour or until tender. Serve with cooked rice and gravy and hot biscuits.

Doves

Olive oil
Dry mustard
Celery salt
Garlic salt
Salt
Curry powder
Pepper
2 tsp. Worcestershire sauce
Juice of 1 orange
Juice of 1 lemon

Roll doves in enough olive oil to get them well greased. Sprinkle curry powder, dry mustard, celery salt, garlic salt, salt and pepper over doves. Put in covered dutch oven with a little water and cook for 1½ hours in 250 degree oven. Add Worcestershire sauce, orange and lemon juice. Cook for 10 to 15 minutes longer or until tender.

Baked Doves

8 doves
1 can consomme
1 tsp. Worcestershire sauce
1 tsp. onion juice
½ c. sherry
Salt and pepper and flour
   to coat

Roll doves in seasoned flour and brown in hot shortening. Remove birds; place in roasting pan. Pour off fat and make gravy, using consomme and drippings in which doves were browned. Add other ingredients; pour over doves and bake in slow oven until tender. Baste frequently, adding water and wine as needed.

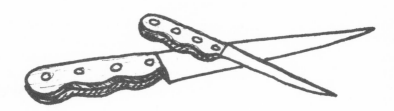

Dove With Wine

12 doves
Salt and pepper to taste
Flour
½ c. oil
½ c. water
1 can cream of mushroom soup
½ c. celery, chopped
½ c. wine

Shake doves in seasoned flour. Brown in oil in skillet. Pour off excess oil. Place in 2-qt. casserole. Combine water, soup, chopped celery and wine. Pour over doves. Cover and bake at 350 degrees for 2 to 3 hours. Serves 6.

Squirrel in Sauce Piquant

4 squirrels
4 Tbsp. olive oil
2 onions, medium size
6 cloves garlic
1 stalk celery, chopped fine
2 Tbsp. flour
1 tsp. tomato paste
Salt and pepper to taste
2 Tbsp. bell pepper
2 Tbsp. chopped parsley

See that squirrels are free of shot and well cleaned. Cut each squirrel into 4 pieces. Sprinkle with salt and pepper, and fry in olive oil. Remove from skillet when brown. Place flour in remaining oil; add onions, garlic, celery and other ingredients. Cook until brown; then place in dutch oven with squirrel. Stir together and cook about 5 minutes. Add hot water to cover squirrels. Cook slowly until done. Serve hot to 8 people.

Pheasant in Casserole

1 pheasant
1 c. flour
1 tsp. salt
½ tsp. pepper
1 c. oil or butter
¾ c. mushrooms
½ c. white wine (optional)
    or
¼ tsp. nutmeg
½ tsp. thyme
1 Tbsp. minced parsley

(I prefer the spices. It brings out the true flavor and the delicate flavor that is different.)

Cut pheasant in serving pieces, usual ¼th. Roll in seasoned flour. Brown lightly in hot butter. (I prefer butter.) Place in casserole or baking dish. Add mushrooms and ½ cup wine. Cover, and bake in slow oven at 300 degrees about 2 hours. Don't forget — if you do omit the wine, you may need ½ cup water and the spices.

Fried Frog Legs

12 pairs of frog legs
Milk
1 c. flour
2 tsp. salt
1 tsp. red pepper
¼ c. corn meal

Soak frog legs in milk for at least 1 hour. Mix flour, cornmeal, salt and pepper. Cover frog legs with this mixture. Heat cooking oil hot enough to ignite a kitchen match, and use enough oil to cover legs. Fry about 4 minutes or until light brown. Do not overcook.

Rabbit A 'La Creole

1 tsp. salt
1 tsp. black pepper
1 tsp. red pepper
1 tsp. garlic powder
1 tsp. onion powder
2 Tbsp. white vinegar
1 3-lb. rabbit, cut into pieces

Mix above ingredients. Pour over rabbit and marinate over night in refrigerator. Add 2 tablespoons of oil to baking pan. Add rabbit and the marinade and bake in moderate oven 450 degrees, for one hour.

While rabbit is baking, prepare mushroom sauce as follows:

1 tsp. Kitchen Bouquet
1 large can whole mushrooms
1 Tbsp. butter
1 Tbsp. parsley
2 Tbsp. bell pepper
2 Tbsp. green onion
½ c. white wine (optional)

Mix ingredients together, pour over rabbit and allow it to continue to cook until tender.

Texas Rock Cornish Game Hens

1 15-oz. can hot tamales
4 Rock Cornish hens
¼ c. honey
1 tsp. chili powder
Salt and pepper to taste

Chop tamales, and using 2 tamales to each bird, fill cavity in each hen. Rub outside of hen with a mixture of honey, salt, pepper and chili powder. Bake uncovered at 350 degrees about 1 hour or until well done. Serves 4.

Baked Rock Cornish Hens

Sprinkle each hen with salt, pepper and MSG. Rub generously with butter inside and out. Place in baking pan with breast down and sprinkle with rosemary. Bake uncovered at 300 degrees for 30 minutes. Turn each hen with breast side up and sprinkle again with rosemary. Continue baking hens about 30 minutes longer, until done and lightly brown. Garnish with kumquats on broiled orange slices.

Soul Food
Relishes
Preserves
Sauces

Soul Food Relishes Preserves Sauces

Turnip Greens

Pick off all stems and wash thoroughly. In a large heavy dutch oven or pot put ¼ lb. of salt pork and fill half full of water; add the washed greens and cook 3 to 4 hours. When the greens are nearly done, add more salt, if needed, and 1 teaspoon sugar.

String Beans
(Bunch or Pole)

I use a ham hock, but you can use salt pork. And you use the same method of cooking as you do for turnip greens.

I add a little sugar to all vegetables. It brings the freshness back to them.

Fried Cream Corn

Cut the corn from 6 ears of corn. Just barely tip the end of the kernel and scrap the rest of kernel to get all the milk. Add 2 cups cold water, salt and pepper to taste, and 1 stick butter. Cook in a heavy skillet. Stir constantly to avoid sticking. Cook very slowly until the kernel is done and well thickened. If corn is real young, you may have to use 2 level tablespoons of flour. If you prefer, you can use 3 tablespoons bacon drippings instead of butter.

Squash
(Yellow or white)

6 small tender squash
1 medium onion chopped
Salt and pepper

Cook in small amount of water until tender. Drain. Melt in skillet 1 stick oleo or butter; add the drained squash and continue to cook very slowly until all water and liquid is out, stirring often. Then add 3 eggs beaten real well, 3 tablespoon sweet cream, 2 tablespoons sugar and 1 tablespoon flour. Keep cooking until very dry. It takes a long time to get all moisture from squash. If you don't like squash, you will like this. You may leave out onion if you prefer.

227

Blackeyed Peas
(Serves 4)

2 c. dried blackeyed peas
4 c. water
2 oz. sliced salt pork
2 tsp. salt
½ tsp. pepper

Soak the peas in the cold water overnight. In the morning, drain off the water. Add to it enough more water to make 4 cups liquid. Add to the blackeyed peas with the salt, pepper and salt pork. Cover. Bring to a boil and let simmer for 1 to 2 hours or until peas are tender, adding more boiling water if necessary. You may use bacon or ham hock, if you prefer. A pod of red pepper will enhance the flavor.

Baked Sweet Potatoes

Select sweet potatoes the size of your arm or fist. They bake better if they are small. Grease each one with Crisco or shortening of any kind. Put on cookie sheet. Put in oven 300 degrees and bake until soft to touch with fingers in open pan.

Candied Sweet Potatoes

Peel and slice thickly, or quartered about ½ inch, 2 sweet potatoes about the size of a man's fist. Place in a casserole and add enough water to half fill the dish. Dot with butter all across the top and sprinkle heavily with sugar. Bake in oven 300 degrees until potatoes are done enough to pick with a fork and syrup is thick.

Okra

Boil the whole pods of okra, leaving the stems on, until tender in enough water to just cover. When done, drain and add salt and pepper and melted butter.

Fried Okra

Cut okra in ½ inch circles, soak in sweet milk until ready to cook. Have your skillet hot with oil and take okra from milk and dip in half corn meal and half flour with salt and pepper. Keep separated and fry until golden brown. Serve hot.

Fried Chicken With Cream Gravy

Cut up one 1½ or 2 pound chicken for frying and soak in sweet milk for several hours. Drain. Place ½ cup flour, salt and pepper to taste into clean paper bag. Drop chicken into the bag and shake until each piece is well floured. Have skillet half full of hot oil or fat, drop chicken in and fry slowly until golden brown with top on skillet. Turn only once until each side is brown. When chicken is tender remove at once to a platter.

Gravy:
Add flour remaining in bag to hot grease and stir until brown. Add enough sweet milk and water to make a thick gravy. The longer you cook gravy the smoother and better it will be.

Baked Hen and Turkey

Roasting time for hen 4 to 5 lbs. - 325 degrees - 50 minutes per lb.
Roasting time for turkey 15 to 18 lbs. - 300 degrees - 18 minutes per lb.

15 lb. turkey will serve 20 people.

Use an uncovered roasting pan for roasting chicken or turkey and all other poultry. Salt and pepper inside and outside to taste. How to roast - tie wings and legs down with string. Place chicken or turkey, breast side up, on a wire rack or trivet, in an uncovered roaster. Brush the skin with oil or melted fat, or lay several slices of bacon over the breast. Roast according to chart at top of recipe. Add no water, do not baste and do not turn during roasting. When done, remove skewers and string from fowl and arrange on a hot platter with neck end to your left. Place the platter before carver in same position.

Turkey or Chicken Dressing

Mix together in a deep bowl: 6 cups of crumbled corn bread and 2 cups of biscuits or dry toast. Add rich hot broth to moisten thoroughly, 2 chopped onions, 2 cups chopped celery, 8 beaten eggs, salt and pepper, ¼ lb. melted butter. This dressing should be the consistency of corn bread batter; add more stock if you need it.

Chicken Stew With Dumplings

1 4 to 5 lb. fowl, cut up
½ c. celery diced
1 bay leaf (optional)
2 tsp. salt
⅛ tsp. pepper
2 Tbsp. minced parsley
1½ qt. hot water
1 medium onion sliced

Combine all ingredients; simmer covered 3 to 4 hours or until tender. Thicken chicken stock if desired. Drop dumplings on top of boiling stew, cover tightly, and cook as directed. Serves 6.

Dumplings:
2 c. sifted all purpose flour
2 tsp. baking powder
1 tsp. salt
4-5 Tbsp. shortening
1 c. milk

Sift dry ingredients together and cut in shortening until it has consistency of coarse corn meal. Add enough milk, while stirring with fork, to make a soft dough that can be easily handled. Roll out very thin and cut into squares. Drop into hot stew; let boil over the dumplings for 5 or 8 minutes and then add a few more until all is used.

Fresh Backbone and Spareribs

Into a heavy dutch oven or roaster add enough water to cover bottom of pot, salt and pepper to taste and 1 pod red pepper. Then add backbone and ribs; put the top on and put in oven at 300 degrees. Cook for 1½ to 2 hours. Check to see if the meat is tender. Add just enough water to keep it from sticking. Take the top off and turn to brown. Use about 1 lb. per person. Delicious with baked sweet potatoes.

Barbecued Ribs and Chicken

Both ribs and chicken are delicious when prepared in this fashion and baked in oven; however, for a superior barbecue they should be over charcoals.

Split chicken down the back so it will lie flat. Grease both sides of the chicken well with butter and brown slowly in skillet.

Boil together the following ingredients for sauce (boil 10 minutes):

1 c. vinegar
1 c. water
¼ c. catsup
¼ lb. butter
1 tsp. sugar
2 Tbsp. Worcestershire sauce
Salt and pepper
Red pepper

Pour sauce over browned chicken or ribs and bake in medium oven (350 degrees) for about 1½ hours, basting and turning chicken frequently, until done.

Fresh Fried Fish

Clean fish and cut, if large, in medium pieces.

Sift:
    1 c. white corn meal
    1 tsp. salt
    ½ tsp. black pepper

Dip fish in meal mixture and fry in deep, hot fat until golden brown. Be sure to serve corn pone or hush puppies with fish.

Pam's Red Beans and Rice
(Short method serves 15 to 20)

1 lb. bacon, chopped
3 bell peppers
3 onions

Sauté until clear and not brown. Add 1 #10 can red kidney beans, or 4 #2½ cans beans, 2 bottles catsup, ½ bottle Lea and Perrin Sauce. Red pepper if desired. Cook until seasoning is all through. If you have a baked ham, it is good to chop up pieces and add to mixture. Just adds a good taste. Simmer all ingredients for 1 to 1½ hours. Serve with steamed rice.

Red Beans and Rice

1 lb. red kidney beans
1 lb. salt pork
2 cloves garlic
1 tsp. Italian seasoning
1 bell pepper
1 chopped onion
1 stalk celery
1 whole red pepper

Boil pork 5 minutes to rid of salt. Put pork in second hot water and add beans; water should be one half inch above beans. Add immediately: One bell pepper, one onion, celery, garlic, Italian seasoning and whole hot pepper. Cook slowly 2 to 3 hours, until gravy is thick and beans tender. Just before dishing out, add another pinch of Italian seasoning. Salt to taste and serve with rice.

Gertie's Brunswick Stew

1 4 lb. hen
4 lbs. beef roast (chuck)
4 cans large tomatoes
3 cans Italian tomato paste
½ bottle Worcestershire sauce
Salt to taste
2 lbs. sliced onions
8 lbs. diced potatoes
3 cans corn
1 12-oz. bottle catsup
4 lemons
Tabasco to taste

Cook hen and roast together until very tender and remove bones from the meat. (If you have squirrels, venison and rabbit to go into this, cook all together and remove bones. (These make it good!) Add all other ingredients to the meat and stock, except corn and lemons, and cook slowly for 3 hours; then add corn and lemons, sliced. Cook another hour. If necessary, cook longer until a thick consistency. Serves about 25 people. This freezes real well. It is delicious to bring out during the holidays.

Beef Pot Roast

Place a 5 lb. chuck roast on a piece of wax paper; salt, pepper and flour both sides; rub in real well. I usually add MSG. Add tenderizers if you think it needs it. I put several cloves of garlic down in the roast. Using oil in roaster pan, brown roast on both sides real well. Add enough water to cover bottom of pan. Place top on roaster and put in a medium oven, 300 degrees. Cook for 1½ hours. Take out and add peeled potatoes, carrots and onions on top of roast and around sides. Cover roaster and cook another 45 to 50 minutes until vegetables and meat are tender. Keep enough water to have sufficient gravy.

Hot Tamales

I have served these to every football team and basketball team in Coahoma County. Makes 200 big ones.

15 lbs. round beef roast
3 lbs. beef fat

Boil together in plenty of water until well done; salt to taste; save broth. Grind meat and fat together with 12 to 15 large onions and 2 whole garlics. Season with salt, black pepper and red pepper. Add 1 can chili powder and 6 to 8 cans Italian tomato paste.

Mix 8 lbs. corn meal (plain), 1 can chili powder, salt, black and red pepper and 4 cans Italian tomato paste with hot broth to make a mush. The quantity of mush is to be about the same as meat mixture.

Then start spreading.

Cut shucks and wash in hot water. Let stand in water while you work so they will stay soft. (This makes wrapping easier.)

Place wrapped and tied hot tamales in the remainder of the beef broth and cook slowly from 4 to 5 hours.

Pepper Relish

12 tart apples
6 red bell peppers
6 green bell peppers
2 hot peppers
3 onions, medium

Put above ingredients through food chopper and add 1 teaspoon salt, 1½ pounds brown sugar and 1 pint vinegar. Let all ingredients come to a boil and boil for 10-15 minutes. Put into sterilized jars and seal. Makes about 6 pints.

Mustard Sauce for Ham

¾ c. sugar
1½ tsp. prepared mustard
½ c. water
¼ c. vinegar

Combine ingredients in saucepan and boil 10 minutes. Finger licking good with ham!

Cranberry Chutney

1 lb. fresh cranberries
2¼ c. brown sugar
1 c. light raisins
1 c. water
½ c. toasted almonds
¼ c. lemon juice
¼ tsp. allspice

Combine all ingredients and cook for 15 minutes. Stir often. Seal in jars. Makes 5½ pints.

Mushroom Sauce

2 chicken bouillon cubes
1 c. boiling water
1 can (4½ oz.) whole mushrooms, drained
3 Tbsp. melted butter
⅓ c. cream
3 Tbsp. all-purpose flour
¼ c. shredded Cheddar cheese
1 Tbsp. chopped chives

Dissolve bouillon cubes in boiling water. Sauté mushrooms in butter. Blend in flour. Gradually add bouillon. Add cream, cheese and chives. Cook over medium heat, stirring constantly, until thickened.

Pepper Jelly

1 c. red and green bell pepper, finely chopped
¼ c. hot pepper, finely chopped
6 c. sugar
1½ c. vinegar
½ bottle certo

Mix peppers, sugar and vinegar and boil for 3 minutes. Strain. Bring liquid to a boil and add 1 tablespoon red and green pepper. When boiling rapidly, add ½ bottle certo and cook 3 minutes. Let set until it begins to jell. Pour into small jars.

Ham Sauce

¾ c. pineapple juice
¾ lb. pitted dates
¼ c. sugar
1 whole stick of cinnamon
½ lemon, sliced real thin

Cook all the ingredients in a pan over low heat and let it come to a slow boil. Serve warm over ham. Makes 2 cups. Will keep in a refrigerator for several days, if all is not used.

Raisin Sauce

½ c. seedless raisins
1 c. water
1 Tbsp. vanilla pudding
1 Tbsp. sugar
1 Tbsp. butter
Sherry

Boil raisins in the cup of water until plump. Add other ingredients and cook on low heat until thickened. Add sherry to taste after sauce is done. Add more pudding if you like a thicker sauce. Good served over baked ham.

Pickled Beans

A good tomato substitute for salads. Empty a can of kidney beans into a strainer; run cold water over them until all the bubbles wash away. Put beans in a jar and season with salt, pepper and garlic salt. Cover completely with garlic or wine vinegar. Screw on lid and store in refrigerator. When you make a mixed green salad and wish to add color and tang, add a few of these beans. Sure gives it a nice tart taste! When you use all the beans, open another can and repeat the process, adding just enough of the same type vinegar to cover beans again. The vinegar mixture can be used repeatedly. I find the beans are a godsend for color when tomatoes are the price of gold nuggets.

Orange Sauce for Beets

1 c. orange juice
⅓ c. sugar
1 Tbsp. butter
2 level Tbsp. cornstarch
Salt to taste
Sliced beets

Mix ingredients well and cook in double boiler 5 minutes. Serve over beets.

Cranberry Ketchup

2½ lbs. fresh cranberries
5 c. vinegar
2½ c. sugar
2 Tbsp. cinnamon
1 tsp. cloves

Cook cranberries in vinegar until they burst open, then press through a sieve. Add sugar and spices and simmer until thick. Pour into sterilized jars and seal. Makes 3 pints. Serve with turkey, chicken, pork and as a glaze on ham.

Pickled Pineapple To Serve With Meats

1 No. 2½ can (8 slices) or No. 2 can (10 slices) pineapple cut in halves
⅔ c. pineapple syrup
⅔ c. cider vinegar
1 c. sugar
6 or 8 whole cloves
3 inch stick of cinnamon
Dash of salt

Drain pineapple and set it aside. Heat remainder of ingredients together and boil gently 10 minutes. Add pineapple and heat just to boiling. Cool. Store in covered jar in refrigerator. Pineapple chunks may replace slices. Especially good with broiled lamb or pork chops.

Pear Preserves

Peel pears and slice; (1 gallon cut pears and 1 gallon sugar.) Put pears in dish pan and sprinkle sugar over them. Let soak overnight to make own juice. Next morning cook over low fire until it is a pretty amber color. Add 2 sliced lemons and cook until juice is thick. Put up in sterile jars.

Ice Green Tomato Pickle

20-30 green tomatoes
1 qt. vinegar
4 c. sugar
1 clove garlic
2 tsp. whole cloves
2 tsp. whole allspice
4 sticks cinnamon
Salt to taste
1 c. pickling lime (Mrs. Wages)

Soak tomatoes (about 1/16 inch slices) in dish pan of cold water with lime over night. Drain and wash thoroughly in collander. Add vinegar, sugar, spices and bring to boil before putting in tomatoes. Cook slowly over low heat, about 1½ hours or until tomatoes become rather clear and slightly candied in appearance.

Ripe Tomato Pickles

1 gal. cabbage
1 gal. ripe tomatoes
½ c. mixed spices
  (tied in cloth)
1 gal. white onions
¾ c. salt
5 c. sugar
3½ pts. white vinegar

Chop vegetables, cover with salt and let stand several hours. Wash thoroughly with clear water. Drain. Put on stove with sugar, spices and vinegar and let cook 1 hour. Stir often, seal in sterile jars.

Strawberry Preserves

1 qt. berries
4 c. sugar

Wash berries; stem. Place in collander and pour boiling water over them. Let drain well, put berries and 2 cups sugar on to boil. Stir carefully until melted. When it comes to a rolling boil, time and boil 4 minutes. Add 2 cups more sugar and boil 3 minutes, (timing from boiling stage). Skim; let cool for 24 hours before sealing in sterile jars.

Sweet Pickled Peaches

To 3 lbs. of fruit, add:
1 tsp. mace
2 lbs. sugar
1 tsp. cinnamon
1 pt. apple vinegar
1 tsp. allspice
1 tsp. cloves

Mix vinegar, sugar and spices together. Bring to a good boil and add fruit. Cook until the fruit is very tender. Seal in jars.

Bread and Butter Pickle

Slice enough medium sized cucumbers, about 16 or 17, to fill a gallon crock; cover with water and add a cup of salt. Let stand 2 hours; drain.

In meantime, heat 1 qt. vinegar, 1 tablespoon white mustard seed, teaspoon celery seed, 1 stick of cinnamon (broken up), 1 tablespoon turmeric and 3 cups sugar. Add all to cucumbers and boil 10 minutes. Put in jars and seal; ready to eat following day.

Chili Sauce

12 large ripe tomatoes
2 large onions
4 green sweet peppers
1 hot pepper
4 Tbsp. sugar
1 Tbsp. salt
2 tsp. cinnamon
½ tsp. cloves
2 c. vinegar

Chop or grind the vegetables and cook 2 hours, or until most of vinegar is cooked out. You have to watch closely or it will stick and burn. Cut blaze down real low and cook in heavy kettle.

Chow Chow Pickle

1 gal. green tomatoes
4 sweet peppers
½ gal. onions
2 hot peppers

Chop all ingredients and put in pan with 1 cup salt. Cover with water and let come to a good boil; take off and put in strainer. Run cold water over it. Then add 1 qt. vinegar, ½ qt. water, 3⅓ cups sugar, 1 teaspoon pickling spices (the kind that has everything in it), 1 tablespoon turmeric (if desired) and cook for 30 minutes. Seal while hot in jars.

Perfect Cranberry Sauce

1 lb. cranberries
1 pt. water
1 pt. sugar

Pick over berries; add water and simmer slowly until all berries pop, about 20 minutes. Cover kettle while simmering; then remove cover and add sugar gradually. Boil without stirring, 20 minutes exactly (without cover). Jells perfectly!

238

Watermelon Pickle

Prepare 3 lbs. rind and soak in lime (Mrs. Wages) water 24 hours. Then soak in clear water 5 hours. Drain and boil until tender in weak ginger water.

Drain and pour this syrup over rinds:

3 c. sugar
1 Tbsp. cloves
1 pt. white vinegar
1-2 whole spices

Bring to hard boil. Seal in jars.

Watermelon Rind Preserves

10 c. peeled watermelon rind
10 c. sugar

Mix watermelon and sugar and allow to stand overnight. In the morning add 10 tablespoons finely chopped orange peel. Cook until it is a clear, rich yellow color. Seal in jars.

Tea Cakes
(Makes 50 old-fashioned cakes)

3 eggs
3 c. sugar
4 c. self-rising flour
1 stick butter or oleo
2 Tbsp. vanilla

Melt butter or oleo and let cool. Beat eggs well. Mix all ingredients except flour, which is added gradually to egg mixture. When dough becomes stiff enough to handle, knead on floured board or cloth. Roll out and cut. Bake in 400 degree oven for 12 to 15 minutes. Remove greased cookie sheet immediately and cool. Store in tins.

To prepare apple rings to serve with sausage, cook the apples in the sausage fat until they are tender; then sprinkle with brown sugar.

239

Joe Frogger's Old-Fashioned Tea Cakes

7 c. sifted flour
1 Tbsp. salt
1 Tbsp. ginger
1 tsp. ground cloves
1 tsp. nutmeg
½ tsp. allspice
¾ c. water
¼ c. wine or rum
2 tsp. soda
2 c. dark molasses
1 c. shortening
2 c. sugar

Sift flour with salt and all spices. Combine water and wine. Combine soda and molasses. Cream sugar and shortening; add dry ingredients alternately with wet ingredients. Blend well together after each addition. Roll out on floured board ¼ inch thick; cut with cutter. Place on greased baking sheet. Bake at 375 degrees for 10 to 15 minutes. Let stand on cookie sheet a few minutes before removing.

I Oatmeal Cookies

¾ c. shortening
1 c. brown sugar
½ c. white sugar
1 egg
¼ c. water
1 tsp. vanilla
1 c. flour
1 tsp. salt
½ tsp. soda
3 c. oats uncooked

Place shortening, sugar, egg, water and vanilla in mixing bowl and beat thoroughly. Sift together flour, salt and soda. Add to shortening mixture, mixing well. Blend in oats and drop by teaspoon onto a greased cookie sheet. Bake in moderate oven 350 degrees for 12-15 minutes. Makes 5 dozen 2 inch cookies. You may add ½ cup raisins and ½ cup nuts; then use a few more drops of water to give moisture.

II Oatmeal Cookies

1 c. shortening
1 c. white sugar
1 c. brown sugar
2 c. flour
2 c. uncooked oats
1 tsp. baking powder
1 tsp. soda
¼ tsp. salt
2 eggs
1 c. nuts
2 c. raisins
1 box coconut (optional)

Mix in order given. Drop by teaspoon on greased cookie sheet. Can add crystallized cherries, pineapple and dates if desired.

Old-Fashioned Egg Custard Pie
(Makes 1 nine inch pie)

4 eggs
½ c. sugar
¼ tsp. salt
3 c. scalded milk
1 tsp. vanilla

Beat eggs until well blended. Stir in remaining ingredients. Pour into a rich pastry pie shell and bake for 10 minutes at 450 degrees; then reduce heat to 300 degrees and bake until firm, about 45 to 50 minutes.

Grandmother Clower's Sweet Potato Pie
(Makes 1 nine inch pie)

1 sweet potato size of pint jar
½ lb. butter
3 eggs, beaten
1 c. sugar
3 Tbsp. sweet cream
1 jigger whiskey or 1 Tbsp. vanilla

Boil potato until real tender. Peel and cream while still hot. Add softened butter, beating constantly; take out all strings. Then add sugar, beaten eggs and cream. Beat real well. This filling will be thin, but it will thicken while cooking. Just before you put in the shell add the whiskey. It is so good!

Apple Pie

6 c. pared, cored apple slices
    ¼" thick
⅛ tsp. salt
¼ tsp. cinnamon
⅔ c. sugar
¼ tsp. nutmeg
1 tsp. lemon juice
1 Tbsp. butter

Line 9" pie plate with pastry, as in making a 2 crust pie. Fill with apples. Mix sugar, spices and lemon juice. Sprinkle over apples and dot with butter. Put second crust on top and pinch or flute crusts together. Make several slits on top of crust. Bake in hot oven for 40 minutes at 400 degrees. Serve warm or cold with cheese, cream or ice cream.

Mince Meat

1 lb. chuck beef, cut up
2 lbs. pared, cored tart apples
2⅔ c. seeded raisins
2½ c. currants
2 tsp. salt
1 Tbsp. nutmeg
2 c. sugar
1 c. strong coffee or wine
1 Tbsp. cloves
1 Tbsp. cinnamon
1 c. meat liquid

Cook meat in boiling water to cover in a covered kettle, until tender. Cool in the meat liquid. Grind the meat and save liquid (1 cup). Put apples, raisins and currants through food chopper. Then add all ingredients together. Simmer, uncovered, slowly for 1 hour, stirring frequently. Pour into jars while hot and seal. Makes 5 pints.

Mince Pie

Make a two crust 9" pie using 3 cups mince meat filling. Bake in hot oven 425 degrees for 40 minutes or until golden brown. Serve with hard sauce. Very good for the holidays.

Ginger Bread

¼ c. lard
¼ c. butter
½ c. sugar
1 egg
1 tsp. ginger
½ tsp. cloves
1 c. molasses
⅔ c. hot water
2½ c. sifted flour
1½ tsp. soda
1 tsp. cinnamon
½ tsp. salt

Cream the shortening and sugar until smooth; add the egg and mix thoroughly; then stir in the molasses. Alternate the hot water with the flour, which has been sifted with the soda, spices and salt. Place in a greased and shallow loaf pan. Bake in a moderate oven 350 degrees. Serve warm or cold with whipped cream or hard sauce:

Hard Sauce

½ c. butter
1 c. powdered sugar
1 Tbsp. boiling water
2 Tbsp. of brandy or to taste

Beat butter in bowl until creamy. Then add half sugar and water. Beat well and add remaining sugar and brandy. Store in a cool place until used.

242

Menus for Entertaining Serving Table Setting

Menus
for
Entertaining
Serving
Table Setting

I have gathered these notes of the next pages from my mother's textbooks, my own college textbooks, and my menus and suggestions for parties that have been a guideline to me through thirty years of club work and specialized catering. In most cases these ideas came from pages that I long ago clipped from books and then somehow lost the books. I have no idea how to give proper credit to the original sources. I have used these suggestions so many, many times that they really seem a vital part of me. Even as old as they are, you can still use each menu and party suggestion. I hope you will enjoy reading and using every holiday menu, as I have.

BREAKFASTS

The breakfasts described here are somewhat formal and are served about the usual time for luncheons. The menus are different from regular luncheon fare in that typical breakfast foods are used.

They can be planned for many different occasions. A wedding breakfast usually is formal with as many feminine touches as possible. However, since most of the guests at a football breakfast are men, there should be nothing dainty about the menu. A substantial meal can be served earlier than the luncheon hour so that the men will not have to rush to get to the game on time. Breakfasts are also popular with people who just like breakfast foods and for some reason prefer to get together at noon.

Table decorations vary. White flowers are usually used for wedding breakfasts. Either fruit or combinations of fruit and flowers can be used for less formal parties.

For very large breakfasts, guests can be seated in groups with the dining table reserved for a special center arrangement of flowers. For a small informal breakfast, guests can be seated around the table using colorful linen placemats and matching napkins. Guests for a wedding breakfast may be seated in groups, but the bridal party all sits together at a long table.

Football breakfasts are often served buffet style, but the men usually like to be seated at small tables.

A fruit course is served first, as for luncheons. However, the main course which follows is vastly different.

Using a wide variety of molds adds greatly to any party, but this is especially true for breakfasts. Ring molds make good "rice or grits rings" to be filled with chicken or turkey hash, but the most attractive of all molds is in the shape of a life-sized hen. Turkey hash garnished with parsley surrounding a rice hen makes an attractive main course. A red comb cut from pimento can be added to the head after the hen has been unmolded. The eyes are made of cloves, and the bill may be painted on with yellow food coloring. There is a big variety of molds for sale. Heart-shaped molds may be used for Valentine or bridal parties and star-shaped molds for Christmas to help give a party a special flair.

Eggs in some form should always be included in the breakfast menu. A delicious but elegant way to include eggs is a cheese souffle ring filled with sweetbreads or creamed ham. Another pretty idea is creamed eggs surrounded by clear fried apple rings. Broiled breakfast link sausages are placed through the center of each apple ring. There are many cheese and egg dish recipes included in this book which would make a suitable party breakfast.

Many good desserts could be served, depending completely on the taste of the hostess. I like to serve crisp waffles layered with guava jelly and dusted with powdered sugar. A square of cream cheese is served with it instead of butter. Molded ice cream waffles served with maple syrup are delicious. Add pecans to the maple syrup for an extra touch. Orange Alaska is made by scooping out large oranges and packing them with ice cream. Seal this with meringue and bake quickly. Cantaloupes and grapefruits may also be fixed this way.

You do not have to wait for a party to use many of these recipes and ideas. They are also suitable for family use.

WEDDING BREAKFAST

Pass Tray of Tomato Juice, Orange Juice and Green Minted Grapefruit Juice
Pastry Cones of Chicken Hash - Baked Stuffed Apple
Creamed Eggs-Cheese Sauce, Surrounded by Broiled Tomato Topped with
Stuffed Mushroom Cap
Individual Coffee Cakes with Rum Butter Top
Blueberry Muffins - Banana Muffins
Coffee
Pass Wedding Cake - Sliced

SMALL WEDDING BREAKFAST

Fruit Bouquets
Individual Rice Rings Filled with Chicken Hash
Baked Stuffed Eggs-Cheese Sauce
Apple Sauce Ring, Tinted Green, Filled with Honeydew Balls
Orange Marmalade Muffins - Coffee
Sliced Wedding Cake and Molded Ices

EASTER BREAKFAST

Fruits on the Half Shell
Rice Hen with Chicken or Turkey Hash
Tomatoes Stuffed with Mushrooms
Parsley Garnish
Goldenrod Eggs
Ginger Muffins - Coffee
Cake Ring "Nest" Filled with Different Colored Ice Cream Eggs
Wine Sauce

FOOTBALL BREAKFAST

Broiled Grapefruit
Broiled Country Ham
Egg Cutlet - Tomato Sauce
Crusty Peaches
Rolls - Coffee
Pineapple Alaska

FOOTBALL BREAKFAST (2)

Orange or Grapefruit Juice
Individual Grits Rings with Turkey Hash
Baked Apple Stuffed with Sausage
Goldenrod Eggs
Rolls - Coffee
Waffle Molded Ice Cream
Maple Nut Sauce

FOOTBALL BREAKFAST (3)

Tomato Juice
Broiled Sweetbreads on Canadian Bacon
Clear Apple Rings Around Creamed Eggs
Corn Fritters
Blueberry Muffins - Coffee
Waffles with Guava Jelly and Cheese

BREAKFAST

Cranberry Juice Cocktail
Frosted Red Grapes
Turkey Hash in Grits Ring
Baked Stuffed Tomato
Broiled Pineapple
Creamed Riced Eggs on Toast
Rolls - Coffee
Big Orange Alaska

BREAKFAST (2)

Ring of Scalloped Biscuit Filled with Chicken Hash
Bell Pepper Filled with Cheese Souffle
Corn Fritters   Baked Peaches
Ginger Muffins   Coffee
Cantaloupe Baked Alaska

BREAKFAST (3)

Tomato Juice   Rosebud of Olive and Cheese
Toasted Cheese Wheels
Broiled Sweetbreads, Bacon and Grilled Pineapple
Broiled Tomatoes Around Creamed Eggs
Clear Apple Rings
Corn Meal Biscuit   Coffee
Fruit Compote with Cheese at Center
Melba Sauce Glaze
Hot Salted Crackers - Buttered

BREAKFAST (4)

Cantaloupe Pond Lily
Pastry Cornucopias with Chicken Hash
Clear Apple Rings with Breakfast Sausage
Eggs with Cheese Sauce
Corn Fritters   Coffee   Marmalade Muffins
Waffle Molded Ice Cream
Maple Syrup Sauce with Chopped Pecans

BREAKFAST (5)

Hot Pineapple Juice
Cheese Souffle Ring with Chicken Livers and Mushrooms in Center
Clear Apple Stuffed with Orange Marmalade
Broiled Tomatoes   Cheese Potato Strings (Canned)
Banana Muffins   Coffee
Grapefruit Baked Alaska

BREAKFAST (6)

Minted Grapefruit Juice
Brain Cutlets-Mushroom Sauce   Rice Balls with Jelly
Goldenrod Eggs   Broiled Tomatoes
Rolls   Coffee
Baked Peach-Macaroon Meringue

BREAKFAST (7)

Orange Juice
Individual Corn Meal Muffin Rings with Turkey Hash
Baked Apple Stuffed with Sausage
Creamed Eggs　　　Broiled Tomatoes
Rolls　　　Coffee
Pineapple Baked Alaska

BREAKFAST (8)

Pineapple Points Served with Powdered Sugar
Big Uncapped Strawberries
Ham and Cheese Rolls on Toast
Baked Eggs Stuffed with Mushrooms
Crusty Bananas　　　Fried Corn　　　Rolls　　　Coffee
Ginger Waffles with Ice Cream Ball

BREAKFAST (9)

Broiled Grapefruit
Stuffed Lamb Chops　　　Grilled Pineapple
Broiled Tomatoes Around Shoestring Potatoes (Canned)
Creamed Riced Eggs
Rolls　　　Coffee
Chocolate Waffles-Whipped Cream

BREAKFAST (10)

Bunch of Honeydew "Grapes"
Cheese Souffle Rings with Creamed Sweetbreads Surrounded by
Shad Roe Balls on Lemon Slices
Broiled Tomatoes　　　Crusty Fried Corn
Rolls　　　Crepes Suzette　　　Coffee

BREAKFAST (11)

Honeydew Sections with Melon Balls
Baked Apples Stuffed with Sausage　　　Egg Cutlets
Broiled Tomatoes and Cheese on Toast　　　Blueberry Muffins
Coffee　　　French Toast　　　Strawberry Jam and Whipped Cream

249

BREAKFAST (12)

Green Minted Grapefruit Juice
Frosted Green Grapes
Individual Rice Rings with Chicken Hash
Broiled Tomato   Goldenrod Eggs
Rolls   Coffee
Party Waffles with Guava Jelly and Cream Cheese

BREAKFAST (13)

Grapefruit Half   Center Filled with Maple Syrup
Cheese Souffle Ring Filled with Creamed Sweetbreads and Ham
Baked Tomato Stuffed with Mushrooms
Clear Apple Rings
Blueberry Muffins   Coffee
Pound Cake "Toast" Slices
Molded Ice Cream Eggs with Wine Sauce

COFFEES AND TEAS

One of the most popular forms of entertaining has long been the afternoon tea because of its charm, graciousness, and informality. In some parts of the country morning coffees have replaced the afternoon tea. Coffees are served from 11:00 to 11:30 A.M. and usually are very similar to teas, because the food is basically the same.

The morning coffee was begun in the South, probably because of the unbearable heat of Southern afternoons; however, many Northern hostesses have begun to favor coffees, because more people seem to have more free time in the mornings than in the afternoon.

Coffees and teas may be as simple or as fancy as you wish, but the serving table should always be arranged attractively. Refreshments may be served either by using a silver service placed at one end of the table or by passing tea to the guests. Guests may serve themselves dainty sandwiches and cakes from the platters on the table. These platters will need to be refilled often so that the table will always look attractive. Napkins and plates should be placed near the tea service. On hot days iced beverages can replace tea or coffee.

The same kinds of sandwiches can be used for teas and coffees; but little sweet rolls, toasted sandwiches, and muffins can also be used for coffees. Canapé recipes can be used for the sandwiches at coffees and teas; so I have listed my canapé and sandwich recipes together. It is helpful to have many different sandwich cutters, since sandwiches cut in many different shapes add to the charm of the party. I usually try to have four different kinds of sandwiches. A good combination is a meat, a cheese, a vegetable, and a sweet sandwich.

Since coffees are served early in the day, it is more convenient to plan several sandwiches which may be prepared in advance. Sandwiches which are to be toasted may even be made a day early. They are brushed with melted butter, covered with a damp cloth, and refrigerated until time to be toasted. Toast rounds, cheese wheels, orange toast, and some others may also be made in advance.

Seasonal menus and special menus for bridal parties are fun to plan and help to make a party more interesting.

The size of sandwiches for a formal party may vary slightly. They should never be large, but a few should be a moderate size to mix with the smaller ones. Decorating the tops of sandwiches also makes them more appealing. Shapes cut from pimento and olive slices are attractive.

Tiny canapé cutters are sold to cut out decorations for sandwiches. First use the cutter to remove some of the bread from the top of the sandwich, then use it to cut the decoration. The tiny pimento cutouts fill in where the bread has been removed. Also, circles can be cut in the tops of sandwiches to allow the filling to show. A pickle ring can also be used to fill in a circle cut from the top of a sandwich. Decorations can be cut in advance and then inserted in the proper place with a toothpick just before serving.

Sandwich making can be made easier by cutting pairs of shapes and putting them together with mayonnaise. They can be covered and filled at a later time. After the filling has been added, they should be covered with damp cloths and refrigerated until serving.

MORNING COFFEE MENUS

MORNING COFFEE
Christmas Season

Individual Oyster Loaves   Tomato Open-Faced Canapés
Cheese Dreams-Christmas Tree Shape
Star Shaped Cinnamon Toast   Coffee
Small Square Individual Cakes, Iced in White and "Tied"
With Red Ribbon Icing to Resemble Christmas Package

MORNING COFFEE (2)
Christmas Season

Christmas Tree Shaped Chicken Salad Sandwich-Pimento Star at Top
Cheese Wheel Christmas Wreath with Pimento "Holly" and Parsley Garnish
Round Tomato Sandwich with Inch Circle Cut from Top
Toast Star with Philadelphia Cheese and Guava Jelly at Center
Cheese Pastry Christmas Trees Filled with Mincemeat
Coffee

MORNING COFFEE (3)

Toasted Tomato Sandwiches   Cheese Puffs
Cucumber Sandwiches   Stickies
Pastry Cups with Cherry Preserves or Lemon Filling
Topped with Whipped Cream
Coffee

MORNING COFFEE (4)

Toasted Mushroom Sandwiches   Open-Faced Tomato Sandwich
Swiss Cheese and Bell Pepper on Rounds of Rye Bread
Rolled Cinnamon Toast
Coffee   Rum or Bourbon Balls

MORNING COFFEE (5)

Toast Cups Filled with Crab Supreme
Tomato Sandwich, Crescent Top
Tiny Sausage Turnovers
Orange Marmalade Muffins
Chocolate Cornflake Cookies
Coffee

MORNING COFFEE (6)

Cheese and Cucumber Sandwich   Ham Squares
Egg and Anchovy Sandwich   Toasted Rolled Asparagus Sandwich
Fudge Cake   Coffee

MORNING COFFEE (7)

Rounds of Toast with Canapé Marguery
Cheese Sandwich No. 3   Spring Sandwich
Small Banana Muffins   Brown Sugar Fudge Cake
Coffee

MORNING COFFEE (8)

Cheese and Bacon Toasted Sandwich   Carrot Sandwich
Ripe Olive and Nut Sandwich   Orange Marmalade and Cheese Toast
Cake Squares with Mocha Icing Covered with Grated Almonds
Coffee

SUMMER COFFEE

Watermelon Cantaloupe and Honeydew Melon Balls on Cocktail Picks
Cucumber Almond Sandwich   Toasted Cheese Dreams
Tomato Sandwich   Orange Marmalade Muffins
Iced Coffee   Brown Sugar Kisses

SUMMER COFFEE (2)

Chicken Salad in Cream Puff Shells   Cheese Puffs
Carrot and Black Olive Sandwich   Orange Bread and Butter Sandwiches
Iced Coffee with Vanilla Ice Cream Topping
Hot Spice Cup Cakes

BRIDE'S TEA

Heart-shaped Chicken Salad Sandwich with Tiny Pimento Heart at Center
Tomato Sandwiches with Large Circle or Heart Removed from Top of Sandwich
Calla Lily Sandwich   Bell-shaped Orange Toast
Petits Fours   Tea

BRIDE'S TEA (2)

Toast Cups Filled with Crab Salad   Heart-shaped Spring Sandwiches
Ribbon Sandwiches with Green Tinted Cheese Filling
Rolled Asparagus Sandwiches
Pale Green Iced "Marshmallow Towers"   Tea

BRIDE'S TEA (3)

Puff Shells of Chicken Salad   Cucumber Sandwiches
Cheese Lily of the Valley Sandwiches
"Valentine" Sandwiches   Angel Food Rum Balls
Tea

CHRISTMAS TEA

Round Turkey Sandwich-Cranberry Jelly Garnish
Philadelphia Cheese and Olive Sandwich Christmas Tree Shaped
Pimento Star Garnish at Top
Open-faced Tomato Sandwich (See Tomato Canapé)
Cheese Wafers-Cut in Christmas Bell and Star Shapes
Small Snowball Coconut Cakes with Holly Spray Iced on Top
Tea

VALENTINE TEA

Valentine Sandwich, Heart-shaped Open-faced
Heart-shaped Tongue and Olive Sandwich with
Pimento Heart Garnish at Center
Round Cucumber Sandwich on Whole Wheat Bread
with Stuffed Olive Center
Heart-shaped Orange Toast
Heart-shaped Teacakes   Tea

HALLOWEEN TEA

Boston Brown Bread Halloween Sandwiches with Jack-o-Lantern Faces
Round Carrot Sandwiches on Whole Wheat Bread with Inch Circle Cut from
the Top-Garnish Tray with Cheese Pumpkins
Ham Squares
Tomato Sandwiches
Chocolate and Orange Cakes   Tea

ST. PATRICK'S TEA

Shamrock-shaped Chicken Salad Sandwiches   Water Cress Sandwiches
Green-tinted Cheese Ribbon Sandwiches
Cucumber Sandwich-Inch Circle Cut from Top and Parsley Spray Inserted
Coconut Ball Cakes-Tops Decorated with Shamrock
Cut from Green Mint Cherries   Tea

GEORGE WASHINGTON TEA

Hatchet-shaped Parmesan Cheese Toast (See Cheese Wheels)
Tomato Sandwiches
Rolled Chicken Salad "Logs" with Tiny Favor Hatchets Across Each One
Cucumber and Almond Sandwich
Tricorn of Toast Filled with Cherry Preserves   Tea

SUMMER TEA

Chicken Salad Sandwich   Tomato Sandwich
Date Bread Sandwich   Cucumber Sandwich
Iced Tea with Pineapple Sherbet Topping
Hot Cup Cakes

AFTERNOON TEA

Shrimp Ovals   Spring Sandwiches
Philadelphia Cheese and Stuffed Olive Sandwiches
Brown Bread and Crystallized Ginger Sandwiches
Small Spice Muffin Cakes   Tea

AFTERNOON TEA (2)

Chicken Mushroom Open-faced Sandwiches
Cheese and Olive Flower Sandwiches
Avocado Sandwiches   Cinnamon Toast Sticks
Date Bars   Tea

AFTERNOON TEA (3)

Hot Rolls Stuffed with Chicken Salad   Cucumber and Cheese Sandwiches
Celery Sandwiches   Nut Bread and Butter Sandwiches
Date Nut Kisses   Tea

AFTERNOON TEA (4)

Rolled Chicken Salad Sandwiches   Russian Cheese Sandwiches
Tomato Sandwiches   Egg and Almond Sandwiches
Caramel Thins   Tea

AFTERNOON TEA (5)

Ham and Olive Sandwiches   Cucumber and Almond Sandwiches
Rolled Asparagus Sandwiches   Brown Bread Wedges
Angel Food Rum Balls   Tea

LUNCHEONS—
PLATE LUNCHEONS

There are several different kinds of luncheons, such as the lap tray, bridge, and very formal luncheon consisting of several courses. This section mainly deals with the formal type, but I have included menus for some less elaborate ones. Buffet luncheons are discussed in another section.

Most of these menus have been used for club parties, but all of them could be used for entertaining at home.

For formal luncheons we use our very best linens, china, and silver and even try to harmonize the color scheme of the first course with that of the floral arrangement and other decorations. For example, if yellow daffodils are used in the centerpiece, the first course could be a grapefruit half on lettuce leaves topped with a daffodil made from varieties of yellow cheese. This cheese daffodil is surrounded by green leaves cut from avocado pear. If yellow day lilies are the centerpiece, the first course could be a cantaloupe cut to look like a pond lily. If the centerpiece is pink, I sometimes use watermelon balls arranged like a bouquet on a paper lace doily with single mint leaves arranged around the outside. Or, sometimes I fill half of an avocado pear with frozen tomato mayonnaise, since it has a nice pink color.

In hot weather I plan cold luncheons. For example, my favorite is a salad platter centered with a salmon mousse in the shape of a fish and with an olive slice for its eye. The fish is surrounded by a pool of green cucumber aspic decorated with pond lilies made from hard-boiled eggs. Leaves for the lilies are cut from green pepper.

The menus for fall luncheons should harmonize with harvest symbols and other symbols of plenty. All other holiday menus should try to fit the food to the decorations of the season.

One of my favorite Christmas luncheons featured a miniature holly wreath for each plate. I cut thick slices of pineapple and left the hull on it. Then I removed the fruit, leaving a circle which looked very much like a wreath. I filled each little wreath with a fruit mixture and topped it with a red cherry. On the top of each wreath I tied a red bow and some real holly berries. This fruit plate was placed on the table before the guests entered the dining room.

Valentine luncheons are no trouble to plan, because the heart theme may be used over and over.

For Easter luncheons I have used the Easter bonnet theme for the dessert course by making little "hat" cakes iced in different pastel colors and accented with tiny flowers, such as lilies of the valley, roses, daisies, and orchids all formed from icing. I used one hat cake for each table, since each cake could serve about ten people. This way each table's dessert was distinctive.

257

My favorite May Day luncheon dessert was a cake shaped like a May basket. The handle was decorated with a ribbon made of icing, and inside the cake were individual ices made in the shape of several different flowers.

These have all been elaborate ideas which I have suggested so far, but I also have many good ideas for simpler luncheons which are just as much fun; in fact the simple lap tray luncheon is always very popular.

Our club's lap trays have borders of red, black, green, yellow, blue and peach; and on them we use brightly colored linen tray covers and napkins. To make things gay, I make the colors of the napkins and tray cover contrast with the color of the tray. For example, on a black tray, I sometimes put a coral cover and a turquoise napkin; on a yellow tray I use a teal blue cover and an orange napkin; and on a red tray I use a dark green cover and a chartreuse napkin. Any number of color combinations is possible. Since the guests are seated in groups, the maids at the club are told to take as many different colors as possible to each group.

Food for these parties consists of two courses. First the meat, such as curried chicken in individual rings, a salad, and a hot roll are served from trays. Usually one side dish is passed, and coffee is served by the maids. Loaf sugar has previously been placed on the table to facilitate service. Rolls are passed again. After all the dishes have been removed, the dessert is served.

One of my favorite lap tray luncheon menus is a salad plate consisting of three kinds of salads. A satisfying luncheon on a warm day is lettuce cups filled with stuffed eggs and olives, hot cheese dreams, iced tea, and a simple dessert. A good combination for this kind of salad plate would be a chicken or crab meat salad, a vegetable salad, and a molded fruit salad. The fruit salad could even take the place of a dessert, since it is sweet.

LUNCHEONS

Many different organizations use our club for morning meetings, and then we serve them a light luncheon. Often we use a salad plate with sandwiches, a drink and cookies.

Because some of these groups meet more than once a month, I plan a wide range of menus. Nothing pleases me more than for someone to say, "You never seem to serve the same thing twice."

The following menus have been used for different kinds of parties at the club.

BRIDE'S LUNCHEON

"Fruit Bouquets" of Melon Balls
Stuffed Squab-Orange Sauce
Clipped Corn   Stuffed Eggplant
Hot Rolls   Peach Pickle
Party Ice Tea   Orange Slices
Mint Bubble Garnish
Individual Ices, Bride and Bridesmaid Designs
Little Cakes Iced in Flowers

BRIDE'S LUNCHEON (2)

Bunches of Honeydew Grapes on Galax Leaves
Pastry Cones Filled with Crab or Shrimp Newburg
Garnish of Green Bell Pepper Slice Filled with Pickle Relish
Cauliflower Bouquet with Carrot Roses   Fresh Garden Peas
Rolls   Pale Green Meringue Hearts Filled with Ice Cream   Coffee

THANKSGIVING LUNCHEON

Grapefruit Juice Cocktail (Minted)
Frosted Grapes on Galax Leaf
Sliced Turkey on Rounds of Turkey Dressing
Mushroom Gravy
Rice Ball on Ring of Cranberry Sauce
Casserole on Hot Fruit Compote No. 1
Green Asparagus   Rolls
Individual Mince Pies   Hard Sauce
Coffee

CHRISTMAS LUNCHEON

Tomato Juice Cocktail   Bell-shaped Cheese Wafers
Olive, Radish "Christmas Tree Garnish"
Sliced Spice Round or Baked Ham   Clear Pickle Rings
Bright Red Bell Pepper Stuffed with Creole Cauliflower
Star-shaped Beaten Biscuit
Two-toned Christmas Salad
Round Slice of Plum Pudding-Molded Bell of Eggnog Ice Cream on Top
Fluffy Bow Red Ribbonzene on Top of Bell

HALLOWEEN LUNCHEON

Golden Salad
Halloween Puff Pastry Shell Filled with Creamed Ham or Sweetbreads
Stuffed Yellow Squash   Green Gage Plum and Apricot Compote
Pass Cabbage Spook Head Filled with Olives,
Celery and Radishes (See Garnishes)
Rolls   Coffee
Sunshine Cake Rings with Uncooked Orange Icing and Garnish of
Pumpkins Made of Icing, Filled with Yellow Lemon Ice Cream
Coffee

SUMMER LUNCHEON

Jellied Bouillon   Assorted Crackers
Sliced Turkey and Fresh Fruits
Hot Blueberry Muffins   Iced Tea
Broken Orange Chiffon Cake with Serving of Pineapple
or Lime Sherbet Garnished with Orange Sections

Sliced turkey breast in center of plate surrounded by Della Robbia wreath of fruits on lettuce hearts. Fruits used are watermelon, cantaloupe and honeydew balls, fresh peach halves filled with red raspberries or blueberries, peeled fresh plums, fresh apricots, sections of fresh pears, tiny bunches of green grapes and black cherries. Celery seed or poppy seed dressing should be passed several times.

SUMMER LUNCHEON (2)

Sandwich plate, consisting of Holland rusk, buttered with anchovy paste, on shredded lettuce, covered in turn with sliced baked ham, sliced chicken breast, thick slice of tomato and two halves of deviled eggs. Cover all completely with Russian dressing. Serve with ripe and stuffed olives and iced tea.

Chilled platter with lime sherbet heaped in center of dessert tray. Around this put fresh apricots, plums and large black cherries. Tuck in ivy leaves under fruit. Allow one of each kind of fruit for each person to be served.

SUMMER LUNCHEON (3)

In center of each plate put a ring of cantaloupe or honeydew melon. Surround this with lettuce leaves, on which are placed small groups of fresh fruit: fresh peach halves filled with raspberries, green grapes, melon balls, blue plums stuffed with cheese balls rolled in nuts, sliced bananas, orange sections, etc. Just before serving fill the center of the melon ring with raspberry or lime sherbet and garnish with mint spray. Serve with "Wine Dressing" and pass buttered "Nut Bread Sandwiches".

CHRYSANTHEMUM LUNCHEON

Orange Chrysanthemum Filled with Molded Fruit Salad
Crackers
Rice Rings with Curried Chicken   Stuffed Yellow Squash
Baked Peach Half Stuffed with Bananas   Coconut Topping
Rolls
Individual Iced Chrysanthemum Cakes Around Apricot Ice Cream
Coffee

ROSE LUNCHEON

Lime Cocktail   Olive and Cheese Rosebuds (See "Garnish")
Tomato-Cheese Rose Salad   Crackers   Baked Country Ham
Eggs and Mushroom, Swiss Cheese Sauce, Casserole
Pickle Rings   Beaten Biscuit
Individual Pink Rose Ices in Cake Basket-Iced in Pale Green   Coffee

CAMELLIA LUNCHEON

Salad of Grapefruit Half with Pink Cheese Camellia on Top Avocado Leaves
French Dressing   Assorted Crackers   Deviled Chicken
Broiled Tomato Slices Topped with Individual Molds of Corn Pudding
Broccoli   Beaten Biscuit   Red Crab Apple Pickle
Tennessee Baked Country Ham
Strawberry Sherbet on Platter Surrounded by
Macaroon-dipped Ice Cream Circles
Fresh Strawberry Garnish   Coffee

DAFFODIL LUNCHEON

Grapefruit Half, Daffodil on Cheese on Top   French Dressing

Crackers

Fish Pudding Ring with Potato Balls   Lemon Cups with Tartar Sauce

Cucumber-Radish Garnish   Cauliflower-Carrot-Rose Bouquet

Stuffed Yellow Squash   Little Corn Meal Muffins

Orange Pudding Ring   Whipped Cream   Coffee

PINK LUNCHEON

Avocado Filled with Frozen Mayonnaise   Crackers

Baked Ham Slice   Creole Crumb Topping   Baked Stuffed Tomato

Casserole of Baked Fruit Compote

Pickle in Pepper Ring (See "Garnish")

Large Ring of Devil Food Cake   Pink Peppermint Stick Candy Ice Cream

Coffee

YELLOW LUNCHEON

Cantaloupe Pond Lilies

Cheese Souffle Ring Filled with Creamed Sweetbreads,

Bordered with parsley and "Carrot Flower Garnish"

Green Asparagus with Riced Egg

Yellow Squash, Fried Whole   Rolls

Golden Charlotte Russe   Coffee

PURPLE LUNCHEON

Purple Grape Juice Cocktail   Frosted Pink Grapes

Pastry Cornucopias Filled with Lobster Newburg

Individual Molds of Bing Cherries and Grapefruit Salad   Rolls

Stuffed Eggplant   Green Peas

Purple Cabbages Stuck with Radish Roses and Carrot Flowers,

Center Filled with Celery Curls and Olives (See "Garnishes")

Black Raspberry Ice Cream on Platter Surrounded by

Individual Chrysanthemum Cakes, Iced in Shades of Lavender and Pink

Coffee

* * * *

This menu was served at a luncheon given at our club for Region Six of the Associated Junior Leagues of America a year or so ago. The guests were seated in groups around the club and the dining room table was used only as a decoration.

The Victorian note of the club furnishings inspired the unusual arrangement and the color scheme blended with the club decor. The large round table was draped in a soft shade of Burgundy velvet which fell from the top of the table to the floor and which extended around the edge of the table, where it was caught down in plaits. A flat plaque of green magnolia leaves came almost to the edge of the table and in the center a two-foot high tripod of wrought iron was hung with specimen bunches of pink Tokay grapes which formed a tree. Small chrysanthemums, shading from pink to lavender, outlined the branches. At the base of the tree, extending almost to the edge of the magnolia leaves, was banked an arrangement of purple eggplant, green artichokes, limes and avocados. The young artist who arranged it was a Junior League member and also a member of the club.

Our menu, as you see, was planned to tie in with the purple and green color scheme.

* * * * * *

MONTHLY CLUB LUNCHEONS

* * * * * *

Our monthly club luncheons are usually attended by 150 to 175 guests seated at tables holding from six to ten. The decorations are planned by the Home Department of the club and many attractive and unusual ideas are carried out by their untiring efforts.

The first course is usually on the table when the guests come into the dining room, and it is always planned to tie in with the table decorations.

The meat is usually put on the plate for the main course, with some sort of garnish, and often one vegetable, such as a stuffed pepper, tomato or squash, is also on the plate. If the salad is served with the main course, it is on the plate with the meat and the vegetable platters are passed. This is an easy way to serve large groups.

The following suggestions show how we plan the different monthly menus:

JANUARY LUNCHEON

Frosty Salad Rings Filled with Grapefruit and Russian Dressing
Crackers　　　Noodle Ring Filled with Tuna Fish Creole
Stuffed Patty Pan Squash Around Green Peas-Parsley Garnish
Green Asparagus, Lemon Butter and Toasted Almonds on Top
Rolls　　　Pickles　　　Green Mint Ice Cream　　　Coconut Balls
Coffee

Decorations for the luncheon were little snow men and snowballs made of styrofoam.

263

FEBRUARY CLUB LUNCHEON
(George Washington)

Tomato Juice Cocktail	Hatchet-shaped Cheese Toast
Olives Celery Curls	Bing Cherry and Grapefruit Salad
Baked Ham Slices	Creole Crumb Topping
Baked Stuffed Tomato	Beaten Biscuit

Chocolate Marshmallow Roll iced in chocolate to resemble a log. Platter decorated with sprays of artificial cherries. Pasteboard hatchet across the roll.

(Pasteboard hatchets about 10 inches long are available at stores specializing in favors.)

Logs 4 inches in diameter and about 14 inches long had three holes bored down the length; these held red candles which were decorated around the base with artificial bunches of cherries. These were used for our table decorations.

MARCH CLUB LUNCHEON
(Saint Patrick)

Green Pineapple and Cucumber Aspic Salad
Individual Rings of Fish Pudding Centered with
Tartar Sauce and Parsley Bud Garnish
Potatoes in Cream Sauce   Riced Eggs
Slice of Lemon on Plate with Pickle Relish on Top of it
Green Asparagus   Little Hot Corn Meal Muffins
Green Meringue Rings Filled with Vanilla Ice Cream
Green Marshmallows-Mint Sauce   Coffee

Decorations for this luncheon were jonquils put into green pasteboard Irish top hats. Little green shamrocks for place cards. Hats can be ordered from a firm who deals in favors.

APRIL CLUB LUNCHEON
(Easter Season)

Pineapple Quarters with Fruit Garnish
Half Deviled Chicken   Orange Slice with Jelly Garnish
New Green Peas   Hot Fig Compote   Rolls
Ice Cream   Pass Easter Bonnet Cakes   Coffee

Decorations for this luncheon were little round bandboxes covered with orchid-covered wallpaper. The tops were off to one side and pale pink tissue paper was fluffed inside the boxes.

In each box was a little toque made of flowers with a pink tulle veil on it. The hats were fashioned of an iris surrounded by rosebuds and weigela. These were made by the club members who decorated the club luncheon tables under the direction of the chairman of the home department.

MAY CLUB LUNCHEON

Grapefruit May Baskets Filled with Fruit
Molded Chicken Salad with Tomato Aspic Top
Stuffed Green Patty Pan Squash
Casserole of Lima Beans and Mushrooms
Crab Apple Pickle   Hot Rolls   Iced Tea
May Basket Cakes Filled with Molded Flower Ices

(Ice cakes in pastel shades and fill with Easter lilies, roses, yellow Calla lilies of ice cream.)

May baskets filled with roses and "baby breath" were on each table.

JUNE CLUB LUNCHEON

Cantaloupe Pond Lilies
Toast Boats Filled with Sweetbreads, Chicken and Mushrooms
Broccoli with Lemon Butter Sauce
Broiled Tomato Slices with Individual Corn Pudding on Top of Tomato
Peach Pickle   Hot Rolls   Iced Tea
Apricot Ice Cream   Broken Sunshine Cake

(Yellow garden lilies in different shades were used for this luncheon.)

JULY CLUB LUNCHEON

Watermelon Balls on Green Ice
Tomatoes Stuffed with Chicken Salad
Corn Pudding   Lima Beans
Iced Tea   Hot Rolls

Platter of Green Mint or Lime Ice with fresh fruits at either end. (See "Summer Delight".)

Shaded pink specimen zinnias were used for this luncheon.

AUGUST CLUB LUNCHEON

Cantaloupe Rings Filled with Fruit
Molded Lamb Ring Filled with Potato Salad-Surrounded by Tomato,
Cucumber and Stuffed Pickle Slices Placed One on Top of the Other
(See "Pickle Garnish")
Stuffed Eggs   Hot Banana Muffins
Frozen Party Iced Tea with Ginger Ale
Frozen Macaroon Pineapple Dessert
(White spider lilies on these tables)

SEPTEMBER CLUB LUNCHEON

Half Grapefruit, Crystallized Ginger Center
Broiled Sweetbreads on Ham-Mushroom Sauce
Squash and Egg Casserole   Broiled Tomatoes Around Green Peas
Iced Tea   Blueberry Muffins   Sunshine Dessert

Yellow and orange colored large fluffy marigolds for table decoration.

OCTOBER CLUB LUNCHEON

Cream of Corn Soup   Crackers   Baked Ham
Tomato-Cheese Artichoke Salad on Plate
Stuffed Eggplant
Crusty Peaches   Rolls   Charlotte Russe Ring-Wine Jelly Top
Coffee

Fall flowers used on these tables.

NOVEMBER CLUB LUNCHEON

Egg Appetizer on Tomato Slice   Crackers
Turkey Ball on Pat of Dressing   Mushroom Gravy
Clear Apple with Orange Marmalade Glaze
Green Asparagus   Little Fried Yellow Squash
Rolls   Pickle
Molded Ices in Fruit Shapes   Broken Sunshine Cake   Coffee

Combine bunches of grapes, apples, pears, peaches, bananas of ice cream
on platters surrounded by galax leaves.

(Small gilded pumpkins filled with yellow chrysanthemums were flanked
with bunches of red grapes. The grapes were highlighted with gold paint.)

266

DECEMBER CLUB LUNCHEON
(Christmas)

Pineapple Ring Christmas Wreaths Filled with Fruit   Holly Garnish
Sliced Turkey on Pat of Dressing   Mushroom Gravy   Cranberries
Star-shaped Mold of Rice with Star of Pimento on Top
Baked Stuffed Tomatoes   Red Crab Apple Pickle   Hot Rolls
Christmas Dessert

Little styrofoam sleds filled with packages tied to resemble Christmas gifts and drawn by "Rudolph the Red-nosed Reindeer" were placed down the center of the tables. (Holly decorations were also used.) The packages were from 1 to 3 inches long and were really small blocks of wood tied in gay wrappings.

SALAD PLATE LUNCH

Bing Cherry and Grapefruit Salad
Chicken Salad in Hot Rolls   Open-faced Tomato Sandwiches
Cheese and Water Cress Sandwich   Tea or Coffee
Canadian Cookies

SALAD PLATE LUNCH (2)

Sweetbread and Cucumber Salad in Tomatoes
Individual Oyster Loaves   Cheese Sandwich
Asparagus Sandwich   Chocolate Cup Cakes   Tea or Coffee

SALAD PLATE LUNCH (3)

Perfection Salad   Tongue and Olive Sandwich   Cheese Sandwich
Egg and Anchovy Sandwich
Brown Sugar Muffin Cakes   Tea or Coffee

SALAD PLATE LUNCH (4)

Molded Jewel Salad   Chicken Salad Sandwich   Tomato Sandwich
Olive Nut Sandwich   Angel Food Rum Balls   Tea or Coffee

SALAD PLATE LUNCH (5)

Tomato Stuffed with Eggs and Caviar

Ham Squares   Carrot Sandwiches   Cucumber and Olive Sandwiches

"Monkeys"   Tea or Coffee

SALAD PLATE LUNCH (6)

Jellied Tongue Ring Filled with Chopped Vegetable Salad

Egg Sandwich   Water Cress Sandwich

Swiss Cheese and Bell Pepper Sandwich on Rye Bread

Peanut Butter Cookies   Tea or Coffee

SALAD PLATE LUNCH (7)

Tomato Aspic with Celery   Crab Mayonnaise

Hot Cheese Dreams   Roll Stuffed with Tongue   Asparagus Sandwich

Tea or Coffee   Spice Muffin Cakes

SALAD PLATE LUNCH (8)

Molded Grapefruit and Pineapple Salad

Chicken Salad Sandwich   Tomato Sandwich   Cheese Dreams

Tea or Coffee   "Rocks"

SALAD PLATE LUNCH (9)

Tomato-Cheese Layer Salad   Tongue and Olive Sandwich

Egg and Anchovy Sandwich   Bacon Twists   Tea or Coffee

Hot Cup Cakes

SALAD PLATE LUNCH (10)

Molded Ginger Ale Salad with Fruit   Tomato Sandwich

Snappy Cheese Sandwich   Tuna Fish Sandwich

Tea or Coffee   Coconut Corn Flake Cookies

SALAD PLATE LUNCH (11)

Crab Salad Molded   Cucumber Aspic Top   Spring Sandwich

Cheese and Bacon Open-faced Sandwich   Asparagus Sandwich

Tea or Coffee   Fruited Cookies

SALAD PLATE LUNCH (12)

Molded Pear and Cheese Salad   Toasted Mushroom Sandwich
Spring Sandwich   Ripe Olive and Nut Sandwich
Tea or Coffee   Brown Sugar Fudge Cake Squares

SALAD PLATE LUNCH (13)

Grapefruit-Asparagus Salad   Red Dressing
Cucumber Sandwich   Cheese Dreams   Hot Sardine Biscuit
Tea or Coffee   Bittersweet Chocolate Cookies

SALAD PLATE LUNCH (14)

Individual Frosty-Salad Rings Filled with Shrimp   Russian Dressing
Cucumber and Tongue Sandwich   Egg and Almond Sandwich
Carrot Sandwiches on Whole Wheat Bread   Tea or Coffee
Chocolate Corn Flake Cookies

SALAD PLATE LUNCH (15)

Chicken-Vegetable Molded Salad
Roquefort Cheese Sandwich on Rye Bread   Tomato Sandwich
Carrot Sandwich on Whole Wheat Bread   Tea or Coffee   Date Bars

SALAD PLATE LUNCH (16)

Molded Apricot Salad   Chicken Salad Sandwich
Philadelphia Cheese and Olive Sandwich
Tea or Coffee   Fudge Cakes

SALAD PLATE LUNCH (17)

Tomato Stuffed with Eggs and Caviar   Ham Squares
Cheese Dreams   Cucumber and Almond Sandwiches
Tea or Coffee   Chocolate Macaroons

SALAD PLATE LUNCH (18)

Frozen Fruit Salad   Rolled Cheese Dreams   Spring Sandwiches
Olive and Nut Sandwich   Tea or Coffee   Torte Cakes

* * * * * *

LAP TRAY LUNCHEONS
* * * * * *

Avocado Half Filled with Crab Meat   Russian Salad Dressing
Molded Perfection Salad   Molded Grapefruit-Pineapple Salad
Ripe Olives   Hot Rolls   Stuffed Olives
Iced Tea or Coffee

Arrange the three salads in separate lettuce cups in clover-leaf shape. Pu
olives between each serving of salad.

LAP TRAY LUNCHEON
Individual Mold of Chicken-Vegetable Salad
Slice of Tomato, Philadelphia Cheese on Top with
Garnish of Artichoke Heart
Molded Bing Cherry and Grapefruit Salad
Olives   Marmalade Muffins   Stuffed Eggs
Iced Tea or Coffee   Individual Chocolate or Lemon Tarts

LAP TRAY LUNCHEON (2)
Individual Mold of Chicken Salad with Tomato Aspic Top
Green Asparagus Salad with Stuffed Egg Garnish
Hawaiian Salad-Cream Cheese Topping
Banana Muffins   Ripe Olives   Iced Tea or Coffee
Individual Iced Cake Rings Filled with Strawberry Ice Cream

LAP TRAY LUNCHEON (3)
Tomato Stuffed with Vegetable Cottage Cheese
Small Mold of Salmon Mousse   Mold of Fruit Salad
Ripe Olives   Hot Rolls   Green Olives
Iced Tea or Coffee   (No dessert necessary unless desired)

LAP TRAY LUNCHEON (4)
Grapefruit Salad in Avocado Pear (on Plate)
Pass Platters of Chicken Valenciana   Toasted French Bread
Tea or Coffee   Individual Chess Pies

LAP TRAY LUNCHEON (5)

Individual Cucumber Aspic Rings Filled with Crab Salad (on Plate)
Baked Stuffed Tomato (on Plate)
Pass Casseroles Creamed Asparagus and Almonds
Hot Corn Meal Biscuits   Iced Tea or Coffee
English Trifle in Individual Compotes
Whipped Cream Topping

LAP TRAY LUNCHEON (6)

Individual Rice Rings Filled with Curried Chicken (on Plate)
Large Red Bell Peppers Stuffed with Creole Cauliflower (Pass)
Individual Mold of Apricot-Cheese Salad (on Plate)
Hot Rolls   Pickle   Tea or Coffee
Meringue Rings Filled with Vanilla Ice Cream
Fresh Red Raspberries

LAP TRAY LUNCHEON (7)

Baked Ham-Creole Dressing (on Plate)
Mold of Tomato Aspic with Celery and Olives (on Plate)
Pass Casseroles of Baked Stuffed Eggs and Mushrooms with Cheese Sauce
Blueberry Muffins   Peach Pickle   Tea or Coffee
Broken Sunshine Cake with Vanilla Ice Cream and Strawberries

BUFFET LUNCHEONS AND SUPPERS

One of the most popular means of entertaining is the buffet party, because this eliminates many problems for the hostess without help. The buffet usually consists of one main dish, a vegetable, and a dessert. All of these are planned so that they may be prepared ahead of time.

The buffet is arranged so that the plates, silver, and napkins are at one end. For a buffet luncheon a central floral arrangement is used, and for a buffet supper an arrangement of candelabra or single candlesticks is used.

Platters of food are spaced along the table with serving spoons and forks by each platter. The food should be plentiful enough so that the guests may have second servings.

Some hostesses provide a small tray for each guest, and the guests are seated at small tables. The coffee may either be poured from one end of the buffet table or poured by the hostess at the small tables while the guests are serving their plates. Dessert may be served by the hostess at each small table or placed on the buffet table for the guests to serve themselves.

If an elaborate buffet is planned, the hostess should arrange to have someone help her.

MENUS

SUMMER BUFFET LUNCHEON
Platter of Cold Sliced Turkey or Chicken Breast
Ring of (Fruit Ball) Jewel Salad
Philadelphia Cheese Thinned with French Dressing   Potato Chips
Nut Bread Sandwiches   Cucumber Sandwiches
Iced Tea   Lime Sherbet   Small Muffin Cakes

BUFFET LUNCHEON
Chicken Breasts with Mushroom Sauce   Rice and Carrot Ring
Philadelphia Cheese Ring Salad Filled with Grapefruit Sections
and Balls Cut from Avocado with Melon Scoop
Crab Apple Pickle   Rolls   Coffee
Frozen Lemon Icebox Dessert

BUFFET LUNCHEON (2)

Stuffed Eggs with Newburg Sauce in Shells
Tomato Aspic with Shrimp in Ring Mold
Beaten Biscuit   Coffee
Orange Chiffon Cake-Center filled with Whipped Cream
Surround Cake with Spoons of Wine Jelly

BUFFET LUNCHEON (3)

Chicken or Turkey Divan   Molded Grapefruit and Pineapple Salad
Watermelon Pickle   Coffee   Rolls
Orange Chiffon Dessert

BUFFET LUNCHEON (4)

Casserole of Scalloped Shrimp
Salad of Avocado Pear Halves Filled with Orange or
Grapefruit Sections-French Dressing
Green Lima Beans in Cream   Rolls   Coffee
Coconut Bavarian with Butterscotch Sauce

BUFFET LUNCHEON (5)

Ring of "Chicken-Vegetable" Salad Surrounded by Slices of Tomato and
Cucumber and Lettuce Hearts   Stuffed Deviled Eggs
Pickle   Potato Chips   Rye Bread and Butter Sandwiches
Iced Tea   Pineapple Sherbet   Muffin Cakes

BUFFET LUNCHEON (6)

Salmon Mousse in Fish Mold Shape   Potato Salad   Pickle
Cucumber and Whole Wheat Sandwiches   Iced Tea
Raspberry Sherbet   Broken Chiffon Cake

BUFFET LUNCHEON (7)

Individual Molds of Chicken Salad with Tomato Aspic Top
Casserole of Cauliflower and Mushrooms
Peach Pickles   Rolls   Coffee
Orange Pudding

BUFFET LUNCHEON (8)

Ring of Tomato Aspic with Bowl of Crab Meat Mayonnaise in Center
Casserole of Stuffed Eggs with Swiss Cheese Sauce
Beaten Biscuit   Pickle   Coffee
Raspberry Chiffon Cake Dessert

BUFFET LUNCHEON (9)

Chicken a la King
Individual Molded Apricot Cheese Salad in Lettuce Cups
Green Asparagus Sprinkled with Riced Eggs
Coffee   Rolls   Rum Charlotte Ring with Whipped Cream

BUFFET LUNCHEON (10)

Crab Supreme in Shells Around Outer Edge of Large Platter
Canned Potato-Cheese Strings in Center of the Tray
Molded Pineapple and Cucumber Salad
Hot Corn Meal Biscuit Brushed with Melted Butter
Golden Charlotte Russe

BUFFET LUNCHEON (11)

Platter of "Eggs and Mushrooms" Surrounded by Border of
Fried Chinese Noodles (Canned)
Molded Vegetable Salad   Casserole of "Fruit Compote"
Rolls   Tea or Coffee   Pineapple Icebox Pudding

BUFFET LUNCHEON (12)

Chicken Tetrazzini   Perfection Salad-Apricot Green Gage Plum Compote
Rolls   Coffee   Lemon Tarts

BUFFET LUNCHEON (13)

Chicken Valenciana   Molded Grapefruit Salad   Green Asparagus
Toasted French Bread   Pickles   Chess Pies   Coffee

BUFFET LUNCHEON (14)

Creamed Ham, Sweetbreads and Black Olives
Tomato Aspic with Celery
Squash and Egg Casserole   Beaten Biscuit   Relish Tray
Rum Charlotte Ring   Coffee

BUFFET LUNCHEON (15)

Tomato Aspic with Crab Mayonnaise   Curried Eggs
Peas and Pimento   Celery Hearts and Carrot Sticks
Rolls   Coffee   Lemon Tarts

BUFFET LUNCHEON (16)

Chicken and Shrimp Casserole   Grapefruit and Pineapple Molded Salad
Cauliflower and Mushroom Casserole   Corn Meal Biscuit   Coffee
Fudge Pie with Peppermint Ice Cream

ELABORATE BUFFET SUPPER OR SMORGASBORD

Platters of Cold Sliced Baked Country Ham and Turkey Breast
Individual Molds of Tomato Aspic with Shrimp
Molded Vegetable Aspic
Crab Salad Molded in Shape of Fish, Surrounded by Green Cucumber
Aspic and Egg Pond Lilies
Potato Salad   Deviled Eggs   Huge Ripe and Stuffed Olives
Celery Hearts and Carrot Curls   Radish Roses and Pickles
Hors d'oeuvre Circles
Rye Bread and Butter Sandwiches   Beaten Biscuit
Cheese Platter of Varieties of Cheese   Coffee
Lime Ice in Watermelon Halves Scooped Out and Cut in Points Around Edge
Garnish of Melon Balls and Fresh Fruits

CHRISTMAS BUFFET SUPPER

Sliced Turkey   Sliced Baked Ham or Spice Round
Pickles, Celery Hearts, Carrot Curls and Radishes
Cinnamon Apples or Cranberry Sauce
Casserole of Lima Beans and Mushrooms or Creole Eggs
Rolls   Coffee
Fruitcake Slices Around a Variety of Cheeses   Christmas Candy or Nuts

BUFFET SUPPER (2)

Chicken Indian Curry with Condiments   Celery Hearts
Carrot Strings   Radishes   French Bread
Coffee   Orange Ice   Cookies

BUFFET SUPPER (3)

Deviled Oysters   Baked Sliced Ham   Cranberry-Pineapple Salad
Asparagus and Cheese Casserole   Rolls   Coffee
Macaroon Pudding

BUFFET SUPPER (4)

Creole Chicken   Bing Cherry and Grapefruit Salad   Rolls
Asparagus and Egg Casserole   Chocolate Icebox Pudding   Coffee

BUFFET SUPPER (5)

Italian Spaghetti   Grapefruit Salad with Cucumber Dressing
French Bread   Coffee   Date Crumble

BUFFET SUPPER (6)

Baked Sliced Ham   Boston Baked Beans   Chopped Vegetable Salad
Toasted and Buttered Boston Brown Bread Slices
Rolls   Coffee   Trifle

BUFFET SUPPER (7)

Brunswick Stew   Slaw No. 1   Hot Biscuit   Rolls
Individual Chess Pies   Coffee

BUFFET SUPPER (8)

Creamed Crab and Rice   Tomato Aspic with Avocado Mayonnaise
Apple Compote   Green Lima Beans   Beaten Biscuit
Coffee   Golden Charlotte Russe

BUFFET SUPPER (9)

Chicken with Sausage Balls   Fluffy Rice   Tomato Aspic with Celery
Casserole of Fruit Compote   Rolls   Coffee

BUFFET SUPPER (10)

Chicken Chop Suey over (Canned) Chinese Noodles
Molded Vegetable Salad   Rolls   Celery   Olives
Chocolate Tarts   Coffee

BRIDGE PARTIES

There are several different kinds of bridge parties. One is the dessert bridge which is served at two or three o'clock. The card playing follows this. The dessert is usually very fancy and rich. Coffee and salted nuts may also be served. This is the simplest bridge party for a hostess without a maid to serve. Another afternoon bridge menu is a salad plate or sandwiches and cookies. A simple luncheon consisting of a salad, one hot dish, a simple dessert, and coffee is also a good idea for a bridge party.

If the hostess prefers morning bridge, a luncheon or salad plate could be served after cards. If the party is at night a dessert is served.

BRIDGE PARTY MENUS

DESSERT BRIDGE

Large Egg Kisses Filled with Vanilla Ice Cream
Strawberry Sauce
Coffee
Salted Pecans

DESSERT BRIDGE (2)

Fudge Pie
Peppermint Candy Ice Cream
Coffee
Salted Almonds

DESSERT BRIDGE (3)

Broken Orange Chiffon Cake
Vanilla Ice Cream
Cherry Jubilee Sauce
Coffee
Salted Mixed Nuts

DESSERT BRIDGE (4)

Vanilla Ice Cream
Eggnog Sauce
Fruitcake
Coffee
Salted Nuts

DESSERT BRIDGE (5)

Almond Macaroon Icebox Pudding
Salted Pecans
Coffee

DESSERT BRIDGE (6)

Large Cream Puff Shells Filled with
Ice Cream-Chocolate Sauce
Coffee
Salted Pecans

DESSERT BRIDGE (7)

Rum Charlotte
Whipped Cream
Coffee
Salted Nuts

DESSERT BRIDGE (8)

Pecan Crisp Cups
Vanilla Ice Cream with Butterscotch Sauce
Coffee
Salted Nuts

DESSERT BRIDGE (9)

Chocolate Cake Ring
Peppermint Candy Ice Cream
Salted Almonds
Coffee

DESSERT BRIDGE (10)

Fruit Icebox Pudding
Coffee
Salted Nuts

DESSERT BRIDGE (11)

Mocha Cake
Whipped Cream
Coffee
Salted Nuts

DESSERT BRIDGE (12)

Strawberry Torte
Coffee
Salted Nuts

AFTERNOON BRIDGE REFRESHMENTS

MENU NO. 1

Cheese and Pineapple Aspic Salad   Tomato Sandwiches
Cucumber Sandwiches   Brown Sugar Fudge Squares   Coffee

MENU NO. 2

Fruit Salad in Aspic   Orange Bread and Butter Sandwiches
Chicken Salad Sandwiches   Tea   Angel Food Rum Balls

MENU NO. 3

Cherry-Orange Salad, Frozen   Nut Bread and Butter Sandwiches
Cheese and Olive Sandwiches   Tea   Chews

MENU NO. 4

Frozen Fruit Salad No. 1   Spring Sandwiches   Cheese Wheels
Tea   Ham Squares   Brown Sugar Kisses

MENU NO. 5

Ginger Ale Salad   Ripe Olive Sandwiches   Cheese Dreams
Tea   Chocolate Thins

MENU NO. 6

Pineapple and Cucumber Salad   Tomato Sandwiches
Toasted Mushroom Sandwiches   Tea   Date Kisses

MENU NO. 7

Pear and Cheese Salad, Frozen
Date and Nut Bread and Butter Sandwiches
Chicken Salad Sandwiches   Tea   Fruited Cookies

BRIDGE LUNCHEON

Apricot Cheese Molded Salad   Stuffed Eggs Newburg Sauce in Shells
Rolls   Coffee or Tea   Chocolate Tarts

BRIDGE LUNCHEON (2)

Frosty Salad Rings Filled with Shrimp   Russian Dressing
Cheese Fondue   Rolls   Coffee   Date Crumble

BRIDGE LUNCHEON (3)

Chicken Vegetable Salad   Creole Eggs   Cheese Biscuit
Coffee   Fudge Cake

BRIDGE LUNCHEON (4)

Tomato Aspic   Crab Mayonnaise   Baked Stuffed Eggs-Cheese Sauce
Rolls   Coffee   Cherry Tarts

BRIDGE LUNCHEON (5)

Frozen Cream Cheese and Jelly Salad with Grapefruit Sections
Asparagus and Egg Casserole No. 1   Blueberry Muffins   Coffee
Corn Flake Cookies

BRIDGE LUNCHEON (6)

Chicken Salad Molded with Tomato Aspic Top   Corn Pudding   Rolls
Coffee   Chocolate-Orange Cup Cakes

BRIDGE LUNCHEON (7)

Molded Vegetable Salad   Creamed Asparagus with Almonds
Banana Muffins   Coffee   Spice Meringue Cake

COCKTAIL PARTIES

Informal cocktail parties are the most popular, because they require less preparation and because the guests may serve themselves. They should be bountiful even though they are informal. At formal cocktail parties canapés and relishes are served by the same waiters who serve the cocktails. A few tomato juice cocktails should always be provided for guests who do not want alcoholic cocktails. The following menus are only for the canapés and other food served at cocktail parties. The choice of cocktails is left up to each hostess.

COCKTAIL PARTY SUGGESTIONS

INFORMAL COCKTAIL PARTY

Cold Sliced Turkey   Sliced Country Ham
Sliced Sandwich Bread (Crust removed)
Sliced Rye Bread   Bowls of Whipped Butter   Prepared Mustard
Small Hot Biscuit   Relish Trays of Olives and Celery Hearts
Bowls of a Variety of Cheese Spreads   Crackers and Potato chips
Jumbo Shrimp on Cocktail Picks   Russian Dressing Stuffed Deviled Eggs
Sliced "Cheese Nut Roll"   Cocktails

LARGE FORMAL COCKTAIL PARTY

Hot Cheese and Bacon Canapés   Beaten Biscuit with Baked Ham
Chicken Salad in Tiny Cream Puff Shells   Shrimp Ovals
Water Cress Canapés   Cucumber or Tomato Open-faced Sandwiches
Relish Tray with Stuffed Eggs, Olives, Celery, etc.   Cocktails

All arranged on attractively decorated platters and passed continuously among the guests.

281

COCKTAIL PARTY

Hot Ham and Cheese Pinwheels   Cheese and Pepper Canapé
Chicken Canapé   Tomato Canapé   Bacon Twists
Stuffed Celery and Olives   Cocktails

COCKTAIL PARTY (2)

Hot Ham Squares   Crab Meat in Toast Boats   Water Cress Canapé
Cheese and Anchovy Canapés   Stuffed Deviled Eggs   Carrot Sticks
Cocktails

COCKTAIL PARTY (3)

Hot Sardine Turnovers   Cheese and Pepper Canapé   Cheese Puffs
Cucumber Canapé   Relish Tray of Olives, Stuffed Beets and Celery
Cocktails

COCKTAIL PARTY (4)

Fish Roe Canapé   Tomato Canapé   Chicken Salad in Toast Cups
Cheese Dreams   Olives   Chipped Beef and Cheese Rolls
Cocktails

COCKTAIL PARTY (5)

Cheese and Bacon Open-faced Sandwiches   Individual Oyster Loaves
Toasted Rolled Asparagus   Crab Meat Canapé
Relish Tray with Olives and Radishes   Cocktails

COCKTAIL PARTY (6)

Anchovy and Cheese Canapé   Water Cress Canapé
Cheese and Poppy Seed Open-faced Sandwiches   Beaten Biscuit and Ham
Relish Tray with Celery and Carrot Sticks   Bacon Twists
Cocktails

DINNERS

Present-day hostesses hardly ever serve six or seven course formal dinners. Therefore, the following series of menus will be flexible enough for some of the courses to be combined or for the salad course to follow the meat course in some cases. The hostess can be the judge, since all the menus are complete enough for most occasions.

Serving the salad first is a way of combining the appetizer and salad course. Cocktails served with canapés in the living room also take the place of one course. A fish course is rarely served now, but fish may be used in the form of appetizer or soup. For informal dinners the salad may be placed on the table with the meat course. This is especially nice if there is limited maid service.

I think most hostesses will prefer the menus I have listed; but I have also included one formal one, simply to show how it should be served.

FORMAL DINNER MENU

Rose Apple Appetizer   Anchovy Circles   Olives
Clear Tomato Soup   Crackers   Shrimp Sea Shells
Tiny Corn Meal Muffins   Chicken Breasts with Wine Sauce
Rice Rings with Pimento Peas   Peach Pickle   Green Asparagus
Rolls   Head Lettuce   Roquefort Dressing   Coffee
Lime Sherbet with Fruits (Summer Delight)

CHRISTMAS DINNER

Grapefruit Halves with Crystallized Ginger   Maraschino Cherry Garnish
Baked Turkey   Cranberry Relish   Celery Hearts
Sweet Potato Ring Filled with Apple Balls
Cauliflower with Tomato Curry Sauce
Green Beans with Toasted Almonds
Rolls   Plum Pudding-Eggnog Sauce   Coffee

THANKSGIVING DINNER

Oyster Cocktail   Hot Tomato Bouillon   Celery, Olives, Crackers
Baked Duck or Goose   Clear Apple Filled with Orange Marmalade
Wild Rice Ring Filled with Green Peas and Pimento
Spinach Souffle or Broccoli with Hollandaise Sauce
Individual Mince Pies with Cheese Pumpkin Garnish
Coffee

DINNER

Avocado Appetizer   Shrimp Bisque   Deviled Chicken
Peach Pickle   Lima Beans with Sour Cream   Clipped Corn
Rolls   Coconut Bavarian Cream   Coffee

DINNER (2)

Crab Salad in Avocado Pear   Russian Dressing   Crackers
Chicken Ring Surrounded by Crusty Peaches
Creole Cauliflower in Bell Peppers   Baby Lima Beans   Rolls
Charlotte Russe   Coffee

DINNER (3)

Individual Tomato Aspic Rings with Stuffed Egg in Center
Chicken Breasts in White Wine
Rice and Carrot Ring Filled with Peas   Green Asparagus
Cherry-Sherry Ring   Broken Orange Chiffon Cake   Coffee

DINNER (4)

Frosty Salad Rings with Grapefruit and Avocado
Fish Creamed with Shrimp Sauce   Baked Stuffed Tomatoes
Potato Balls   Corn Meal Muffins
Peach or Strawberry Meringue   Coffee

DINNER (5)

Frozen Consomme with Shrimp   Creamed Chicken in Noodle Ring
Broccoli with Lemon Butter Sauce   Fig and Ginger Compote
Salad can be added here (Optional)   Rolls
Macaroon Pudding   Coffee

DINNER (6)

Grapefruit and Black Grape Salad
Cream of Mushroom Soup (Optional)
Stuffed Squab   Crab Apple Pickle
Corn Timbales on Broiled Tomatoes   Stuffed Squash   Rolls
Macaroon Meringue Ring with Vanilla Ice Cream   Coffee

DINNER (7)

Tomato and Egg Appetizer (Optional)   Sliced Baked Country Ham
Clear Pickle Rings   Casserole of Deviled Oysters
Snap Beans with Toasted Almonds   Rolls
Peppers Stuffed with Cheese and Tomato Catsup
Rum Charlotte Ring   Coffee

DINNER (8)

Grapefruit Half with Ginger (Optional)
Cream of Celery Soup   Carrot Sticks   Radishes   Fish Cutlets
Tartar Sauce   Cauliflower with Tomato Curry Sauce
Green Peas-French Style   Corn Meal Muffins   Slaw No. 1
Strawberry Torte   Coffee

DINNER (9)

Tomato Juice   Bacon Twists   Chicken Cutlet-Mushroom Sauce
Hot Fruit Compote   Asparagus and Almonds
Salad may be added here (Optional)
Chocolate Icebox Pudding   Coffee

DINNER (10)

Soup (Optional)   Canapé Marguery   Creole Chicken   Rice Balls
Green Asparagus with Toasted Almonds   Sweet Potatoes and Pears
Trifle   Coffee

DINNER (11)

Shrimp Cocktail   Crackers   Lamb Chops Stuffed with Mushrooms
Pear Garnish   Asparagus with Almonds   Baked Stuffed Tomato
Salad can be added here (optional)   Rolls   Pickles
Almond Macaroon Icebox Pudding   Coffee

DINNER (12)

Cream of Corn Soup   Crackers   Sweetbreads Broiled   Tomato Sauce
Lima Beans Creamed   Stuffed Squash   Baked Bananas   Rolls
Salad (optional)   Apricot Ice Cream   Orange Chiffon Cake   Coffee

DINNER (13)

Tomato Juice Cocktail   Bacon Crisps   Stuffed Celery
Blue Cheese Canapé   Turkey Balls   Cranberry Relish
Asparagus in Bell Peppers   Sweet Potato Ring   Salad (Optional)
Mocha Cake   Coffee

DINNER (14)

Oyster Soup   Crackers   Celery   Radishes   Olives
Sweetbread Cutlets   Lima Beans and Mushrooms   Broiled Tomatoes
Apricot and Green Gage Plum Compote   Salad (Optional)
Pecan Crisp Rings   Ice Cream   Butterscotch Sauce   Coffee

DINNER (15)

Avocado Appetizer   Crab Bisque (Optional)   Crackers
Barbecued Chicken   Snap Beans with Mushroom Sauce
Baked Stuffed Tomato   Hot Fig and Ginger Compote   Rolls
Strawberry Torte   Coffee

DINNER (16)

Individual Cheese Rings with Grapefruit Sections
Shrimp Creole in Rice Ring   Green Peas with Pimento   Rolls
Stuffed Squash   Frozen Lemon Icebox Dessert   Coffee

SETTING THE TABLE

SERVING THE PARTY

Formal parties should be planned so that the decorations, china and linens harmonize. The taste of the hostess determines the floral arrangement. One rule to follow, however, is that the arrangement should be low enough for the guests to see each other. If a long table is used and candelabra are a part of the decoration, the centerpiece should be tall enough to balance with them.

Candlesticks and candelabra are used for teas, dinners, and buffet suppers, never for breakfasts or luncheons. They should always be lighted. Compotes of candies or nuts can also be part of the decoration.

Tablecloths of damask, lace, or linen are used for dinners, while place mats and runners are used for luncheons.

Each guest should be allowed twenty-four inches, and his plate should be in the center of this space. Plates should be spaced so that each plate will be directly opposite from the ones on the other side of the table.

Glasses are placed to the right and slightly above the service plate. The bread and butter plates are to the left and slightly above the service plate. Bread and butter plates are hardly ever used for formal dinners but may be used for luncheons. The butter knife is placed at right angles to the other silver at the top of the bread and butter plate.

One rule to follow in placing the silver is that all knives and spoons are placed to the right of the service plate with the cutting edge of all knives turned to the plate and all forks except the cocktail or oyster fork are placed to the left of the service plate. The cocktail or oyster fork is placed to the right with the knives and spoons. The lower edge of all silver should be in a straight line one inch from the edge of the table. To avoid the look of too much silver on the table at one time, the dessert spoon and fork are sent with the dessert and the after dinner coffee spoon is sent with the coffee. Silver is placed in the order of its use from the outside toward the plate.

Napkins are folded on the service plates if the first course is to be soup which is served after the guests are seated; but if the first course is already on the table when the guests are seated, the napkins are folded in a rectangular shape and placed to the left of the dinner fork and in line with the lower edge of the silver.

Place cards are customary for a formal dinner. The hostess seats a woman guest of honor to the right of the host and a man guest of honor to her right. At an all-women luncheon the guest of honor is to the right of the hostess.

In order to have good service for a formal dinner there should be one maid for each eight guests if she does nothing but serve. If the maid also must cook, the dinner should be more simple and the number of guests should not exceed six.

Black uniforms with white collars and cuffs for the maids are in good taste, but white uniforms may be used in the summer.

The guest of honor should be served first. If more than one maid is serving for a large dinner, they should begin serving at opposite ends of the table. If the first course is soup, it is served after the guests are seated; but if it is an appetizer, it may be placed on the service plate before the guests are seated. The soup plate is placed on top of the service plate. A service plate should always be before each guest except when it has to be removed for the dessert. Each course until the main course is placed on the service plate. Each plate is brought on a serviette, a square lace-edged envelope with a quilted pad inside it. When serving the main course, the maid removed the service plate and soup bowl with her left hand and with her right hand immediately replaces it with a hot plate. All the dishes are removed and crumbs cleared with a folded napkin before the dessert is served.

Next, a dessert plate covered with a lace doily is placed before each guest. A finger bowl is placed on the doily. A flower matching the floral arrangement may be floated in the finger bowl. The dessert fork is placed on the plate to the left of the finger bowl and the dessert spoon to the right of it. The guest puts the silver on the table and the doily and finger bowl to the left above his plate. Then the dessert may be served either by passing a platter and letting each guest remove his own or by letting the maid bring in from the kitchen filled dessert plates. She removes the original dessert plate with her left hand and serves the filled plate with her right hand. All dishes are served from the left of the guest except for the cup, saucer, and glasses which are served from the right.

Coffee may be served either by bringing it in from the kitchen or by having the hostess serve it from the table, or in the living room. If the hostess serves it, coffee is brought to her on a large silver tray. She passes the filled cups to the guests or has a maid pass it.

SILVER ARRANGEMENT

The silver arrangement for a formal dinner is placed from the outside toward the plate in the following manner: on the right side, cocktail fork, soup spoon, fish knife (breakfast knives can be substituted if fish knives are not available) and dinner knife; and on the left, fish (or breakfast fork), dinner fork, and salad fork. Silver is placed from the outside toward the plate in the order it is used. Dessert forks and spoons and after dinner coffee spoons are sent in when they are to be used.

For a less formal dinner the silver is arranged from the outside to the plate in this manner: on the right, fruit spoon and dinner knife and on the left, the dinner fork. Dessert and coffee silver are sent in later. For a breakfast the smaller breakfast knife and fork are substituted for the larger dinner ones.

Special Helps

Special Helps

RECIPES FOR SERVING 50 PEOPLE

COFFEE

4 full c. of coffee
9 qts. water

COCOA

1½ c. cocoa
2 c. sugar
½ tsp. salt
1 qt. boiling water (optional)
8 qts. warm milk

CHICKEN SALAD

6 five pound chickens
1 can pimento
4 tsp. salt
½ c. butter
4 bunches parsley
1½ lbs. mushrooms
1 lb. white sauce

BAKED BEANS

7 lbs. Navy beans
⅓ c. soda
¾ c. molasses
1½ tsp. mustard
⅓ c. sugar
1½ tsp. paprika
4 Tbsp. salt
1½ lb. pork
2 c. water

MACARONI AND CHEESE

5 lbs. macaroni
2 gals. water
¼ c. salt
½ c. butter
6 quarts of white sauce
2½ lbs. cheese

FOR SERVING ONE HUNDRED PEOPLE

2 20 lb. to 24 lb. turkeys
20 lbs. hamburger
5 large cakes
3 gallons vegetables
6 dozen lemons, 4 lbs. sugar,
   5 gallons water
2½ pounds of coffee
6 gallons milk
20 pounds meat
30 pounds of potatoes
15 large cans of peas
4 gallons of soup
3 lbs. of butter
8 loaves of bread
1¼ lbs. of olives
25 heads of lettuce
100 ears of corn
50 cantaloupes
25 lbs. smoked ham
20 lbs. boiled boneless ham
100 ribs of beef (raw)
10 lbs. cheese, brick American or Swiss
16 quarts of ice

WEIGHTS, MEASURES AND EQUIVALENTS

EQUIVALENTS

A few grains . . . . less than ⅛ teaspoon
1 coffee spoon . . . . ¼ teaspoon
3 teaspoons . . . . 1 tablespoon
2 tablespoons. . . . . 1 fluid ounce
1½ ounce . . . . 1 jigger
½ jigger. . . . . 1 pony
16 tablespoons. . . . . 1 cup
1 cup . . . . ½ pint
2 pints . . . . 1 quart
4 cups. . . . . 1 quart
4 quarts . . . . 1 gallon
8 quarts . . . . 1 peck
4 pecks . . . . 1 bushel
16 ounces . . . . 1 pound
1 pound flour. . . . . 3 cups
1 pound butter. . . . . 2 cups
½ pound butter . . . . 2 sticks
1 stick butter . . . . ½ cup
¼ pound grated cheese . . . . 1 cup
1 pound cheese. . . . . 4½ cups
1 pound brown sugar (1 box). . . . . 2⅔ cups
1 pound confectioners (1 box). . . . . 2½ - 3 cups
1 pound granulated sugar . . . . 2 cups
1 pound lump sugar . . . . 55-70 lumps
1 pound seeded raisins. . . . . 2½ cups
1 pound seedless raisins . . . . 3 cups
1 pound coffee . . . . 5 cups - yield 40-50 cups of coffee
1 pound rice. . . . . 2 cups - yield 3-4 cups cooked rice
1 square chocolate . . . . 1 ounce or 3 tablespoons grated chocolate
½ pound marshmallows. . . . . 16 marshmallows
1 pound crab meat. . . . . 2 cups
1 pound pitted dates . . . . 2 cups
1 pound figs (chopped) . . . . 3 cups
1 pound nut meats (chopped) . . . . 4 cups
1 cup noodles . . . . 1½ cups when cooked
1 egg. . . . . ¼ cup
5 eggs . . . . 1 cup
9 eggs . . . . 1 pound
8-10 egg whites . . . . 1 cup
16 egg yolks. . . . . 1 cup
1 lemon, average size . . . . 3 tablespoons juice, 3 tablespoons rind

1 orange. . . . . ½ cup juice
4 medium tomatoes. . . . . 1 pound
3 large bananas (skin on). 1 pound
2 quarts apples . . . . 3 pounds
4 medium potatoes . . . . 1 pound
1 pound peas, in pod. . . . . 1 cup when shelled
12 quarts punch . . . . 96 punch glasses
1 gallon punch. . . . . serves 20
12 pound ham . . . . serves 20
20 pound turkey (or chickens). . . . . serves 20 generously
1 gallon ice cream . . . . serves 30 if scoop is used
11 inch casserole . . . . serves 8 amply
A 4 pound chicken. . . . . yields 4 cups diced chicken

SUBSTITUTIONS

1 sq. chocolate. . . . . 2⅔ tablespoons cocoa plus ½ tablespoon butter
1 tablespoon cornstarch . . . . 2 tablespoons flour (for thickening)
1 teaspoon baking powder . . ¼ teaspoon soda and ½ teaspoon cream tartar
1 cup sugar . . . . 1 cup honey and ½ teaspoon soda (reduce
               liquid in recipe ¼ cup)
. . . . 1 cup maple syrup and ¼ teaspoon soda
               (reduce liquid in recipe ¼ cup)
. . . . 1 cup molasses and ½ teaspoon soda (reduce
               liquid in recipe ¼ cup)
. . . . ½ cup maple syrup and ¼ cup corn syrup
               (reduce liquid in recipe ¼ cup)
1 cup molasses . . . . 1 cup honey
1 cup milk . . . . ½ cup evaporated milk and ½ cup water
. . . . ½ cup condensed milk and ½ cup water
               (reduce sugar in recipe)
. . . . 4 tablespoons powdered milk and 1 cup water
1 cup butter . . . . ⅘ cup bacon fat (clarified) (increase liquid
               in recipe ¼ cup)
. . . . ⅔ cup chicken fat, clarified (increase
               liquid in recipe ¼ cup)
. . . . ⅞ cup cottonseed, corn, nut oil (solid or liquid)
. . . . ⅞ cup lard and salt
. . . . ½ cup suet and salt (increase liquid in recipe ¼ cup)
1 cup sour milk. . . . . 1 cup sweet milk and 1 tablespoon lemon
               juice or vinegar

SIZES OF CANS

No. 1 can . . . . 1½ cupfuls used for baked beans, meats, soups, fruits and vegetables

No. 1 (tall). . . . . 2 cupfuls

No. 2 can. . . . . 2½ cupfuls used for beans, peas, and corn

No. 2½ can . . . . 3½ cupfuls used for tomatoes, spinach, beets and pumpkin

No. 3 can. . . . . 4 cupfuls

No. 10 can . . . . 1 gallon used for both fruits and vegetables

No. 5 can . . . . 7 cupfuls (almost ½ gallon) used for fruit juice

OVEN TEMPERATURE CHART

	Degrees Fahrenheit
Slow oven	250-325
Moderate oven	325-375
Quick or hot oven	400-450
Very hot oven	450-550

TERMS USED IN COOKING

BLANCH — To immerse fruits or nuts in boiling water to remove skins; also, to dip fruits and vegetables in boiling water in preparation for canning, freezing or drying.

BRAISE — To brown meat or vegetables in small quantity of hot fat, then to cook slowly in small amount of liquid.

CLARIFY — To clear a liquid, such as consomme, by adding slightly beaten egg white and egg shells. The beaten egg coagulates in the hot liquid and the particles which cause cloudiness adhere to it. The mixture is then strained.

COATS SPOON — When a mixture forms a thin even film on the spoon.

FOLD IN — To combine two ingredients or two combinations of ingredients by two motions, cutting vertically through the mixture and turning over and over by sliding the implement across the bottom of the mixing bowl with each turn.

FLAMBÉ — Sprinkled with brandy or liqueur and ignited.

JULIENNE — Food cut in very thin strips.

LARD — To insert strips or pieces of fat into uncooked lean meat for added flavor and juiciness; or slices of fat may be spread on top of uncooked lean meat or fish for the same purpose.

MACEDOINE — A mixture of fruits or vegetables.

MARINATE — To let foods stand in a marinade, usually an acid-oil mixture of oil and vinegar or wine, often flavored with spices and herbs.

MINCE — To cut with knife or scissors into very fine pieces.

PAN-BROIL — To cook uncovered on a hot surface, usually a skillet. The fat is poured off as it accumulates.

PAN FRY — To cook in a small amount of fat; synonymous with sauté.

PARBOIL — To boil until partially cooked.

PURÉE — To force vegetables, fruits and other foods through a fine sieve to remove skins, seeds and so forth, and to produce a fine-textured substance.

RAGOUT — A thick, well-seasoned stew.

REDUCE — To evaporate some of the liquid in stock or sauce by boiling.

RENDER — To heat meat fat, cut in small pieces, until fat is separated from connective tissues.

SAUTÉ — To fry lightly in a small amount of hot fat, turning frequently.

SCALD — To heat a liquid to just below the boiling point. Milk has reached a scalding point when film forms on surface.

SCORE — To cut narrow grooves or gashes.

SEAR — To cook at a very high temperature for a short time in order to form quickly a brown crust on the outer surface of meat.

SIMMER — To cook in a liquid that is kept below the boiling point. Bubbles form slowly and break below the surface.

STOCK — A liquid in which vegetables or meat has been cooked.

index

300

301

305

307

bon mélange®

*The Bon Mélange family of products is capable of
providing a complete gourmet meal.*

Items 1–6 .... *appetizers*
    7–15 .... *main courses,
        side dishes,
        and soups*
  16–20 .... *breads and biscuits*
  21–25 .... *desserts*
  26–32 .... *gift baskets*

How To Order Bon Mélange Products

Call toll-free 1-800-647-8170

Before you phone in your order, we suggest that you fill out the Order Form. Total the items ordered for yourself and as gifts, along with the shipping charges...and have your total ready when you call. Also, have your Visa or MasterCard information handy

Order by Mail

Complete the Order Form. Send signed check or money order for the total amount of your order including shipping charges, to: Precision Foods, Inc., P.O. Box 2067, Tupelo, MS 38803. Don't forget to stamp your envelope. (If you are charging your order, be sure to provide Visa or MasterCard data.)

Ordering Gifts?

We'll ship your Gift Orders to another address. Give us shipping instructions when you order by mail or phone in your order. Shipping charges will vary with each order. For example, if you ship a $15.00 Gift Order, shipping will be $4.50. For a $10.00 Gift Order, add $3.00 shipping.

Precision Foods, Inc.
P.O. Box 2067•Tupelo, MS 38803
1-800-647-8170

Retail Price List & Order Form

Quantity	Cat. No.	Bon Melange Product	Price Each	Total Price
	1	Cheesebal Garlic/Herb	$ 2.95	
	2	Cheeseball Onion/Herb	2.95	
	3	Cheeseball Bearnaise	2.95	
	4	Salsa	2.95	
	5	Jezebel Sauce	3.49	
	6	Jalapeno Black-Eyed Pea Dip	3.49	
	7	French Market Soup	4.95	
	8	Split Pea Soup	4.95	
	9	Baton Rouge Bean Soup	4.95	
	10	Bayou Black Bean Soup/Dip Mix	4.95	
	11	New Orleans Red Beans/Rice	4.95	
	12	Mississippi Caviar	4.95	
	13	Hoppin' John	4.95	
	14	Cock-A-Noodle Soup	4.95	
	15	Italian Bean & Pasta Soup	4.95	
	16	New Orleans French Bread	4.95	
	17	Lazy River Herb Bread	4.95	
	18	Lazy River Dill Bread	4.95	
	19	Creole Criscuits	4.95	
	20	Salsa Cornbread	4.95	
	21	Orange Liqueur Fudge	4.95	
	22	Cinnamon Raisin Rolls	4.95	
	23	Poppy Almond Cake	6.95	
	24	Old Tyme Tea Cakes	4.95	
	25	Mississippi Mud	6.95	
	26	Sunday Supper (A) #7/17	16.95	
	27	Sunday Supper (B) #7/18	16.95	
	28	Sunday Supper (C) #11/20	16.95	
	29	Sunday Supper (D) #10/18	16.95	
	30	Supper for 8 (A) #7/17/23	24.95	
	31	Supper for 8 (B) #10/18/25	24.95	
	32	Mississippi Basket #4/12/20/25	29.95	

UPS SHIPPING CHARGE		
0-$10.00 . . . . .3.00	Subtotal	
10.01-20.00 . . . . .4.50	Sales Tax (IL residents 1%) (MS residents 7%)	
20.01-30.00 . . . . .5.50	Shipping, Gift A	
30.01-40.00 . . . . .6.50	Shipping, Gift B	
40.01-50.00 . . . . .7.50	Shipping, Gift C	
50.01- 9.00	Total Amount of Order	

NEED ADDITIONAL COPIES?
Use This Handy Order Form

The Southern Gourmet Cookbook
P.O. Box 2067
Tupelo, MS 38803

Please send me _____ copy(ies) of

        The Southern Gourmet Cookbook @ \$13.95 each _____

Please send me _____ copy(ies) of

        Mrs. Wages Home Canning Guide @ \$ 5.95 each _____

        Postage and handling per book   @ \$ 2.00 each _____

        Illinois residents add 1% sales tax   _____

        Mississippi residents add 7% sales tax   _____

        My check or money order is enclosed for   Total_____

Name _____

Address _____

City _____ State _____ Zip _____

- -

The Southern Gourmet Cookbook
P.O. Box 2067
Tupelo, MS 38803

Please send me _____ copy(ies) of

        The Southern Gourmet Cookbook @ \$13.95 each _____

Please send me _____ copy(ies) of

        Mrs. Wages Home Canning Guide @ \$ 5.95 each _____

        Postage and handling per book   @ \$ 2.00 each _____

        Illinois residents add 1% sales tax   _____

        Mississippi residents add 7% sales tax   _____

        My check or money order is enclosed for   Total_____

Name _____

Address _____

City _____ State _____ Zip _____

Re-Order Additional Copies